INSPIRED

INSPIRED | LIFE IN PENLAND'S RESIDENT ARTIST AND CORE FELLOWSHIP PROGRAMS

Editor: Jean McLaughlin
Editorial committee: Robin Dreyer, Kathryn Gremley, Leslie Noell
Project manager: Kathy Sheldon
Writers: Robin Dreyer, Kathryn Gremley, Jean McLaughlin,
    Deborah Morgenthal, Caitlin Strokosch
Interviewer/interview editor: Deborah Morgenthal
Research assistance: Carey Hedlund, Jasmin McFayden
Design and layout: Ele Annand, 7 Ton Co., Asheville, NC, 7tonco.com

© 2016 Penland School of Crafts

All rights reserved. No part of this book may be reproduced or transmitted in any form or by any means whatsoever without express written permission from Penland School of Crafts, except in the case of brief quotations embodied in critical articles and reviews. Inquiries should be directed to Communications, Penland School of Crafts, PO Box 37, Penland, NC 28765.

First Printing, 2016
ISBN 978-0-9769110-1-2

Penland School of Crafts
PO Box 37
Penland, NC 28765-0037
www.penland.org

Front cover: Penland resident artist Tom Shields working in his studio at The Barns. Photo by Robin Dreyer

Back cover: Penland core fellow Angela Eastman creating a site-specific piece made of braided grass in the Penland meadow. Photo by Wes Stitt

Penland School of Crafts receives support for its programs from the North Carolina Arts Council, an agency funded by the State of North Carolina and the National Endowment for the Arts, which believes that a great nation deserves great art.

CONTENTS

- **6**   PREFACE
- **8**   DIRECTOR'S INTRODUCTION
- **10**   A SHORT HISTORY OF PENLAND SCHOOL OF CRAFTS
- **24**   PENLAND RESIDENT ARTIST PROGRAM
- **36**   PENLAND CORE FELLOWSHIP PROGRAM
- **50**   CONVERSATIONS WITH THIRTY-TWO ARTISTS

    CORE FELLOWS
- 54   Meredith Brickell
- 58   Critz Campbell
- 62   Susan Chin
- 66   Daniel Essig
- 70   Alida Fish
- 74   Seth Gould
- 78   Douglas Harling
- 82   Andrew Hayes
- 86   Amy Jacobs
- 90   Julie Leonard
- 94   Sarah Loertscher
- 98   Jack Mauch
- 102   Ronan Peterson
- 106   Linda Foard Roberts
- 110   Holly Walker
- 114   Dave Wofford

    RESIDENT ARTISTS
- 120   Peter Adams
- 124   Adela Akers
- 128   Stanley Mace Andersen
- 132   Junichiro Baba
- 136   Vivian Beer
- 140   Cristina Córdova
- 144   Stephen Dee Edwards
- 148   Susie Ganch
- 152   Hoss Haley
- 156   James Lawton
- 160   Anne Lemanski
- 164   Marc Maiorana
- 168   Mark Peiser
- 172   Christina Shmigel
- 176   Evon Streetman
- 180   Amy Tavern

- **184**   CORE FELLOWS, 1971–2016
- **186**   RESIDENT ARTISTS, 1963–2016
- **188**   INSPIRING INSTRUCTORS AND COMMUNITY ARTISTS
- **190**   ACKNOWLEDGMENTS
- **191**   INDEX

PREFACE

TIME AND SPACE: ARTIST RESIDENCIES AND THE EVOLUTION OF NEW CREATIVE WORK

Caitlin Strokosch

Executive Director
Alliance of Artists Communities

At this very moment, all around the world, thousands of artists—painters and poets, composers and choreographers, filmmakers and sculptors and novelists and others—are stepping into an artist-in-residence studio, with precious time and space to wonder and to work. You may know some of their names already, though most will be unfamiliar to you. And while their creative output may end up on the stage or the page, on the walls and in the halls of countless cultural institutions, every work begins with this leap of faith.

For centuries, artists have sought time and space dedicated to creating new work. In the late 1800s and early 1900s, these visions began to formalize into artist colonies in Europe and the northeastern United States—including the American Academy in Rome, Byrdcliffe Colony, Étaples, The MacDowell Colony, and Yaddo—offering artists creative immersion, unfettered by the demands of everyday life and with limited interaction with the public. By the 1930s, similar residencies had arisen across the United States—including Hambidge Center in Rabun Gap, Georgia; Montalvo Arts Center in Saratoga, California; and Ox-Bow in Saugatuck, Michigan—as rural outposts for artists seeking temporary escape from the chaos and commercialism of city life.

In the 1960s and '70s the nonprofit sector as a whole expanded in the United States and, with it, the artist residency field. New models encouraged collaboration and exchange; sought synergy between an artist's studio practice and opportunities to share, teach, and learn; and emphasized communal living and environmental stewardship. In the 1980s and '90s, as boundaries between disciplines were breaking down, residencies adapted their selection processes, facilities, and technical support to serve artists working in new ways. An increase in urban residencies offered artists a significantly different experience, challenging the idea of residency as retreat. As funding for individual artists all but disappeared in the 1990s, residency programs banded together, with eighteen lead organizations (including Penland) and seed money from the MacArthur Foundation, creating the Alliance of Artists Communities to serve as a collective voice for the field. At this critical turning point, residency programs moved out of the shadows and developed stronger advocacy for the essential role residencies play in the ecosystem of artist support.

Since then, the field has continued to evolve in response to the most critical issues of our times, with residencies serving artists whose work revolves around the sciences, environmental art, and social justice. New models may be deeply rooted in a specific place, fostering collaborative art-making between artists and the public. Some focus on international exchange, fostering a community of cultural inquiry and forging connections across boundaries. Others are experimenting with thematic and project-based residencies, balancing tangible expectations with an open-endedness that has been a hallmark of the field since its inception.

From emerging artists discovering the joys and challenges of being self-directed for the first time, to established artists longing for fresh ideas, to those returning to their art-making after years or decades of other jobs, raising families, and serving others, this abundance of models offers artists of every stripe a place to call home. Today there are more than 500 artist residency programs in the United States and more than 1,500 worldwide, located in remote rural areas, small towns, suburbs, and cities, supporting one artist at a time or dozens, for a week, a month, a year, or more. Despite all these differences, the field upholds its core beliefs that artists are valuable and worthy of support, that dedicated time and space are essential to incubate ideas and develop new work, and that investing in an artist's process and practice is necessary for the creation of new work.

Indeed there is no one-size-fits-all model for a residency, and each program seeks to offer artists the right mix of solitude and solidarity: a community of like-minded peers and a room of one's own, external inspiration and personal reflection, the opportunity to exchange ideas and the contemplation to let them take root.

Often misunderstood as retreats, artist residencies are more about advancing than retreating, serving as research-and-development laboratories where our most innovative thinkers are encouraged to experiment, to tinker, to take creative risks. The sculptures and paintings, plays and dances, books and music and films often emerge months or years later, and yet residency programs trust artists to make their way from inspiration to implementation, from process to product.

We can point to the works created, the awards won by alumni, the boxes checked on an evaluation form, but the true impact of an artist residency is the transformation that occurs when artists are provided with support to incubate and explore new creative work. Artist residencies are essential to our cultural landscape, providing a critical connection between dreaming and making at a time when outcomes are especially uncertain and ideas most fragile—before the gallery, the publisher, or the stage. And truth be told, if no alumni ever went on to fame or supplied us with an impressive scorecard, residencies would keep doing what they do. Because trust lies in believing that artists transform their experience into something that will leave the world better for it, whether or not we read about it in the *New York Times*.

The pages of this book are filled with such stories of transformation—the breakthroughs that come from complete creative immersion, a chance meeting with another artist that leads to years of collaboration, a career blossoming out of the discipline and focus required during a residency.

What this field does—and, indeed, Penland does exceptionally well—is invest in artists. This is risky business: it requires trust in individuals, patience, and faith, with few tangible tools for assessment. And at a time when we all feel pressure to expand our breadth—serving more artists, offering more programs—Penland's residencies represent depth, in what amounts to an extraordinary investment in a relatively small number of artists over the span of years.

The residency field is rapidly growing and changing to meet the needs of a variety of artists, communities, and institutions. There has been an increase in residency programs in urban settings, residencies embedded within museums and universities, shorter residencies to support artists juggling families and multiple jobs, and residencies that engage the public in issues of social change. And in this context, Penland continues to play a critical leadership role, offering artists the opportunity to nurture their ideas, techniques, and professional development over time; to grow and evolve; to gain the discipline, focus, and community to sustain a creative career for a lifetime. The magic of Penland is the environment it creates, an environment that embodies the essence of craft: the inspiration of its physical site, the spirit of curiosity and learning that underlies all of Penland's programs, the engagement of others to share ideas, and the remarkable generosity of time.

There is no doubt about Penland's impact, reflected in the abundance of new ideas explored, the techniques mastered and reworked and mastered again, the lives transformed, the careers born and built, and the audiences reached as Penland artists have scattered across the globe and shared their work with countless others. In this way, we are all recipients of Penland's gifts, and we celebrate in Penland's success together.

Core fellow Kreh Mellick working on a large drawing, 2008.
Photo by Robin Dreyer

Resident artist Dustin Farnsworth with sculpture components in his studio at The Barns, 2014.
Photo by Robin Dreyer

DIRECTOR'S INTRODUCTION

Jean W. McLaughlin
Executive Director
Penland School of Crafts

When Bill Brown became Penland's director in 1962, he introduced into the school's culture a new perspective on the needs of contemporary artists in America. He recognized that artists required uninterrupted time to experiment and develop ideas, the space to work alone and in collaboration, and the opportunity to be in a supportive community of other artists. He saw a growing number of young artists from across the country with a desire to put their skills, ideas, and ingenuity to work, and he recognized that Penland was a place, in an extraordinary and inspiring setting, that could respond to these needs in an open and engaging manner. What evolved through his vision were two unique programs: Penland's Resident Artist Program (founded in 1963) and Core Fellowship Program (founded in 1971.)[1] Through these programs, scores of artists found grounding and motivation to place the making of art at the center of their lives.

Recording our history is important to Penland and to the field of craft. Our work as an organization is informed by the accomplishments and contributions of so many artists, leaders, and thinkers who preceded us. With this book, *Inspired: Life in Penland's Resident Artist and Core Fellowship Programs,* our aim is to acknowledge the remarkable near-fifty-year history of these two programs and begin to document this history through the stories of participating artists. We wanted to hear how the programs affected the course of their lives, to learn about their mentors, and see where they are today. We wanted to test assumptions about how the programs influenced studio practice, discipline, balance and focus, paths of discovery, career development, and leadership skills.

Relationships are central to Penland's story. Throughout the conversations with artists for this book, the connections between Penland and other schools, universities, and organizations came forward. Similarly, many personal and professional relationships developed as artists' formative years in the programs grew into lifelong artistic careers. Mapping would reveal expanding links and paths between artists, communities, and spheres of influence as these programs have evolved. Professors, fellow artists and students, neighbors and parents drew connections that led artists to these Penland programs. Penland's resident artists and core fellows, in turn, have become guides and inspiration to other students, artists, curators, and collectors. Interconnected webs of relationships, begun with the school's founder, Lucy Morgan, and the founder of these programs, Bill Brown, have continued to evolve through the years. Penland and artists closely affiliated with the school thrive on these mutually supportive connections with other institutions such as Haystack, Arrowmont, Peters Valley, Pilchuck, and Anderson Ranch, the American Craft Council, North Carolina State University, Maine College of Art, the University of Wisconsin–Madison, the University of Illinois–Carbondale, Columbia College Chicago, the University of Iowa, the University of Alabama, California College of the Arts, the University of Georgia, Virginia Commonwealth University, Rhode Island School of Design, The University of the Arts (Philadelphia), and the School of the Art Institute of Chicago—just to name a few.

We invited thirty-two artists—representing a span of years and range of media—to describe the impact these two programs had on their work, careers, and personal lives. Their stories reflect the experiences of many of the 373 artists (at the time of this publication) who took a leap of faith to become part of a new community and part of an experiment in serving the educational and professional needs of artists. We are grateful to these resident artists and core fellows for taking the time to share with us their candid recollections and reflections.

Of course, this book could not begin to encompass all the equally compelling stories of the other participants in these programs. It does, however, open the door for future research and consideration of questions yet to be asked and stories left to be told. Some questions that we have posed include the role of bartering for education, how leadership roles and responsibility were nurtured at Penland and then manifested themselves in the lives of these artists, how longer residencies (two and three years in the case of these Penland programs) compare with shorter ones in other places, the specific nature of the conversations that bonded artists in these programs, the very ideas and works of art that emerged during these years, and how these ideas influenced later bodies of work. Each interview opened the door for longer conversations.

With this publication, we have begun to explore the impact of these two distinct programs on the work and careers of their artist participants. From the outset of the Resident Artist and the Core Fellowship Programs, Penland has asked, "What can happen when artists are offered the opportunity to expand their knowledge, build their skills, and launch careers in a total-immersion environment designed to foster creativity?" The artists featured in *Inspired: Life in Penland's Resident Artist and Core Fellowship Programs* demonstrate how varied the responses to this question can be and also how many themes are shared. Most importantly, this book underscores how, through commitment and generosity of spirit, each individual can influence the work and lives of many others. Truly these two innovative programs have advanced creativity and demonstrated successful models of craft education in America.

[1] In interviews about the program, Jane Brown places the founding date of the Core Fellowship Program at 1970. However, Alida Fish, considered to be Penland's first core fellow, reports her work at Penland began in 1971.

Resident artist Shoko Teruyama working on a form while teaching in the Penland clay studio, 2007.
Photo by Robin Dreyer

Penland core fellow Angela Eastman creating a site-specific piece made of braided grass in the Penland meadow.
Photo by Wes Stitt

A SHORT HISTORY OF PENLAND SCHOOL OF CRAFTS

Robin Dreyer
Communications Director
Penland School of Crafts

"I was taking a jewelry class with Gary Noffke who has done some blacksmithing himself. He had us making stakes—jewelry tools. I had such a big time doing it that I thought I'd like to make a hammer. So I went up to the iron studio and asked Doug Wilson if I could make a hammer and he said, sure, and handed me a big chunk of steel. I had no idea what I was doing, and after I had worked on the thing for about ten hours I had the worst headache of my life. I went back to the dorm and I sat down on the bed. I took a couple of aspirin and I told myself, well, this was something that you wanted to do but you've found that you're just not capable of doing it, so just forget it, go back to jewelry. Then I decided I'd take a shower and get all that crud off of me. While I was in the shower I thought of about ten more things I wanted to make in the iron studio, so I went right back up there the next morning, and I've been going back ever since."

—Blacksmith and sculptor Elizabeth Brim (pictured on page 36), who lives near Penland School of Crafts and has been a Penland student, core fellow, iron studio coordinator, and instructor, from an interview in 1990

Weaving Institute on the porch of the first Ridgeway Hall, 1930s.
Photo by Bayard Wootten

Although she was a woman of great vision, Lucy Morgan was probably not imagining Elizabeth Brim and her chunk of steel when she arrived in the North Carolina mountain community of Penland in 1920. She had come to accept a teaching position at the Appalachian School, an Episcopal mission school founded by her brother Rufus. She had no definite plan for how long she would stay.

During the forty-two years Morgan lived and worked at Penland she established an educational experiment that continues to this day. During its long history, Penland School of Crafts has nurtured the personal and creative lives of thousands of individuals; it has helped establish an alternative model of education; it has contributed to the growth and development of a major area of aesthetic expression; and it has established a distinctive niche for itself in the cultural life of our society.

These accomplishments have been led by the vision of a few key people and supported by the creative and financial contributions of many more. Guiding the school through its remarkable history has been a persistent adherence to a few basic ideas: the value of lifelong education, the power of aligning mind and body in the execution of challenging and creative tasks, a love of handmade objects, the importance of community, and the significance of place.

Elizabeth Brim's discovery of steel, its effect on her life, and her multifaceted relationship with the school are a good story, but not a rare one. Hundreds of similar stories make up the fabric of Penland's history.

BEGINNINGS: THE PENLAND WEAVERS

The early history of Penland School is intermingled with that of two other institutions: the Appalachian School and the Penland Weavers. The story is driven by the relentless energy and adaptable vision of the school's founder.

Lucy Morgan was born in Macon County, North Carolina, in the far western end of the state. The daughter of socially active Episcopalians, Morgan was educated at Central State Normal School (now Central Michigan University). After graduating in 1915, she taught public school in Michigan, Montana, and Chicago.

Opposite page:
Penland's founder, Lucy Morgan, weaving, 1930s.
Photo by Bayard Wootten

Lucy Morgan examining handwoven goods at the Weaving Cabin, 1930s.
Photo by Bayard Wootten, North Carolina Collection, University of North Carolina Library, Chapel Hill

She also attended summer school at the University of Chicago, and worked at the U.S. Children's Bureau, a social welfare agency.

Chicago in that era was a seedbed for the development of progressive education and social work in the United States. John Dewey, the philosopher and advocate of experiential education, was a major influence at the University of Chicago. Hull House, founded by Jane Addams and Ellen Gates Starr, was a pioneer in providing social services to the poor. The Children's Bureau, where Morgan worked, was run by Julia Lathrop, who was involved in the development of early child labor laws. It was from this social climate that Morgan went to Penland in 1920.

Morgan's brother Rufus had talked to her of his dream that the Appalachian School's vocational program could be expanded to include handcrafts, particularly weaving. He had sought out the very few women in the vicinity of the school who still practiced this craft and had hoped to reintroduce it through the Appalachian School. By the time Lucy Morgan came to Penland, however, her brother had moved on.

In the winter of 1923, Morgan was asked to accompany a local girl named Bonnie Willis who was traveling to Berea, Kentucky, to continue her education at the Berea Academy and Berea College. They were joined by Howard "Toni" Ford, a young Appalachian School teacher also enrolling at Berea. The college offered weaving classes, and Morgan had decided to spend her nine-week vacation studying the craft. The teacher, a Swedish weaver named Anna Ernberg, had developed a lightweight loom that was easier to operate than those used by Appalachian weavers of earlier generations. In addition to learning the basics of weaving, Morgan also saw Berea's program that placed looms in the homes of local women and purchased and marketed their woven goods. She returned to Penland with new skills, several looms, and an idea for a weaving program aimed not at her students, but at the surrounding community.

Back at Penland, Morgan set up looms and invited local women to try them out. She wanted potential weavers to experience firsthand the improved technology she found at Berea. "Everybody who came in to see these little looms marveled at how much smaller and lighter they were than the cumbersome old ones they remembered seeing their grandmothers use," Morgan wrote in her memoir, *Gift from the Hills*.

The first person to begin weaving was Bonnie Willis's mother, Adeline. With Morgan's help and instruction, she began to weave rugs in the Log Cabin pattern. When Morgan paid her $23 for the first rugs, word began to spread, and soon Morgan had to commission local woodworkers to make more looms. She had initiated the project with no plan for marketing and was paying for the goods with her own money. When she was finally $2,000 in arrears, she turned to the Episcopal Church for help. The bishop agreed to place the project under the sponsorship of the Appalachian School. The school paid Morgan a salary, and the church provided a Ford pickup truck for transporting and marketing the goods.

She began selling woven items at mountain resorts, at agricultural fairs, through church gift shops, and Episcopal Church conventions. A trip to the North Carolina State Fair in Raleigh put Morgan in contact with the administrator of the state's vocational education program. He found that her weaving program qualified for support under a federal program that subsidized vocational training.

This government funding provided half of Morgan's salary. The terms of the subsidy required the weavers to meet regularly in a central location, so Morgan established Wednesdays as "Weaving Day," and the women gathered at the Appalachian School for instruction, socializing, to pick up materials, and to deliver finished work. In 1926, with seventeen weavers producing, the weavers' families constructed a dedicated building, called the Weaving Cabin, on church property.

Lucy Morgan and Howard "Toni" Ford with the Travelog, which took Penland goods to the 1933 Chicago World's Fair.
Photo by Bayard Wootten

The next evolution of Morgan's project revolved around a man named Edward F. Worst, who was considered the country's leading expert on hand weaving. The director of manual education in the Chicago public schools, Worst had authored several instruction books on weaving and established a cottage industry based on the craft. Morgan invited him to visit Penland in the summer of 1928. According to *Gift from the Hills,* an account of that visit in a small publication called *The Handicrafter* produced letters of interest from other parts of the country. When Worst returned in 1929 to work with the Penland weavers for a week, a few guest students joined the local women for instruction. Morgan would later date the workshop in the summer of 1929 as the birth of Penland School. In 1930, Morgan formally announced a summer "weaving institute" under the direction of Edward Worst, and again a number of students traveled to Penland to join the local weavers.[1]

Edward Worst instructing a student on the porch of the first Ridgeway Hall, 1930s.
Photo by Bayard Wootten

The Penland Weavers organization grew in size until the late 1920s, when it peaked with about sixty women weaving. Although an attempt to add pottery production was a failure, Morgan was able to introduce hammered pewter alongside the weaving. As her attention was increasingly taken up by her fledgling craft school, the management of the Penland Weavers was turned over to others, and, although production continued for several decades, the numbers of weavers and metalworkers began to decline. Jessie McKinney, who ran the program during its final days, reported in a 1993 interview that as factory work and other cash-producing jobs became available, it was difficult to persuade the next generation of women to take up weaving. In 1967, the Penland Weavers finally ceased operation.

PENLAND SCHOOL OF HANDICRAFTS

In 1931, Bonnie and Toni Ford returned to Penland. Bonnie Willis Ford was the same Bonnie Willis who had traveled to Berea in 1923, accompanied by Lucy Morgan and Toni Ford. Willis and Ford had completed their studies and married. Although he worked elsewhere during the rest of the year, Toni Ford was a lively and integral part of the Penland summer sessions. Bonnie Ford quickly became the de facto manager of both the production and educational programs at Penland; she continued working at the school until her death in 1976. She was steady, levelheaded, and a good writer. Morgan described her as "Penland School's Rock of Gibraltar."

Positioning logs during the construction of the Craft House, May, 1935.
Photo by Bayard Wootten, North Carolina Collection,
University of North Carolina Library, Chapel Hill

By 1935, the summer program had expanded so that students in the weaving institute were offered the option of one or two weeks of weaving classes before Worst arrived, plus instruction in a number of other crafts including pottery, basketry, and leather work. The Penland weaving institutes had always borrowed space from the Appalachian School, but in May of 1935, with a small amount of donated money (a $2.50 contribution paid for one log), whatever funds Morgan could borrow against her life insurance, and materials given to the project against the promise of future payment, logs were raised for a fifty-by eighty-four-foot structure on land Morgan owned. It was named the Edward F. Worst Craft House, and it was the first building built at Penland exclusively for the summer craft workshops. More construction followed as the program grew. In 1938, Penland School of Handicrafts was registered as a nonprofit corporation, and in 1940 the property and buildings were transferred to this new entity.

By 1947, the Penland brochure would describe the school this way: "The Penland School of Handicrafts is a small but well-known school with an excellent staff, adequate equipment, and a desire to serve. It is a nonprofit educational corporation directed by a Board of Trustees, and is operated for one purpose only—to instruct all who wish to come in the craft skills of their choice. Its students are a cross section of America, with mountain folk, college presidents, home makers, teachers, and occupational therapists learning together.... There are no entrance requirements excepting the desire to learn."

A pottery student loading a kiln, 1930s.
Photo by Bayard Wootten, North Carolina Collection,
University of North Carolina Library, Chapel Hill

The summer was now divided into four three-week sessions. The main areas of instruction were weaving (including tapestry), metalcrafts, and pottery. Along with these areas were "related crafts," which in various years included spinning, carding, dyeing, silkscreen, block printing, leathercrafts, candle making, doll making, bookbinding, shoemaking, plastics, chair seating, felt crafts, wood carving, drawing, basketry, stenciling, lampshade making, corn shuckery, and the making and playing of shepherd's pipes. There were also classes in color and design. The flyer asked students to indicate their major area of interest, but said, "You may take any crafts you wish or all of them." Students were also cautioned against working too intently and were encouraged to take advantage of field trips and other recreation.

Morgan moved with the times and was always on the lookout for new ways to attract students and special groups. Penland organized workshops for blind students, for home demonstration agents, and for college groups. Special efforts were made to serve occupational therapists. At the end of World War II, she was quick to get Penland approved for GI Bill students. She also arranged, beginning in 1961, for students to be able to receive college credit for Penland classes, an option that has been available ever since.

Penland's promotional materials during this time, while charming and folksy, convey principles that remain important to this day: Admission was on a first-come, first-served basis, and classes were open to all levels of skill. There was no set curriculum and no grades; teaching revolved around the transmission of skills and ideas to people who were interested in them. A noncompetitive, community feeling and the spectacular physical setting were described as essential components of the experience. And, most importantly, learning to make things was deemed to carry a value to the individual apart from that of the objects produced. Morgan's own writing in *Gift from the Hills* and the school's newsletter stresses this final point over and over again.

By the late 1950s, however, the school had gradually begun to decline. Enrollments were down, government subsidies ended in 1954, and board meetings were dominated by discussions of expenses, indebtedness, tactics for attracting students, problems with the physical plant, and Morgan's desire for retirement. At the 1961 board meeting a search committee was appointed to find a new director. The committee found William J. Brown. Morgan was enthusiastic, and Brown was offered the job.

Lucy Morgan retired in 1962 and moved to Webster, North Carolina, where she lived until her death in 1981. She never gave up weaving, which she had continued to practice during her years running the school. She received two honorary doctorates, and, in 1993, the Women and the Craft Arts Conference at the National Museum of Women in the Arts gave her a posthumous lifetime achievement award.

IT NEEDED SOME KIND OF A JOLT

As Morgan's successor, Bill Brown was a spectacular choice. Plainspoken, witty, and charismatic, he is remembered by many as a person reluctant to judge or criticize—a man whose special genius was empowering others to follow their passion. "There is no way to educate anyone," he once said, "they have to do it on their own." He had an MFA from Cranbrook Academy of Art in Michigan. He had taught at the University of Delaware, the New York State Teachers College at Oswego, and the Worcester Center for Crafts in Massachusetts. But most importantly, from 1951 to 1962, he had spent summers teaching and assisting the director at the Haystack Mountain School of Crafts in Maine.

Haystack was founded by philanthropist Mary Bishop, whose specific intent was to create a school similar to Penland. She invited printmaker and Flint (Michigan) Museum of Art director Francis Merritt to run the school. Haystack's written material described the school in terms that echoed Penland's combination of artistic and social goals. Its educational format, however, evolved

Opposite page:
Penland's second director, Bill Brown, with his wife, Jane, and their sons, Jerry and Bill Jr., in front of the Lily Loom House on the day they arrived at Penland, September 1962.

Bill Boysen, who built the first Penland glass studio, working in that studio, circa 1965. Glass, photography, and blacksmithing were important expansions to the Penland program made during Bill Brown's tenure as director.

quickly towards single-subject, total-immersion workshops taught by a rotating group of guest instructors. This was the model Brown brought with him to Penland.

In a 1979 interview, Brown remembered his first day at Penland. It was September 1962, and summer classes were just ending. "The first breakfast we had here," he said, "there was only one person who was under fifty years old. It was quite quiet. . . . It was a very nice place, but it needed some kind of a jolt."

Brown invited all of the regular faculty to return, and his initial changes were subtle but significant. Most important was increased studio access. At Haystack, studios were available twenty-four hours a day. At Penland, they opened at nine in the morning, were closed during mealtime, and the lights went out at nine or ten in the evening. A studio monitor was always present to keep track of materials sold to students. Brown unlocked the studios and put sales on an honor system. "Now the lights were on all over the place," he said, "all night long, nobody went to bed."

By 1969, the program was completely transformed. The school was now referred to as Penland School of Crafts. Almost all of Lucy Morgan's instructors were gone. Summer had been extended to seven sessions, two or three weeks in length, with a total of sixty-three individual classes listed. Most instructors taught a single session. The topics were ceramics, glass, wood, weaving, plastics, enameling, metals, lapidary, photography, graphics, sculpture, tapestry, and dyeing. Rotating special classes in this time period included workshops in soft sculpture, banner making, and guitar building. Students enrolled in a single class for the duration of the session, which, combined with unlimited studio access, allowed them to cover a seemingly impossible amount of material in a few weeks. The instructors were a mix of university teachers and full-time studio craftspeople, including graduates or faculty members from Parsons School of Design, University of Wisconsin, Cranbrook Academy of Art, the School for American Craftsmen, Cleveland Institute of Art, Kansas City Art Institute, and Alfred University.

While the basic media areas had not expanded much since 1963, photography, which had been taught informally in the 1950s, became a regular program in 1968, and the addition of glass to the lineup was especially significant. Glass did not emerge as a craft that could be practiced in small studios until 1962, when Harvey Littleton and Dominick Labino demonstrated a small-scale glass furnace at the Toledo (Ohio) Museum of Art. In 1965, Brown arranged for Bill Boysen, one of Littleton's students, to set up a glass studio at Penland. This early embrace of the craft led to Penland being the site of the founding of the Glass Art Society in the early 1970s, and the school has remained strongly identified with the development of contemporary glass.

Another significant addition to the program was blacksmithing, which was added in 1981 with help from Brown's son, Bill Brown Jr. Penland's first iron class was taught by Brent Kington, a sculptor who started the first university program in ironwork, and the Penland program has been largely shaped by instructors influential in the development of iron as an expressive and sculptural medium.

The Penland board gave Brown complete autonomy in running the school, and he gave this same freedom to his faculty. He did not publish class descriptions, and after 1968 he didn't even publish biographical information about the teachers. When instructors asked him what they should teach, he told them to teach whatever was important to them. Despite his art school training, Brown had no use for formal critique, which he saw as destructive, and he thought competition only made sense in sports. He saw the close proximity of different media and the potential for friendly cross-fertilization as essential components of Penland's structure. The collaborative, community learning atmosphere promoted by Lucy Morgan was extended and solidified during Brown's tenure.

Brown's management of the school benefitted from the experience and good sense of Morgan's stalwart assistant Bonnie Ford, who served as business manager, bookkeeper, and registrar. His wife, Jane Brown, supervised housing

Photographer Bea Nettles teaching at Penland, early 1990s. Photography was added as a regular program in 1968 under the guidance of Evon Streetman, who brought important art photographers to Penland as instructors. Bea Nettles, who has taught at the school since the 1970s, was prominently involved in exploring printmaking processes and nineteenth-century photographic processes in the context of contemporary art.

and the kitchen and managed the school's work-study scholarship program. Also important to Brown's management were the uncountable personal relationships he and Jane Brown developed with students and faculty.

There is scant information about scholarships in Morgan's time, although the 1946 brochure describes a work scholarship arrangement similar to what exists today. Under Brown, work-study scholarship students became integral to the school's operation, with fifteen or more students in each session working three or four hours a day under Jane Brown's direction. This program made Penland financially possible for hundreds of students who might not have attended otherwise.

Enrollment at Penland increased throughout the 1960s, slowly at first and then in quantum jumps. Brown reported to the board in 1969 that the school was running at maximum capacity with about a hundred students per session. The school began receiving support from new sources, especially the Hanes and Reynolds families of Winston-Salem. Instructors were paid equally and received—more or less as in Morgan's time—room, board, travel money, and a tiny honorarium. Penland, however, had become a crossroads for craft information, and despite minimal compensation, Brown had no trouble attracting first-rate instructors.

Wendell Castle in the Penland wood studio, 1969. Castle is one of the most important furniture designer-builders of the twentieth century and was part of the network of contemporary craftspeople introduced to Penland by Bill Brown.
Photo by Doug Stewart

While the caliber of the faculty and the nature of the classes had changed dramatically, Penland's open door policy had not. In 1975 Brown wrote: "Thousands of people from North Carolina, from every state in the Union, and from over sixty foreign countries have come to this mountain community to learn to weave, to make pottery, and to work with wood, metal, glass, and stone. Some of these students have become professional craftsmen; many hundreds of others have developed an avocation that has been meaningful to them and their families. . . . We have college and art school students, grandmothers, doctors, lawyers, teachers (and they come in all colors)—anyone who wants to learn."

Brown did not limit himself, however, to transplanting the educational model he and Francis Merritt had developed at Haystack.[2] Other programs established during the first decade of his tenure would give Penland a singular character all its own.

RESIDENT ARTISTS

At the first board meeting Brown attended as director, in June 1963, he talked about his ideas for using the facility when classes were not in session. Chief among these was his plan for a residency program, an opportunity he saw missing in the craft world. Potter Ed Brinkman and woodworker Skip Johnson came in 1963, and by the fall of 1965, there were four artists living at Penland and using the studios to produce their work during the nine months of each year when they were not being used for summer workshops.

Then in the spring of 1965, the Appalachian School decided to close its doors, and its 220 acres of land and all of its buildings were being offered for sale for $100,000. Brown knew that Penland School couldn't afford this price, but he was convinced that buying the property was essential. "I wanted the place to hold onto itself and have enough room around it," he said years later.

Industrialist Philip Hanes committed to raising $25,000, and Brown sent a letter to everyone on the school's mailing list asking for help. Eventually, he convinced the Episcopal Diocese to reduce the price to $40,000, and, with support coming from all directions, Penland School was able to buy the land. In 1968, with a grant from the James G. Hanes Memorial Fund, the Appalachian School's livestock barns were renovated to make studios and apartments, which meant that resident artists no longer had to vacate their workspaces when classes began in May.

Woodworker Skip Johnson, who was in the first group of resident artists at Penland, working in the Penland wood studio, 1960s.

One of Brown's stated goals for the residency was to foster an artistic community at Penland. In 1967 Ed Brinkman bought property in the area, and by the late 1970s the school was surrounded by craftspeople, many of whom had first come as resident artists. The presence of the resident artists and the complex and

lively relationship between the school and the craft community that has grown up around it would become distinguishing features of Penland's program.

CONCENTRATION

With the Resident Artist Program moved to the renovated barns, Penland's teaching studios were again vacant for eight months each year, and this opened the way for several more educational innovations. In the fall of 1970, Penland began a program called concentration, with potter Cynthia Bringle and her sister, the weaver Edwina Bringle, as the first two instructors. These were eight-week classes built on the same workshop model as the summer sessions. There was, and is, no other program quite like it in craft—almost as long as a college semester but with the focused attention of a total-immersion workshop.

The first year, only ceramics and weaving were offered; by 1972, the program stabilized with workshops in ceramics, glass, metals, photography, and textiles. The concentration extended Penland's class schedule from March through November, which opened the way for another Penland program that has never been duplicated elsewhere.

CORE STUDENTS

The Browns were working with a small staff, and Jane Brown's workload included cooking on weekends along with supervising housing and the work of the scholarship students. With the newly extended season, it became possible to offer a few students a year-round scholarship in exchange for their taking over some of the ongoing responsibilities at the school—in effect becoming part-time members of the staff. This evolved into the Core Student Program (later renamed the Core Fellowship), providing several years of room, board, and tuition and an opportunity for students to focus on one medium with a succession of instructors or to explore the entire range that Penland offers. The Core Fellowship has become part of the distinctive signature of Penland School of Crafts.

THE END OF AN ERA

Bill Brown was a man for his time. His management style might accurately be called familial, and much of the school's development in this time period was built on the personal loyalty of dozens of brilliant craftspeople. Brown visited the studios every day. He had daily instructor gatherings at his house. He and Jane Brown hosted parties for faculty, students, and visitors. He depended on a cadre of close friends who, unpaid, helped manage the studios and line up each summer's instructors. The instructors themselves were paid almost nothing, a fact that Brown referred to with some pride. He selected the resident artists, and they stayed as long as he felt they were benefiting. Although Brown successfully secured some funding from foundations and government agencies, much of his fundraising was done by letting wealthy supporters know of his needs and trusting they would come through. In addition to guiding the school's program, he made decisions about finances, the physical plant, and matters of policy with little input from his board, which met once a year to endorse his leadership.

These same qualities would contribute to Brown's conflicts with his board at the end of his career. In 1979, a fiftieth-anniversary campaign raised over $600,000 for much-needed building renovations and to create a scholarship endowment. Some of the funds were restricted and also required substantial matching money, and this brought a new level of fiscal scrutiny from the board. The board recruited several successful businessmen to serve, began to meet twice a year, set up a committee structure, and began to assert its prerogative to set policy. Brown expressed reservations about all of this. Penland had, throughout its history, operated without a budget or an endowment, but some board members felt that these things would be important to the future of the school.

Ceramic artist Robert Turner working at Penland, 1971. Turner was an influential figure in twentieth-century ceramics who taught at Black Mountain College in North Carolina and Alfred University in New York. While he didn't begin teaching at Penland until 1969, it was at Penland, in 1946, that he first worked with clay.

Opposite page:
Potter Cynthia Bringle at Penland, 1970. Cynthia and her twin sister, the weaver Edwina Bringle, were Penland resident artists, and they taught the first concentration workshops in 1970. They live nearby and have been involved with Penland from that time until the present.

Students building a wood-fired ceramics kiln, 1982.
Photo by Ben Simmons

None of these expectations would seem extraordinary by today's standards for nonprofit governance, but they were unprecedented at Penland. Brown felt that his achievements were directly related to his ability to make unencumbered decisions, and he chafed under the unaccustomed level of supervision. "I have had some success as the skipper of a P.T. boat," he wrote to the board. "I may not have the qualifications nor the desire to be in charge of a battleship." His relationship with the board deteriorated, and in October 1983, he was asked, at age sixty, to take early retirement. This move sent a shock wave through the Penland community—both the school's artist neighbors and the much wider community of students and instructors whose lives had been touched by the Browns. Letters of inquiry, complaint, bewilderment, and protest came from all over the country. Brown was given a modest pension, and he lived the rest of his life in a house he and Jane had built near the school.[3]

Brown was made an honorary fellow of the American Craft Council in 1979, and in 1991 he received the North Carolina Award in recognition of his work at Penland. He died in 1992. His grave is marked by an uncut boulder with this inscription: "He gave us the strength to believe in ourselves." After Bill Brown's death, Jane Brown taught the Alexander Technique at Appalachian State University and tutored dyslexic children for several decades. She now lives in a retirement home in Chapel Hill, North Carolina.

Brown's lasting influence is such that, with a few significant additions, Penland's program in 2015 is essentially the one he established between 1963 and 1972. The program's philosophical underpinnings, developed by both Morgan and Brown, guide the school to this day.

SUSTAINABILITY

Bill Brown's immediate successors were Verne Stanford (1984–1989), Hunter Kariher (1989–1992), and Ken Botnick (1993–1997). These relatively short tenures following two directors who had served the school for thirty-three and twenty-one years, respectively, may reflect a society in which long, linear careers are less common. It is also typical of the difficulties many organizations have in finding stable leadership in the wake of charismatic, visionary founders (Penland had two of these).

This third era of Penland's history has been one in which directors, staff, trustees, contributors, students, and instructors have worked in various ways to create a sustainable future for Penland's educational and social ideals. This concern has particularly characterized the leadership of Jean McLaughlin, who has been the director since 1998. It has also been a time of a general opening up—of the program, the instructor group, the engagement of its board, the school's base of support, and its relationship to the public.

Between 1985 and 1993, under directors Verne Stanford and Hunter Kariher, there was a significant expansion in the media offered. Books, paper, painting, and drawing all became regular programs. A second clay studio added more classes in handbuilding and sculpture. Flameworking took its place beside hot glass. Graphics was redefined as printmaking. This expansion culminated with the construction of a new studio complex—for books, paper, photography, printmaking, painting, and drawing—and a new kitchen, which allowed the maximum number of students attending a single session to rise from 100 to 167. (In recent years this capacity has risen to 187.) In 2007, letterpress printing became a separate program with a dedicated studio.

Starting in the mid-1980s, Penland began offering considerably more information about what was being taught and who was teaching. Class content is still primarily determined by the instructors (in consultation with a program director), but workshop descriptions and instructor bios are published for each class.

The flexibility of the workshop format and a succession of creative program directors—most notably Dana Moore, who ran the program for nineteen years—have

Czech glass artist Martin Janecky and assistants working in the Penland glass studio, 2007. Penland has attracted international instructors throughout its history.
Photo by Robin Dreyer

resulted in consistently innovative workshop content. Special workshops in recent years have included stone carving, casting—in glass, bronze, iron, paper, concrete, and other materials—performance, site-specific sculpture, classes based on gathered materials and found objects, classes that incorporate writing and text with traditional materials, and workshops that straddle several media. A recent summer included both the deeply traditional technique of hand-welted shoemaking and a workshop that combined glass with performance and video. Theme sessions, cutting across all media areas, have been offered in site-specific work, figurative art, and public art. In the summer of 2015, one session was taught entirely by faculty members from Australian National University.

Exhibition and community education programs added in the past twenty years have expanded the school's reach beyond workshops and residencies. Penland has developed a network of teaching artists who provide art experiences in the Mitchell County school system, at community events, and in partnership with other local organizations. Subs with SuitCASES is an innovative, art-based training program for substitute teachers, Kids Camp provides creative summer workshops for children, and the school hosts an annual open house that welcomes 400 to 500 visitors into the teaching studios. A small gallery and visitors center was opened in the mid-1980s, and it has grown into an impressive showcase for contemporary craft that attracts about 10,000 visitors each year. The Penland Gallery and Visitors Center provides information about the school and area artists, and it works from a mission statement that challenges its staff to expand its visitors' understanding of craft.

Potter Kevin Snipes talking glazes in the outdoor area of the Penland clay studio, 2012.
Photo by Robin Dreyer

The facility has also received considerable—and much-needed—attention. Director Ken Botnick had a background in landscape design and worked with several gardeners to give the school's landscaping the same care and attention students were bringing to their studio work. Botnick also supervised the design and construction of a new glass studio. Jean McLaughlin expanded this concern by creating a master plan for the buildings and grounds that emphasizes renovation, preservation of the school's existing aesthetic, and new construction to meet program needs. This plan, led by Edwin F. Harris, FAIA, has guided the location and design of new studios for book arts, drawing and painting, iron, print and letterpress, and wood, along with new housing. It also set a direction for dealing with the thorny problem of improving accessibility at a campus built over an eighty-year period on the side of a hill.

Care for the campus is not just a matter of offering excellent studios and comfortable rooms. Since Lucy Morgan's day, the place itself has been deemed integral to the experience. In the 1999 campus master plan, there is a statement addressing the importance of place that includes this: "Although the connection is hard to define, there is universal agreement that the landscape at Penland is an inspiration for the work created in the studios. Some of this inspiration is direct: there is no shortage of work depicting the landscape or incorporating materials from it. Of equal importance, however, is the spiritual nourishment provided by a physical environment that is infinitely textured in its natural features and artfully cared for by its stewards."

Penland's base of support has expanded considerably since the year 2000. The annual fund is strongly supported by hundreds of consistent donors. Auctions of donated artwork produce well more than a half-million dollars annually. The school also receives regular support from foundations, corporations, and government agencies. Jean McLaughlin has spearheaded two successful fundraising campaigns, one completed in 2004 and the second in 2016, which have increased the school's endowment from 2 to 17 million dollars, expanded scholarships, funded the new studios, addressed housing needs, improved accessibility campus-wide, and allowed for renovation of many of Penland's older buildings.

Cutting the ceremonial ribbon at the opening of the Paul Hayden Duensing Letterpress and Print Studio, 2007. This building was part of a series of important upgrades to the Penland campus undertaken between 2000 and 2016 under the leadership of Jean McLaughlin. Left to right: facilities director Scott Klein, printer and philanthropist John Horn, program director Dana Moore, board chair Dan Bailey, executive director Jean McLaughlin, printer and studio coordinator Lisa Blackburn, printer and instructor Steve Miller.
Photo by Robin Dreyer

Ensuring Penland's future has required an increased level of organization and accountability, new kinds of expertise, a more active board, and a larger and more professional staff. While this has taken away some of the extraordinary looseness of the school's earlier years, the overwhelmingly positive feedback from students, instructors, resident artists, and others suggests that the school

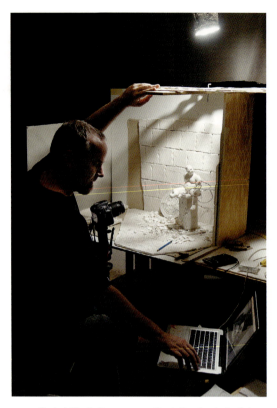

Student Charlie Evergreen working in the clay studio during a 2015 workshop in figurative sculpture and stop animation taught by Cristina Córdova and Arturo G. Córdova. This workshop, in which articulated, fired ceramic sculptures were animated using digital cameras and animation software, is indicative of the kind of innovative programming Penland has been bringing to the craft world for many decades.
Photo by Robin Dreyer

Opposite page:
Student Grace Kim pulling sheets of paper in the books and paper studio, 2012.
Photo by Robin Dreyer

has maintained its commitment to its mission while responding to the changing needs of its constituents. Penland remains a flexible and creative organization dedicated to both personal and artistic growth.

HANDICRAFTS OF THE SPIRIT

Although casual observers sometimes assume that Penland's impact is felt mostly through the objects that are created, participants and close observers know that Penland School is more importantly about an experience—an experience that is routinely described as life changing or transformative. Frequent student Carola Jones, for example, wrote this: "There are places on earth that have the power to open your soul to possibilities, train your hands to be creative, and uplift your heart through friendship and community. Penland does all that for me plus more."

It's easy to hear echoes of words written by Lucy Morgan, decades ago: "I am quite convinced that we cannot hold in our hands, we cannot run sensitive fingers over, we cannot study with discriminating eyes the textures or forms or colorings of our most beautiful and most useful Penland productions. I say these are the Penland intangibles, the wondrous handicrafts of the spirit, things impossible to feel in your fingers or examine under a magnifying glass but real, nevertheless, and tremendously important and of value inestimable. These are the things not made, but won, earned—received, at any rate—in the making of things."

...

Author's note: This chapter is a shortened and updated version of an essay I wrote in 2003 for the book *The Nature of Craft and the Penland Experience*, which was published by Lark Books in conjunction with the school's seventy-fifth anniversary. It's worth noting that I have been Penland's communications director since 1995, and the school has had a profound impact on my personal and professional life. Although I have tried hard to approach the subject from a journalistic rather than a promotional point of view, there is no question that I have a bias and it is this: I love the place.

Notes

1   Besides *Gift from the Hills*, I was unable to find any accounts of what actually took place in 1929. *The Handicrafter*, according to *Gift from the Hills*, was published by Paul Bernat, and he accompanied Worst on his visit to Penland in 1928. Two accounts of the Penland Weavers written by Bonnie Ford make no mention of the 1929 workshop but talk quite a bit about the first Weaving Institute in 1930.

2   In addition to Haystack and Penland, residential craft workshops are now offered by a number of excellent schools, notably Anderson Ranch Arts Center (CO), Arrowmont School of Arts and Crafts (TN), John C. Campbell Folk School (NC), Peters Valley School of Craft (NJ), and Pilchuck Glass School (WA). Countless other institutions offer similar programs in music, dance, theater, personal growth, and other subjects. The total-immersion workshop is used worldwide as a method for teaching languages.

3   My account of this controversial moment in the school's history is based primarily on the records of the Penland board of trustees and the personal papers of John Ehle. I am also grateful for conversations with Cynthia Bringle, Jane Brown, Susan Larson, Mike Page, and Doug Sigler. (Bringle, Larson, and Page were on the board in 1983.)

PENLAND RESIDENT ARTIST PROGRAM

Deborah Morgenthal

The Resident Artist Program at Penland School of Crafts offers artists in every craft medium the chance to spend up to three years living and creating work in Penland's school community. During the residency, artists have an unimpeded opportunity to develop their studio practice, explore new ideas, expand their technical abilities, and hone the business and life skills they will need to become professional artists. Between 1963, when the program began, and 2016, when this book was published, 148 artists benefitted from this distinctive residency. Although the program's structure and selection process have evolved over five decades, its mission has remained remarkably consistent: to provide talented and motivated individuals with the time and space to mature as artists and become an integral part of a community that fosters mutual respect, creativity, and collaboration.

Although the residency directly serves a limited number of artists at one time, their presence on campus has a significant and positive impact on the school; they serve as role models for Penland's core fellows and the more than 1,400 annual workshop students who see the commitment required to become a self-supporting artist. Moreover, when the residents leave the program and pursue careers as studio artists, teachers, or arts-related professionals, they have the potential to influence and inspire hundreds of other artists. Their work is included in public and private collections and museums around the country and abroad, exhibited in nationally recognized exhibitions, and represented by prestigious galleries. Thanks to an endowment gift from the Windgate Charitable Foundation in 2013, Penland's Resident Artist Program will thrive for years to come.

Bill Brown with Penland resident artists, 1965.
Left to right: Ron Burke, Bruce Bangert, Pat Bangert, Skip Johnson, Bill Brown.

SELECTION PROCESS

Resident artists are selected from every category of traditional and nontraditional craft: including books, papermaking, clay, drawing and painting, glass, iron, metals, photography, mixed media, printmaking and letterpress, textiles, and wood. Although there is no bias for one media over another and no bias for functional over sculptural work, the selection committee aims for a balance of different media and styles of working. There are also practical matters to consider—some studios are more suited to certain media, scale, processes, and equipment; some studios are flexible and can be outfitted to suit the individual resident's needs. Only the glass studio, a stand-alone facility, is dedicated to that medium because it provides appropriate ventilation and fire protection.

The selection process is competitive. Currently, between sixty and seventy artists apply for Penland's residency openings. The program has space and funds for seven residents during each three-year period. Occasionally two artist collaborators have shared one residency. The selection committee is headed by the school's program director and also includes one current resident artist who represents the current resident group, one former resident artist, and a respected artist who is active and knowledgeable in the field. This is often a Penland artist-trustee or instructor. Applicants submit work and an application, which includes a statement of intent outlining how they plan to spend their time during those three years and how the opportunity will affect their professional trajectory. The committee recommends candidates to Penland's executive director.

Key selection factors include the applicants' interest in living and working as part of a close-knit community, as well as evidence that they are at a pivotal or transitional time in their work or career. Hoss Haley, for example, arrived as a blacksmith, who primarily made architectural and functional work; when he left the program, he was a sculptor, using metal, concrete, and a range of metal-working techniques. Some residents shift from sculpture to functional work, or from production to one-of-a-kind work. Although this is rare, a few artists have explored a new medium: David Chatt entered the residency as a respected craft artist known for his intricately constructed beaded jewelry and objects; he

"The residency changed my life. It gave me the time to develop the strength to know I could do it—be an artist."

Adela Akers, 1968–1970

Opposite page:
Resident artist Rachel Meginnes working in her studio at The Barns, 2015.
Photo by Mercedes Jelinek

Ceramist Jerilyn Virden working at her studio in The Barns in 2002. Photo by Dana Moore

"I am a huge advocate of the Resident Artist Program. The biggest thing I tell people is you have to be realistic about your financial situation. If you're stressed out just trying to pay the bills, the program may not be the right fit."

Anne Lemanski, 2004–2007

spent his residency focused on glass casting, building equipment as needed and exploring significant shifts in both scale and process for his studio work.

Although some candidates have prior Penland experience, either as a student or core fellow, studio assistant or coordinator, visiting artist or instructor, others come to Penland for the first time as a resident. The school's rural, mountainous location, the "eclectic" nature of the housing and studio spaces, and a community lifestyle are tangible features of the residency experience, and applicants need to be comfortable living in a cohesive, vibrant, communal setting that values friendship and the sharing of ideas.

FINANCIAL SUPPORT

During the three-year residency, Penland's resident artists pay a nominal amount ($185 a month in 2016) for unfurnished housing and studio space, plus their own utilities, which can run about $150 to $200 per month. The school's famously delicious meals are provided free of charge when classes are in session. Residents are also offered one free summer workshop during their residency, can take any workshop on standby for half tuition, and are invited to participate in all other aspects of life at Penland, such as slide nights when instructors show their work, talks by visiting artists, movement classes, gallery events, etc.

The low cost of the residency reduces, but does not eliminate, the financial pressures residents face as they create new work and develop professional relationships for its sale and exhibition through museums, galleries, craft shows, and commissions. Resident artists are expected to be able to pay their bills, including the cost of materials and equipment. When they arrive for the residency, they must equip their studios; fortunately, when they leave the program, they will have the equipment they need to establish their own studios. Penland helps residents supplement their income in a number of ways. Those interested in teaching are considered for Penland workshops. Some have been invited to lead the school's Kids Camp workshops. Others have been selected as visiting artists for partnership programs with the University of North Carolina School of the Arts and Heart of Los Angeles (HOLA). Some, like Peter Adams and Marc Maiorana, were commissioned by the school to build furniture or metal railings.

PROFESSIONAL SUPPORT

Resident artists benefit from local as well as national exposure. They are encouraged to show their work in the Penland Gallery throughout the year, are often invited to participate in invitational exhibitions at the gallery, and are included in its online shop. Frequently, their work is featured in the gallery's national advertising. This exposure gives gallery staff the chance to talk to visitors about the resident artists' work as well as the program itself, and to encourage visitors to drive up the road to see what the residents are working on in their studios in The Barns.

From 1998 until 2011, the Penland Gallery programmed biennial exhibitions of the work of the current resident artists. These on-campus exhibitions afforded residents the opportunity to share their work in a more formal setting outside their studio spaces, to work with gallerists, and to interact with the community, media, and visitors. These group exhibitions have given the artists a chance to reflect on the residency's effect on their work's growth and evolution, to view their work alongside their peers, and to engage in dialogue around their ideas within a creative community.

The gallery's support is important in other ways, too. "Over the years," gallery manager Kathryn Gremley explained, "the gallery has involved the residents in off-campus exhibitions, or we have assisted in some way to facilitate them. More often, the residents have found those opportunities themselves, and I serve as an advisor as needed." She sees her role as a sounding board for a variety of questions pertaining to the marketplace, patrons, pricing, shipping, grant writing, and image selection. Gremley elaborated, "When asked, I give the residents straightforward answers and honest opinions about their work—both finished and in progress. It is a two-way street: they are navigating the ever-changing playing field of exhibitions and galleries, negotiating new and unique challenges. Their collective experiences provide me with a broader insight into the current issues they are facing."

Because resident artist studios are open to the public, the artists have the opportunity to show and sell their work directly to visitors from the region and across the country. Over the course of a year, resident artists have the chance to meet many of the school's 14,000 visitors, more than 1,400 students, and special touring arts, educational, and collector groups. During each session, resident artists host an open house, welcoming students into their studios. Each August, the school holds a "Coffee at The Barns" on the weekend of the Penland Annual Benefit Auction, inviting up to 500 guests into their studios. It is common for residents to sell work and receive commissions as a result of connections made during these events.

As residents promote their work, they experience the prestige the residency conveys, which can provide a strong advantage in the competitive art world. The networking opportunities on campus are advantageous, too: residents get to know the accomplished artists who live in the community and Penland's highly regarded instructors, who come from all over the world to teach workshops at the school. It is not uncommon for residents to form enduring professional connections, mentorships, and lifelong friendships with the artists they meet at Penland.

Gremley, a former core fellow (1983) and resident artist (1984–1987), recalls the impact the residency had on her life: "At the end of three years, I was making the bulk of my living from weaving. I had such great resources as a resident. Early in my residency, I recall being accepted into my first major craft show. I had the work to sell, but no experience with building a booth or creating the marketing tools. Fellow residents and community members loaned me everything I needed and shared their expertise in dealing with the wholesale market. That was the beauty of the experience. Former resident Dan Bailey photographed my work. Textiles instructor Randall Darwall recommended my work to important galleries. This wouldn't have happened if I wasn't a resident artist and didn't have contact with this level of artists."

With all its opportunities, the residency can be a big adjustment. According to Leslie Noell, program director, "Although residents are intentionally given a lot of independence, many have recently come from graduate programs or other residencies, where they were intensely involved with other artists, classwork, and critique. When they first arrive at Penland they can feel somewhat adrift without constant conversation and structure."

Noell, a graphic designer, artist, and former core fellow (1994–1996), provides residents welcome and important support. "I am their primary contact before, during, and after their residency," she explained. "I am available to them as a resource, advisor, and sounding board. I encourage them to seek out opportunities to support their individual goals. This varies from person to person and can include teaching or taking classes—either at Penland or elsewhere—exhibiting work, strengthening the business side of their career, and exploring new concepts or ways of working."

Noell also offers residents feedback on their work, slide presentations, writing, and applications. She often writes letters of support as they apply for grants or future projects. She also facilitates opportunities for residents to interact with core fellows, former resident artists, instructors, and visitors to the school. These connections to the larger community can prompt conversations from the practical—strengthening business practices and setting specific career goals—to the philosophical challenges of making work.

"During the first four months, I was hunting down galleries, sending proposals to publications. Rather than being prolific in the work itself, I did this major PR push. That was hard, because people asked, *So what are you doing?* I was afraid I was promoting work that no one was ever going to see. I didn't realize then how many people were going to come to me. I didn't appreciate then the visibility of being at Penland with 200 people coming to my studio every two weeks."

Vivian Beer, 2005–2008

Bead sculptor and glass artist David Chatt working in his studio in The Barns in 2009.
Photo by Robin Dreyer

Penland resident artists outside The Barns, 2007. Left to right (back): Matt Kelleher, Vivian Beer, Shoko Teruyama, Angela Bubash, Jenny Mendes, Anne Lemanski; (front): Jennifer Bueno, Thor Bueno, Pinkerton.
Photo by Robin Dreyer

PEER SUPPORT

The support residents give one another may be the most essential and distinctive aspect of Penland's Resident Artist Program. Although value is placed on individual responsibility and self-motivation, residents benefit greatly from peer support and the cross-pollination of ideas. Artists enter the residency with different experiences and expertise; some arrive from graduate school, others from apprenticeships or teaching, some from running studio businesses of their own. Often, they are at different stages in their careers. They offer each other all kinds of feedback, technical advice, and emotional support. They influence each other's studio practice—and sometimes the conceptual development of the work itself.

PROGRAM REQUIREMENTS

The residents' main responsibility is to be actively engaged in their work, setting and meeting their own goals. They maintain an open door policy to welcome students, instructors, and the general public into their studios. Although they can invite feedback from their peers, staff members, and others, they are crafting their own use of the residency.

It can take residents that first year to establish a routine for making work and the contacts to show and sell it. Although Penland attracts collectors and customers, resident artists need to keep momentum going on their own to promote their work on a regular basis. This may mean creating a website, developing marketing materials, talking to instructors, negotiating commissions, or reaching out to curators. Each resident grapples with the weight of time and the pressure of possibility in his or her own way. Each finds a way to discover what it takes to be a working artist.

ASSESSING THE PROGRAM'S IMPACT

Clearly, the program has the potential to benefit the work and life of individual resident artists. However, its positive influence extends far beyond the residents in the program in several ways. On an informal basis, residents interact with Penland's core fellows, who regard them as role models for a future professional life; some residents become their mentors. Regardless of their varying levels of experience, residents and core fellows share common interests and goals and they often form lasting friendships, supporting each other's creative endeavors.

Resident artists also have an impact on workshop students, who visit their studios and are inspired by their work and their studio spaces. In addition, many residents teach at Penland during the residency or after, which gives them the opportunity to directly influence students. Moreover, some residents go on to teach in academic art programs and in workshops in the United States and abroad, where their work, experience, and teaching styles have a deep and far-reaching influence on emerging and next-generation artists.

Most concretely, the impact of resident artists is evident in the creation and shaping of the larger community of artists in the Penland area. Since the 1960s, residents have bought homes and set up studios in close proximity to the school after they leave the program. Their presence, in turn, has attracted numerous other artists to live and work in the "neighborhood." Of the nearly 200 studio artists in the area, more than 50 are former resident artists.

This community of artists makes significant contributions to the region's economy. Not only do the artists support the tax base, local schools, and businesses, they collaborate to create vibrant retail opportunities that benefit area restaurants, hotels, and stores. Several co-op galleries have been organized by artists (including former residents), and group sales events attract customers and collectors who travel to the area to buy work directly from artists. Particularly successful are the Spruce Pine Potters Market, which is held every October, and the twice-yearly

"I learned the heart of contemporary crafts during my immersion at Penland. Most importantly, I learned that I could contribute to it—make a living with the work I enjoyed. I went into the residency with uncertainty, and when I left, I was confident that I could create a life doing this."

Marc Maiorana, 2002–2005

Opposite page:
Resident artist Richard Ritter blowing glass, 1970s.
Photo by John Littleton

Resident artist Adela Akers working with a loom, 1970.

"Those years at Penland were an exploration for me as an artist. They gave me time. Most of the young craftspeople were there to improve their skills so they could make a living as an artist. I was there to quit making art for other people and learn to make it for myself."

Evon Streetman, 1971–1975

Toe River Arts Council Studio Tour. This studio tour is the largest, longest running studio tour in the country, attracting hundreds of visitors who create their own self-guided trips from studio to studio through Mitchell and Yancey Counties.

The reach of the program is extended as current and former residents show their work. They are represented in galleries, museums, and cultural centers throughout the United States and abroad. For example, three former Penland resident artists—Vivian Beer, Cristina Córdova, and Marc Maiorana—were featured in *40 under 40: Craft Futures*, a landmark exhibition at the Renwick Gallery of the Smithsonian American Art Museum that showed work by 40 artists born since 1972. The work of former resident artists is in prestigious museum collections, including the Renwick Gallery, the Art Institute of Chicago, New York City's Museum of Arts and Design, the Whitney Museum of American Art, the Metropolitan Museum of Art, the San Francisco Museum of Modern Art, Glasmuseet Ebeltoft in Denmark, and the Victoria and Albert Museum in London.

As with a stone tossed in a pond, the talent and experience of these artists continuously ripple outward, impacting the careers and work of many others.

HISTORY OF THE RESIDENT ARTIST PROGRAM

During his first months as Penland's director in 1962, Bill Brown saw an unmet need to serve artists who wanted to develop studio-based careers and formulated a residency program that he initially called The Winter Craftsman's Residency. The practical objective was to make use of housing and studio spaces that were empty from September to May when summer workshops were over. Brown wanted to invite young artists to spend an extended period of time developing their skills and learning to make a living as professional craftspeople. Brown's vision went further: he viewed the residency as an innovative approach to building a community of crafts people in the area, a way to distinguish Penland from other craft schools in the country, and an opportunity to influence the field of craft itself.

Brown wanted the program to give artists the gift of time, much like a professional internship or apprenticeship. He imagined that "visiting specialists" would offer residents seminars on marketing, simple bookkeeping, how to obtain loans for equipment, and other relevant topics. Speaking in a taped television interview in 1979, he said:

> *A doctor or a lawyer, when they get out of school, can get a job in a law office as a junior partner or they can go to a clinic and be a doctor until they build up their clientele and then they have their own office. Well, a craftsman needs space and he needs a lot of tools or equipment.... Here it was dormant during the wintertime. And I thought, well, we should use the equipment and facilities and bring people who are trained—most of them have a master's degree or equivalent—and have them learn to produce and market their work.*[1]

Brown outlined this model in the rough draft of a grant application, comparing craftsmen with doctors or lawyers who could readily transition by working with other doctors or lawyers. Brown wrote: "The craftsman has no such opportunity because of the limited number of craftsmen working in their own studios, because of the wage laws which prohibit the apprenticeship system, and because each of these individuals is a trained creative person who must work out his own problems and his way of working."[2]

The program officially launched with the arrival of two residents in 1963: woodworker C.R. "Skip" Johnson and Ed Brinkman, a ceramicist. By 1965, Bruce and Pat Bangert, Ron Burke, and Judith Barrow had joined them. Many early residents came into the program from academia; others arrived after working in design and nontraditional craft fields.

BARNS RENOVATION

The most pressing need in these first years was year-round studio space for the residents. Penland's workshops were offered only in the summer, which meant residents were able to work in the workshop studios from September to May but had to vacate them when workshops resumed. This abrupt annual transition was at odds with the continuity of time and focus needed by the resident artists. Brown knew that an uninterrupted amount of time to make work would better enable the residents to become self-sufficient studio artists. And without dedicated studios and housing, the program would always be limited in its focus.

An amazing opportunity presented itself in 1965. Penland's neighbor, the Appalachian School, closed its doors and was selling 220 acres of land and all its buildings. With support from industrialist Philip Hanes, and individual donations personally solicited by Brown, Penland purchased the land and buildings, which not only included housing and a chapel, but pony and dairy barns as well. Brown envisioned converting these barns into permanent studios spaces and apartments for residents. In 1968, with a grant from the James G. Hanes Memorial Fund, the two barns were renovated to provide residents with year-round studios and housing.

Gordon Hanes[3] suggested the studios, then and now fondly referred to as "The Barns," be dedicated as The Terry Sanford Center for Producing Craftsmen. Sanford served as governor from 1961 to 1965, and his administration founded several educational and arts-oriented initiatives, including the University of North Carolina School of the Arts in Winston-Salem.

Now that residents had their own studios, Brown launched concentrations—eight-week intensive workshops—offered in spring and fall. And, with workshops taking place three-quarters of the year, it became necessary and practical to have some long-term scholarship students, who could be in classes March through November, live at the school all year, and help with day-to-day jobs in the dining hall and elsewhere on campus. This was to become the Penland Core Fellowship Program. (See page 37 for more about the origins of the core program in 1970.)

GROWING THE RESIDENT ARTIST PROGRAM

The admission process during Brown's tenure was relational and intuitive: he excelled at choosing artists who were talented, self-reliant, and willing to do whatever was required to maximize the residency opportunity. From 1963 to 1968, about twenty residents benefitted from the program; about five or six artists were residents each year. Some stayed three months, others several years. Mark Peiser, Penland's first glass resident, was one of several artists who brought to fruition Brown's goal of encouraging the residents to remain in the area. Peiser has lived and worked down the hill from the school for decades. Ed Brinkman, Cynthia Bringle, Jane Peiser, Richard Ritter, Jan Williams, Rob Levin, William and Katherine Bernstein, Norm Schulman, and Stanley Andersen are among the early residents who settled in the community. By 2015, fifty-six resident artists had remained in the area after the program, establishing businesses that are vital to the local economy. From the artist pioneers of the '60s and '70s to the program's newest residents, a stable, collaborative, creative community of craftspeople has coalesced to become a dynamic resource and a magnet for other artists.

FACING CHALLENGES

In spite of the obvious benefits of the residency to the individual artists, the school, and the larger community, the cost of subsidizing the program presented on-going financial challenges for Brown and the four directors who followed his tenure. Fundraising to support the program was a constant necessity.

"I think the basic thing I learned from my time at Penland as a resident was that if you extend trust to people, you will not be disappointed. As soon as you got out of your car at Penland, there was a sense that your future was your own responsibility. Bill and the instructors and staff were there to help you in any way they could, but it was up to you to show up."

Mark Peiser, 1967–1970

The Appalachian School dairy barn, 1950s. This building was converted into resident artist studios in 1968. A nearby horse barn was converted into apartments for the artists.

Penland's residency program faced other challenges and growing pains. There was a lack of clarity around the length of the residency; whether residents were obliged to have open studios; how best to evaluate if residents were meeting their goals; how to define whom the program could best serve. Resident artists often functioned somewhat separately from the Penland school community, unclear about what was expected of them apart from the production of their own work. However, the residency program persevered, and directors looked for innovative ways to illustrate its value.

For example, in 1992, director Hunter Kariher helped to mount an exhibit called *Penland Overlook* at the Asheville Art Museum, the debut show of the newly renovated museum. Frank Thomson, the museum's curator, chose 180 objects from forty-eight artists who had been residents from 1963 to 1990. When the exhibition closed in Asheville, it traveled to six other venues on the east coast. The quality of the work validated the strength of the program and called attention to the school's long commitment to serving artists through this residency program.

PURSUING CLARITY

Director Ken Botnick's decision in 1993 to hire Dana Moore and put her in charge of the residency program represented a crucial time of recalibration for the program. Moore clarified the length of the residencies, established professional selection procedures, and created routine annual reviews. Most importantly, for the first time, the school defined the program as serving artists "at transitional points in their careers." As a result of this redefinition, a more diverse group of artists began to apply to the program. According to Moore, "People come into the residency from so many different points. It is equally relevant for people fresh out of grad school, for those who are older and are coming back to making after years of teaching, and for those who have been doing commission work that hasn't allowed for their personal expression. We wanted artists who wouldn't just continue doing the production work they'd done for the past ten years, but who genuinely wanted to make changes."

Going forward, the selection process continued to consider how the program might benefit the individual artists, but also focused on how Penland would benefit from the involvement of these individuals in the larger school community. Moore emphasized, "We wanted someone who wanted to be part of the community at Penland and wouldn't just be alone in her studio."

Dana Moore continued to oversee the residency program for the next nineteen years, and under her watch, and with input and support from director Jean McLaughlin, other refinements were made, such as setting a three-year time frame for the residency (rather than two years with a possible third upon request), clarifying the role of the residents as ambassadors for the school, encouraging residents to explore materials and process through Penland workshops, creating routine open studio events for students, and assessing the impact of having studios open to the public.

Clarity in terms of what the school provided for and expected from the resident artists was also a part of this period. McLaughlin felt strongly that they needed to be fully integrated into the life of the school. She explained, "When I arrived, there was a sense from some of the resident artists that they were hovering on the outskirts of the school. Some preferred this perceived autonomy and independence; others wanted more direct inclusion, engagement, and involvement. One example I noticed is that we described the residents as being 'adjacent to the school.' While this could have meant 'adjacent to the workshops on the core campus,' the residency had become perceived as being disconnected from the heart of the organization. I believed the Resident Artist Program needed to be fully embraced, integrated smoothly, and understood as central to the mission of the organization. It may sound like a small thing, but we began offering the residents all meals in the school's dining hall as a benefit of the residency and a direct way to connect the residents with daily campus activities. And, we began talking about the program as integral to the

"Though Karen and I hadn't originally intended to settle in North Carolina, in the end that's exactly what we did. We bought an old farm about fifteen minutes from the school. I built a studio and settled into the life of a full-time studio potter. It has been satisfying to be surrounded not only by old friends we've known since 1979, but by the gentle yet constant influx of new artists, new friends, drawn to the area in the past thirty-five years by the presence of Penland School."

Stanley Mace Andersen, 1979–1983

Resident artist Ann Marie Kennedy dyeing handmade paper, 2002.
Photo by Dana Moore

Opposite page:
Resident artist David Eichelberger preparing clay, 2012.
Photo by Wes Stitt

Resident artist Mercedes Jelinek conducting an informal photography workshop with a group of clay students, 2014. Photo by Robin Dreyer

school. Providing a residency program for the professional development of artists fit appropriately within Penland's mission and fully met the historic role of the Resident Artist Program."

McLaughlin and Moore articulated the expectations of the program: resident artists were to be full-time artists testing ideas and making choices that would have a lasting effect on their work and their lives. They would be developing their studio practice, while working out the practicalities of earning a living as artists. Although the primary expectation of resident artists was to focus on the development of their work, they were also required to have an open door policy, welcoming students, instructors, and the public to their studios. This would be done informally and through open houses during each workshop session and at the benefit auction. Residents would be ambassadors for the school and share information about the school with visitors. They were welcome to attend demonstrations in the workshop classes, attend slide lectures, and be involved in all special offerings of the school. Moreover, they would be encouraged to plan resident group exhibitions and would be invited to talk about their work when opportunities arose. They could also take a free class of their choosing and were eligible for any class on a standby scholarship basis.

In 2013, Leslie Noell, who managed the educational component of the Core Fellowship Program, became director of programs and advisor to the resident artists and the core fellows. One of her goals has been to strengthen the mutually beneficial relationships between these two groups. According to Noell, "Resident artists and core fellows naturally have a lot in common. Core fellows look to the resident artists as people at the next stage in the career they imagine for themselves."

Residents, for the same reason, have an easy understanding of where core fellows are in their evolution, having been in a similar place earlier in their life. Noell explained, "If residents are looking for ways to connect with the school, they may choose to go see what the core fellows are doing in a class, which then gives them a way to meet instructors and other students. Most residents are keen to have that interaction, so they develop an interest in what core fellows are up to. I find them to be incredibly generous with core fellows, often taking them under their wing and assuming a dual peer/mentor role."

SECURING A CREATIVE FUTURE

Due to the vision and commitment of Penland's directors, staff, and participating artists, the Resident Artist Program continues to be a vital part of Penland School of Crafts. Under McLaughlin's leadership, the Resident Artist and the Core Fellowship Programs received endowment gifts in 2013 from the Windgate Charitable Foundation to fund these programs in perpetuity. "The resident artist endowment gift reinforced the power of this program to affect the lives of artists in deeply significant ways," McLaughlin stressed. "The Windgate Foundation wants to encourage creativity in all its exuberant, spontaneous, and innovative aspects."

In Windgate board president Robyn Horn's words, "The residency produces a valuable group of alumni who help promote the school because of the positive experience they've had there. The opportunity offered to residents is pretty overwhelming, and because of it, residents have gone out into the larger craft community and either taught or spread the word about Penland in their preferred way, and this has an enormous impact on others."

Since the beginning of the Penland residency and continuing to the present day, artists have acknowledged the critical role the program played in their lives as artists, educators, and professionals in a range of crafts-related careers. Dana Moore underscored one key benefit of the residency: "In other contexts for craft, such as some university fine arts programs, a student can easily feel that *the idea* is the thing—and once the idea is complete, creating a tangible piece based on

> "By nature, artists are experimental, and that was the idea behind the residency program—to take some of the financial pressures off, so you could stretch your wings and fly, and not have to worry as much about having to sell work. There was no way you could fail!"
>
> Stephen Dee Edwards, 1980–1983

that idea is almost redundant. In the Penland residency, not only is the object essential to conveying the idea, but the object, and the process itself, become the sources for new ideas."

EMBRACING THE LIFE

Fiber artist Rachel Meginnes, who completed her residency in 2015, makes tangible what Moore was describing. Meginnes can cite an impressive list of accomplishments and activities that detail how she spent her three years expanding her skills as an artist and educator, and how her talent and dedication benefitted other residents and core fellows. She created an outstanding new body of work, examples of which were included in more than a dozen exhibitions around the country. She was featured in the 2014 winter issue of *Surface Design*. She taught a range of classes: a one-week class at Penland in 2014; a three-day workshop at Maiwa in Vancouver, Canada; textile workshops at Haystack and Arrowmont; and material exploration workshops at the Heart of Los Angeles, an afterschool program for underserved children in LA. She mentored core fellows as part of an ongoing seminar in professional practices. She served as the juror of the national fiber exhibition EXCITE, which showcased contemporary fiber work based on the work of Anni Albers at Black Mountain College. She received numerous commissions from private collectors. Meginnes will be teaching a fall concentration at Penland in 2016.

As she reflected on her time-intensive, multifaceted experience, Meginnes said, "The residency is about having a life—you have to focus on everything: making work, selling work, making money, exploring your artistic expression, connecting with your peers, finding time for your partner, eating, and sleeping." The most valuable aspect of the residency for her was the connection to other artists and the opportunity to push her work. "I worked very hard to make the most of the residency," she said. "I had to make hard choices about how to spend my time—and most of it was in my studio making work so that I could grow as an artist."

Following her residency, Meginnes accepted a one-year teaching position at her alma mater, Earlham College, in Richmond, Indiana. "In graduate school, I was planning to teach," she explained, "but I wound up being more interested in making work. Now I know I can combine teaching with maintaining a studio practice. I learned I could do both as a result of all my experiences while I was a Penland resident."

1 Transcribed from *Penland Summer 1979*, a television feature, produced by WTVI, Charlotte, NC, 1979.

2 Penland Archives, John Ehle correspondence.

3 Gordon and Phillip Hanes were part of the Hanes family that founded the Hanes Corporation, based in Winston-Salem, NC. They were important donors to the University of North Carolina and the North Carolina Museum of Art.

"I've since forgotten exactly how many footsteps there are between the Upper Farmhouse where I lived as a resident and The Barns studio. But something about that distance is an ideal, representing the need for reflection coming and going from the studio. This has stayed with me. Also, the importance of maintaining forward momentum in the shop no matter how crazy and distracting the world outside is."

James Lawton, 1983–1985

Flameworker Micah Evans working in the glass studio at The Barns, 2015.
Photo by Robin Dreyer

PENLAND CORE FELLOWSHIP PROGRAM

Deborah Morgenthal

For more than four decades, Penland's Core Fellowship Program has offered talented, self-motivated, and energetic young artists the opportunity to live, study, and work at the school as they explore their artistic interests, skills, and professional options. This unique two-year fellowship provides nine students with a mutually beneficial arrangement: in exchange for working twenty-five hours per week for eight months completing essential jobs for the school, core fellows receive room, board, and a small stipend, and five summer workshops each year, choosing from more than one hundred classes, as well as two eight-week concentration workshops—one in the spring and one in the fall. In addition, they exhibit their artwork in the annual Core Show, work in their own studios, and learn relevant professional skills. Some participants view the fellowship as an alternative to graduate school; some see it as a way to prepare for graduate school; others use the time to learn the basics of production crafts; many experiment in a new medium or further their skills in an existing one. Unlike any other member of the Penland community, core fellows are integrated into every aspect of life at the school.

All nine core fellows live together in a large house on the Penland campus. Over the course of two years, they form a community of creative peers, offering each other true fellowship—a linchpin of this challenging program. The complexity and intensity that arises from living and working together invites problem-solving opportunities that help them mature as artists and individuals.

HANDS-ON LEARNING

Penland's ever-changing learning environment, which includes world-class artists and instructors in dozens of media, allows core fellows to tailor their experience to meet their individual goals as they prepare for careers in studio art, education, and arts-related fields. Often, they are mentored by Penland's instructors, resident artists, and local artists, who demonstrate what the life of a studio artist looks like and encourage the fellows to learn and grow. This interaction provides an unprecedented opportunity to network with outstanding artists in every field of contemporary craft. The atmosphere of the program, like the school itself, is one of support, collaboration, hard work, mutual respect, shared enthusiasm—and play.

In practical terms, the daily tasks core fellows perform for Penland are essential to the school's ability to meet the needs of students, instructors, staff, and visitors. Working as weekend cooks, dining hall managers, gardening assistants, and entertainment coordinators places them at the heart of Penland's operations and helps them develop leadership and time-management skills. Moreover, their dual role as workers and students has a positive impact on others: they model the dedication, hard work, and curiosity of makers, while demonstrating a commitment to the daily well-being of the school. Their engagement in the sessions helps generate the creative momentum and esprit de corps that is a vital part of the Penland experience and ethos.

The only two-year work-study program of its kind in the country,[1] the fellowship has evolved over time to reflect the changing needs of the school and the participants. To date, 224 individuals have participated in the program and about 70 percent continue to practice as artists or work in art-related fields after the fellowship. A 2013 endowment from the Windgate Charitable Foundation ensures that dozens more talented young artists will be able to contribute their insights and fresh ideas to the Penland community.[2] Robyn Horn, board president of the Windgate Charitable Foundation and a strong advocate for the program, reflected that, "These students help the school in so many important ways. They are the face of the school. The program has earned well-deserved recognition, and is attracting talented, better-prepared applicants. The fellowship is valuable to the school and to the artists who are chosen to participate."

Instructor Beth Ross Johnson and core fellow Zee Boudreaux in the textiles studio, 2012. Photo by Robin Dreyer

"When I reflect on my time as a core student, what strikes me most is the wholeness of the experience, the joy of always being busy, of always working productively, whether at my job or in class. It was like being awake all the time, seeing and feeling how the things I was learning to do with my hands and body and mind in the dish room fed straight into the things I learned to do in the studio, and vice versa."

Wes Stitt, 2008–2009

Opposite page:
Core fellow and studio coordinator Elizabeth Brim in the old Penland iron studio, 1986.

Penland core fellows, 2009. Left to right (back): Jessica Heikes, Christina Boy, Wes Stitt, Marianne Dages, Leah Frost; (front): Beth Schaible, Joshua Kuensting, Mark Warren, Jason Bige Burnett.
Photo by Robin Dreyer

"Working with that group of core students, I had to learn to get along and engage and build relationships. We created a family of artists. We relied on each other. You pick your friends, but this group is just handed to you. You're thrown together by chance, and then these people become your closest friends for a lifetime."

Daniel Essig, 1992–1994

SELECTION PROCESS

Over the years, the selection process has become more formalized and competitive. In 2014, 112 applicants applied for four openings compared with only nineteen in 2006. One reason for this increase is that, since 2006, core fellow candidates are no longer required to have previous experience at Penland. With each ensuing year, the number of strong candidates with impressive artistic skill and clearly articulated goals has risen.

Today's applicants come from all over the country, with different educational and work backgrounds. However, those selected share common traits: "Penland is looking for talented, self-motivated, and service-oriented artists who have reached a moment in their lives when the program will be a pivotal experience," explained program director Leslie Noell, herself a former core fellow (1994–1996). A solid foundation in creative practice is important, as is interest in working with the materials and processes that comprise Penland's workshop sessions.

Candidates also are assessed for their willingness to be part of a close-knit community of their peers. Core fellows need to be independent and self-directed, but they also need to have or to develop the ability to work and live in a communal setting that values collaboration, friendship, and the sharing of ideas. Applicants submit images of their work, along with a written statement of intent in which they describe their goals for the fellowship and their understanding of the program's value to them. They also submit two letters of recommendation: one from someone who can address the candidate's work ethic and strengths as an employee or volunteer, and one from someone who knows the candidate's studio work well and can address his or her ability to take advantage of the educational benefits of the program.

Penland's program director leads the core selection process and brings together a knowledgeable review panel. The process includes current core fellows and the school's services manager, who oversees the core fellows' daily work responsibilities and evaluates the work experience of applicants. Former services manager Taylor Shelton emphasized, "I look at their work experience to see if they have had jobs that are similar to what we need. They don't need to be master gardeners to be assigned to the garden crew, but they have to be willing to learn, and be accountable, flexible, multitaskers, who can smile, even when they are stressed." The program director and the selection committee review the candidate's portfolio and written materials. Final recommendations are then made to Penland's executive director.

Applicants arrive with varied intentions and prior educational and life experiences. According to Noell, many candidates express the desire to work in a variety of media. Someone may have a background in clay but want to come to Penland to take clay, iron, and wood classes. Others may have studied history or music and along the way discovered a love for making jewelry or furniture. Many candidates want to learn and evolve as craftspeople but aren't interested in earning another degree. Noell explained, "There are also many students who come to us from strong academic programs in art, craft, and design. Although they have a highly developed conceptual foundation, they say 'I have all these great ideas, and I feel like I've received a lot of critical feedback, but I don't know how to make what I want to make. I want to spend two years gathering skills so that I can make anything I can think of, and then my ideas will never be limited by my technical understanding.' The fellowship program allows them to do just that."

THE SERVICE SIDE OF CORE

Penland's program director and services manager share oversight of the program; one focuses on the fellows' educational development and the other supervises their work duties. New core fellows arrive ten days before the start of spring sessions for orientation and training with the services manager and the core fellows who performed that job the previous year.

When classes are in session, core fellows complete their work assignments over an average of twenty-five hours each week. In most cases, they keep the same job for a year. A handbook details the responsibilities of the available positions, which include jobs such as weekend cook, dining hall manager, garden assistant, driver, and entertainment coordinator.

Work hours are scheduled for a set time frame each day to help instructors know when core fellows are available for class activities and to help fellows manage their time. According to Shelton, "Core fellows are expected to balance their workload with their sessions and their studio time to get their work for the school done and done well. They are really good at finding creative solutions to meet their core obligations and stay on top of their classes."

In addition to their scheduled duties, all core fellows participate in "changeovers" between sessions, when they lead crews of work-study students in preparing the campus for students and instructors for the next session—cleaning rooms, changing linens on the beds, etc. Their help is also called upon during community open houses, board meeting weekends, fundraising events, and holiday activities surrounding the annual Easter egg hunt and July 4th parade.

Although the core jobs are not difficult, they require attention to detail, dedication, and accountability. As Shelton pointed out, "Compared to other students, core fellows are ambassadors for the school—and they are artists—so they are always making the switch between their multiple roles, from service to education. It's quite challenging."

In spite of these multiple and sometimes conflicting demands, core fellows deeply appreciate their life at Penland. They enjoy the feeling of ownership that comes with being an essential part of Penland's day-to-day operations and take pride in the jobs they perform. Many describe these responsibilities as providing a much-needed balance to the artistic challenges they face in workshops; helping set up an instructor's slide presentation is sometimes less stressful than learning a new metals technique or preparing to show your new work to visitors. The rigorous schedule they maintain requires them to stay focused and juggle the business of Penland with the business of making art. This prepares core fellows for the reality of what it means to make a living as an artist—they learn how to prioritize, set goals, and apply their energy in the right place at the right time. This serves them long after the fellowship ends and is an essential skill former core fellows often mention when they talk about the lasting benefits of the program.

FINANCIAL SUPPORT

Core fellows today receive tuition-free classes and room and board, plus a stipend of $40 every two weeks to help cover the cost of materials for workshops, gas for their cars, and other incidentals. However, the program can be a challenge for fellows who do not have enough money to meet their various expenses. During the interview process, Noell encourages applicants to total their monthly expenses—cell phone, car insurance, gas, student loans, credit card payments—and then add an estimate for studio fees and materials. The best scenario is to come into the program with that amount saved up or to accept that they will incur some level of debt during the two years. "Most core fellows need a way to come up with additional income," Noell said. "I try to be really upfront with them about this, so there are no surprises. Some can find freelance work to do remotely during the winter. Others make production work to sell throughout the year. We try to help them partner with artists in the area who might need a short-term assistant. The price of this opportunity is to struggle with the reality of the financial challenges, which is not unlike the price of any other artistic pursuit, where you're not in a nine-to-five salaried situation."

"I think I really internalized the idea that I am able to do anything and get along with anyone. I met so many different people while at Penland and tried so many different things. When you're a core fellow, you bounce around a lot: one minute you're welcoming a world-renowned artist to campus and the next minute you're scrubbing a shower curtain with a toothbrush. These kinds of discrepancies have led me to be flexible, friendly, and jump into just about any project that I need to undertake."

Benares Angeley, 2000–2002

Core fellows Jamie Karolich and Daniel Garver working as weekend cooks in the Penland kitchen, 2015.
Photo by Robin Dreyer

> "The freedom and flexibility of the core program helped me find my own sense of direction and forced me to become more self-disciplined in my art/craft practice. Being surrounded by other artists working in a diversity of media was eye-opening and has vastly benefitted my ability to think creatively and critically about my work."
>
> Liz Koerner, 2012–2014

EDUCATIONAL OPPORTUNITIES

At the heart of this hands-on work and educational experience is the unprecedented opportunity for core fellows to take tuition-free workshops in well-equipped, professional studios, taught by outstanding instructors across all media—traditional and nontraditional, plus two eight-week concentrations. Although many classes are materials- and technique-based, others are more concept-oriented. Without the external pressure of grades or formal critique, fellows feel free to select workshops that match their individual artistic journey, motivated by the desire to expand their creative experience. They can choose to develop skills in one medium or in several. The wide variety of workshops invites cross-disciplinary experimentation and creative risk-taking. Moreover, being exposed to so many different instructors gives fellows the chance to experience a range of teaching styles—a close-up view of the craft of teaching.

Living on campus year-round presents a predictable set of challenges that core fellows learn to accommodate. Summer workshops and Penland activities keep them busy and engaged. Fall and spring concentrations allow sustained immersion in one media. During the winter, they have time to process ideas, assimilate learning, and work independently in the teaching studios, where they can take advantage of the space and equipment. Their core work for the school is suspended from late November to late February, allowing them focused time in the studio.

PROFESSIONAL DEVELOPMENT

To supplement what they learn in workshops, core fellows attend professional development seminars organized by the program director every spring and fall during the two-month concentrations. Led by a volunteer community or staff member, the group meets every Monday night for eight weeks to discuss a range of relevant topics, from philosophical discussions about the creative process to professional practices, such as writing and marketing. For instance, in February, when new core fellows join the program and team building is important, the topics are open-ended, such as "Why do I make work? Who are my influences? What do I struggle with? How do I get unblocked?" Then, in the fall, the topics are more concrete, including how to apply for grants or residencies, strategies for acceptance into shows or galleries, and ways to develop and manage a website.

Noell's oversight of the fellowship program provides core fellows with emotional as well as professional support; her past experience as a participant gives her insight as their advisor, sounding board, and champion. She meets with them as a group weekly to discuss school-related updates and events, make plans for upcoming projects, and help address issues that may arise. She also meets with them individually to explore more specific questions or concerns.

One of Noell's main missions is to encourage core fellows to pursue opportunities that support their individual goals. She described, "This varies from person to person and can include choosing classes, seeking exhibition opportunities, negotiating commissions, and identifying professional intentions. I help them with whatever they need, whether it is putting together a slide presentation, evaluating a portfolio, or deciding whether to pursue graduate studies or not. I write many letters of recommendation or support for grants, future projects, or academic programs. And I offer feedback and critique about their studio work."

In addition, Noell finds and facilitates networking prospects between current fellows and other artists, including former core fellows, resident artists, instructors, and visitors to the school. She conducts annual reviews and exit interviews, which help core fellows assess how well they are meeting their goals and how well the program is meeting the needs of the school.

She is also a tireless advocate: "I promote the program and the core fellows on a national scale," Noell explained. "I encourage the core fellows to think beyond Penland and help them make connections with people in the field when-

Core fellow Jake Chamberlain working in the wood studio, 1996.
Photo by Dana Moore

Opposite page:
Core fellows Molly Spadone and Rachel Garceau making slip-cast porcelain forms in the clay studio, 2013.
Photo by Robin Dreyer

> "I never expected to be so challenged on so many levels. I'm still sorting through it all. I learned that to be a self-employed creative person is all about endurance and patience. If you just keep making things, things will happen, slowly but surely."
>
> Marianne Dages, 2008–2009

ever I can. I also keep the school informed about the core fellows, their accomplishments, classes, projects, and exhibitions. I initiate conversations about the program with Penland staff, resident artists, and colleagues, and garner support for change as needed—whether that has to do with facility improvements or modifying the selection criteria."

Other Penland staff and board members offer encouragement and support, too, as do the resident artists who often become mentors of individual core fellows. Local artists are a resource, as well, providing a realistic view of the life of professional studio artists. From these artists, fellows can learn how to develop studio practice, run a production line, deal with galleries, balance work and personal life, and much more.

ANNUAL CORE SHOW

Another important component of the fellowship program is the annual Core Show held in the fall. Originating at Gorelick Social Hall in the Northlight building in the early 1990s, the exhibition and the satellite activities honoring the fellows have, over the years, become part of core fellowship lore. From 1999 to 2014, the show alternated between the Penland Gallery and Northlight, and in the 1980s a more low-key version took place at Ridgeway Hall.

Core fellows plan, curate, and install the exhibition when the show is held in Northlight—a complicated but rewarding group activity. This exhibition is their opportunity to formally share the artwork made in and out of Penland classes throughout the year with their family, friends, and the community. An important element of the exhibition experience is working on the professional practices required for an exhibition: delivering the work on time and ready to hang; preparing an invoice, writing descriptions that list materials and techniques; creating a résumé and artist statement. Responsibilities for the event are divided among the group: invitations, preparing the space with freshly painted pedestals and white walls, installation, and the creation of the core book—an artistic record of the year's participants that has taken many different and inventive forms over the decades.

Director Jean McLaughlin with core fellows at the annual core show, 2001. Left to right: Matthew Thomason, April Franklin, Jeannine Marchand, Darryl Maleike, Jean McLaughlin, Eric Dekker, Ronan Peterson, Celia Gray, Meredith Brickell, Benares Angeley, Kelly O'Briant. Photo by Robin Dreyer

Kathryn Gremley, director of the Penland Gallery, has served as an informal advisor for the Northlight show for many years. As she described it: "I may be asked to weigh in on practical issues, such as editing or curating their body of work, pricing, the placement of pieces, or to share my thoughts on ways to incorporate disparate works. The idea of the Northlight exhibition is for core fellows to conceptualize and facilitate it on their own."

The core fellows benefit from Gremley's knowledge as a curator, exhibition designer, and retailer. She meets with them as a group early in the year to clarify the expectations and then meets with them individually prior to the exhibition to discuss the works they want to include in the show. She always encourages them to retain the strongest work from their summer classes, knowing they often complete much of the work for the show in the three-week break between summer and fall.

Gremley aptly described the unique situation of these annual shows: "We encourage core fellows to immerse themselves in classes, learn new techniques, step out of their comfort zone, risk failure, and change gears every two weeks all summer. And then we ask them to present some of their work to their peers, family, and patrons. The conditions under which the work is made are unique, and the work is, most often, quite remarkable."

Many staff and community members help to achieve this special evening—volunteering time, expertise, and support in various ways. The exhibition also provides opportunities for critiques with mentors and occasional commissions that result in studio work for the winter ahead. The Core Show is a highlight of each year, a time when the whole community celebrates the fellows and the program.

PEER SUPPORT

In addition to what core fellows learn in workshops, seminars, and from the Core Show, their peers become an important source of ideas and inspiration. In fact, many core fellows regard their collaborative and supportive interaction with one another to be the most valuable aspect of the program. In their shared studio on the top floor of Ridgeway, the nine work spaces showcase the distinct interests and talents of each individual. Core fellow Will Lentz (2012–2014), when only months away from completing his second year, described the scene: "Often, several of us are working in the studio at the same time, listening to music, and we're very engaged with what we're doing, but we're also tossing ideas back and forth. It's great to be up there working together like that."

A visit to the core fellows house also reflects this communal creativity. Each bedroom announces the occupant's unique aesthetic. The walls and shelves of the shared spaces are decorated with artwork purposefully left behind by previous core fellows. The kitchen features foods that are labeled for common use, as well as food the owners would prefer not to share. According to Lentz, "When we're relaxing at the house, we talk about what we're working on in sessions, what might be stressing us about our core jobs, what we're thinking about doing when we leave the program. These conversations are really important to me."

Core fellows Ele Annand and Ian Henderson working in the outdoor area of the clay studio, 2010.
Photo by Robin Dreyer

The sharing of food, ideas, and experiences creates a supportive environment, in which core fellows feel safe to explore their artistic goals. They support each other with their service work, too; if one fellow has to be away for a few days, others will pitch in to cover those tasks. As artists, they offer each other consistent feedback and encouragement. They observe one another's studio work evolve from sample to prototype to series. They witness the process from experimental beginnings to confident finish, and everything in between. In contrast to this continuity in the studio and in their core tasks, they experience the frequent arrival and departure of instructors and classmates. The constant in this mutable environment is each other, and they build, over time, a trusted creative peer group. After a while, there is no need to provide history or context—this exists easily and lasts long after the fellowship. "My own core group," says program director Leslie Noell, "more than twenty years later, is still an important part of my internal benchmark system. As I evaluate my work and progress, they are present either actually or in spirit. They remain important colleagues, sources of inspiration, and friends. I warn current core fellows that their core group may not be easily shed, and I hear again and again that this turns out to be true."

"I learned how sweet it is to be friends with people that aren't just like you. So many of the people I would never have known in the 'real' world are now my most cherished friends."

Dana Fehsenfeld, 2007–2008

Living, working, and learning together for two years, they become a community of distinct individuals who share the goal of pursuing creative expression. The back side of Morgan Hall, the house currently used by the core fellows, graphically illustrates this point: from this vantage, most of the bedroom windows are visible. Despite the eclectic nature of the individual rooms, this family of windows, when seen from the outside, conveys order, connection, and intimacy, mirroring the relationships the core fellows have with each other.

MEASURE OF SUCCESS

At a time when the percentage of art majors in the United States who continue to remain active as artists is below 10 percent, it is a remarkable accomplishment that more than 70 percent of Penland's core fellows continue to pursue the arts as a career. They teach in colleges and universities across the country; they make a living as studio artists or designers for industry; they work for arts nonprofit organizations. Many former core fellows combine arts-related jobs with work as studio artists. Many return to Penland as studio assistants and instructors. Sixteen have later become resident artists, while forty-eight have settled in the Western North Carolina area and set up studios.

Morgan Hall, 1960s. Built in 1916 by the Appalachian School and named in honor of Lucy Morgan's brother, Rufus Morgan, this building has served for many decades as the group living quarters of the core fellows.

In September 2014, a grant from the National Endowment for the Arts enabled Penland to host its first core retreat and reunion, a one-week open studio residency for seventy-five core fellows. All current and former core fellows were invited to apply, and participants were selected on a first-come, first-served basis. Penland hired three former core fellows, Courtney Dodd, Rachel Garceau, and Jason Burnett, to help with the planning, facilitating, and documenting of the event. The school also hired studio assistants in each area to facilitate the work of participating artists. Former core fellows from every decade (the 1970s to the present) attended, some people returning to Penland for the first time in more than twenty years. The theme of the week was focused studio time; artists arrived in the studios early Monday morning and barely broke for meals until Saturday morning. The week provided a chance for old friends to reconnect with Penland and each other. It was also a chance for core fellows from a span of many years to meet one another and connect as alumni of this influential and singular program. The retreat was a success by all measures—it was experimental, productive, surprising, and meaningful to its participants—and requests were immediately received for a repeat performance.

HISTORY OF THE CORE FELLOWSHIP PROGRAM

In 1970, Penland's director, Bill Brown and his wife, Jane, were looking for ways to expand scholarship opportunities for dedicated students and also address Penland's operational needs as the number of sessions and students grew. These goals led to the creation of the core program, so named because students performed core jobs that helped the school run. Jane Brown, describing the program's origins said: "We noted quite quickly that the scholarship students seemed to develop a truly loving, cooperative spirit for the welfare of the school and that their presence gave an inspiration to the entire school community. The longer they stayed on the grounds, the more they grew in active devotion to the projects, cooked up and volunteered new adventures for us; they literally and figuratively became part owners and protectors of the Penland dream."[3]

To reward this energy and commitment, Bill Brown annually invited four or five work-study students—who later were called core students—to return for another season and stay from March through November. In exchange for working about twenty hours a week, they received room and board, and could take—tuition free—any of the summer sessions that appealed to them, plus a fall and spring concentration. Jane Brown scheduled and supervised their core work.

These early core students were an interdependent group, sharing their creative ideas and helping one another with core duties. Although there was no formal program to support their professional development, they sought feedback from instructors and community area craftspeople on an individual basis. Some core students focused on several media, others on just one. As Linda Foard Roberts, a core student in 1982, noted: "I took only photography classes while I was a core student, but I gathered inspiration by wandering through other studios to see what students in other disciplines were studying."

ONGOING EVOLUTION

When the Browns left, interim director Richardson Rice hired Susan Chin, a former core student, to oversee the core students' work for the school. When Chin left, she passed the baton to Geraldine Plato, who had been a core student in 1983. Plato continued in this role when Verne Stanford took the reins as Penland's director in 1984. When Stanford's wife, Joy, arrived several months later, Plato and Joy Stanford divided up the mounting responsibilities and created another job for Plato, called services coordinator (now services manager), to work closely with the core students on their work tasks. In the following years, a number of dedicated people, including Tim Veness, Nita Forde, Robert Chiarito, and Mark Boyd, served in this capacity.

Over the next decade, important refinements were made to the program. Core student work hours were established at twenty-five hours a week. The length of

Penland core fellows, 1991. Left to right: (back) Gretchen Oubre, Susan Hutchinson, Rosie Sharpe, Mark Tomczak, Mare Schelz; (front) Whitney Nye, Lucille, Jennifer Joyce, Bradley Walters, Chuck DeWolfe.

Opposite page:
Core fellow Elmar Fujita working on a piece of furniture in the wood studio, 2015.
Photo by Robin Dreyer

"Jane and Bill treated us like an extension of their family. They wanted us to behave in a manner that reflected the school in a positive way, to work hard, and make the school coherent with their vision."

Susan Chin, 1983–1984

Core fellow Daniel Beck working in the iron studio, 2010.
Photo by Robin Dreyer

the fellowship was set at two years. The number of summer sessions core students could participate in was set at five—and they were allowed to pick whatever classes they wanted. The requirement that applicants have previous work-study experience at Penland was eliminated. And, a commitment was made to core students that they could live on campus and work in the studios during the winter.

PRESENTING AND MARKETING THEIR WORK

Over the years, core fellows have had various formal and informal opportunities to present and market their work. At each session's close, students across the studios bring their work together in an informal "show and tell" exhibition. In addition, scholarship auctions each session provide core fellows with a chance to see how their fellow students and the community respond to their work. Trading and bartering has also been an active part of Penland's culture.

During the 1990s, a core fellows gallery was created in a room adjacent to the Penland coffee house, then located in the Craft House. When the coffee house moved to the Pines in 2009, the core gallery moved with it. Core fellows are in charge of the upkeep and layout of this space. Beginning in 2009, they were also invited to sell their work in the Penland Gallery. Since 2006, core fellows have organized an open house during the annual Penland Benefit Auction, giving them an opportunity to meet auction guests and talk with collectors about their work and the program. These opportunities to show and sell their work not only provide fellows with much-needed income, they also give them an opportunity to test-market their ideas.

One special exhibition has been held to recognize the remarkable achievements of Penland's previous core fellows. In 1999, Penland Gallery director Kathryn Gremley curated *Alida to Zack: 28 Years of Penland's Core Program*. For the exhibition, she contacted all former and current core fellows, inviting those who were makers to submit a piece, and 80 percent participated. The name of the exhibit refers to Alida Fish, who was the first core fellow, and Zack Noble, who was in the group of core fellows in 1999. This impressive exhibition demonstrated the talent of past and present core students and presented the commitment of core fellows to maintaining artistic careers.

INCREASING PROFESSIONAL DEVELOPMENT

From its earliest inception, Penland staff recognized the need to enhance the educational component of the core program. As part of that goal, Geraldine Plato and others advocated for a staff person to be in charge of the core students' development as craftspeople and professionals. Progress was made in this direction in 1993 when director Ken Botnick hired Dana Moore and Geraldine Plato to be assistant directors. Moore's area of responsibility was programming of workshops and supervision of the Resident Artist Program; Plato was responsible for daily operations, which included the core student program.

During the seven years that Plato worked in this capacity, she was aided by several services managers in structuring the daily workload of the core students, enabling Plato to address such strategic issues as guiding students in their choice of sessions. She also headed up the selection process, which evolved as the school expanded. Plato explained, "When the new glass studio was built, we were then able to accept core students who were interested in pursuing glass. As sessions came to represent the diversity of contemporary crafts, with additions such as letterpress and book arts, we were able to invite candidates with interests in those areas."

Professional support for core students was further bolstered when Jean McLaughlin became Penland's director in 1998. She recalled thinking the program was skewed towards service, and not strongly enough towards art and education. "I believe the program is an important alternative route to what academia offers. The historic bartering of work for education is quite relevant today, especially given the high cost of graduate school," she explained.

> "Being a core student opened my eyes to the idea of making a living with clay, not trying to get a server job or work in a bookstore. Technically, the core program gave me the ability to be a professional studio potter."
>
> Ronan Peterson, 2000–2002

When Stacey Lane was hired as director of studios and student affairs, she began inviting different area artists to mentor core students. Visiting artist Christina Shmigel developed this idea into a two-month seminar. Since that time, area artists have led core seminars every fall and spring. Then, in 2005, Laura Way, Penland's director of operations and finance, asked Leslie Noell, who was working part-time for the school as a graphic designer, if she would be interested in becoming core program coordinator. Noell agreed to work one day each week in this capacity and became the first person contracted to serve as an educational advisor.

In that capacity, Noell assessed how core fellows were functioning individually and as a group. She offered critiques of the work they were doing in classes. Based on their stated goals and their progress, she advised them to take certain classes and identified mentors in the larger craft community. When, in 2013, Noell became Penland's director of programs, oversight of the core program was incorporated into her new job. According to McLaughlin, "Leslie deserves credit for the incredible success of the core program as it functions today. It wouldn't have evolved into the dynamic educational experience it is without Leslie's work."

Noell had a clear agenda: "I felt the core program was as influential in my education as my undergraduate and graduate degrees. But when I listed it on my résumé, no one knew what I was talking about. It just sounded like I was a weekend cook. There was no description yet of the program that communicated the ways the program mattered to me."

She suggested a new name: the Core Fellowship Program. Noell stressed, "I didn't want to lose the 'core' part, but I wanted to add gravitas. I also wanted it to be a program young artists could find as they researched fellowship and residency opportunities." In 2006 the new name was adopted.

MOVING OUT INTO THE WORLD

After two years of concentrated work, learning, and communal living, core fellows leave Penland to establish their own studios, engage in residencies, tackle graduate school, work for other artists to gain deeper skills, and embark on other career-focused activities. Noell describes the relationship between core fellows and Penland: "We see them grow for two years. We reach a point when we adore them and never want to see them go, and then they go. And the only thing that makes it possible for us to bear is that we are so proud of who they are."

The transition from core fellow to core alumni is not "one size fits all," but there is consistency in how these artists look back upon their experiences and forward to the next chapter of their life.

Approaching year two of her core fellowship in 2014, Jamie Karolich felt she was on track to achieve her goals: "I came here to develop skills in printmaking, letterpress, and bookbinding and learn as much as I can about running a studio, so when the program ends, I can make a living with my custom stationery business." She finds that the classes she takes outside of letterpress feed her creativity. "I didn't come to Penland to hold back; I'm here to learn and get better." To help her manage the intensity of the program, Karolich developed what she calls her "rules" that guide how she spends her time: "I donate work to the scholarship auctions because I want to pass forward the opportunity I've been given by helping raise money to support scholarship students; I go to all the openings at The Barns because the resident artists are such great mentors and I want to show them my appreciation. The support we get from resident artists and staff here is amazing. As a part of this generous community, you feel you can take risks, grow as an artist, and then have a good chance to become a professional maker. I also try to keep a structure to my day; it helps to have a mini-routine to stick to, when I'm being bombarded with so much stimulation every day."

"I wanted the experience of the core program more than grad school where I figured I'd have the opportunity to make a larger body of work, but I wouldn't be exposed to as many people and different philosophies."

David Wofford, 1995–1996

Core fellow Elizabeth Stokes, like many core fellows, returned to Penland in a different role after her fellowship. Here she's making a mixed-media piece in the textiles studio when she was a studio assistant in 2009. Photo by Robin Dreyer

"Because I'd been out of school a few years and had worked at jobs like waitressing to support myself, I was so appreciative that I could simplify my life and not worry about money. The trade part—that we could work for opportunity—was ideal for me."

Holly Walker, 1979–1980

In early 2015, Sarah Rachel Brown was anticipating with mixed emotions the completion of the core program. During those two years, she had advanced her skills as a metalsmith and jeweler, while also taking classes in other media, such as glass. She had launched her own website, experienced encouraging sales from the Penland Gallery and other venues, and was reminiscing about her core job as dining hall manager. Although she described the fellowship as very intense, sometimes bordering on overwhelming, she rarely lost sight of its importance: "This opportunity is unique and so valuable. One challenge for me was to balance the desire to learn new materials and techniques with the goal of having finished work to show in my portfolio and at the Core Show. Although I got frustrated not always having finished work after a session, I recognize that the core program has given me the chance to explore a wide range of materials and techniques as well as my own artistic expression. I feel ready to go to the next level as a working studio artist."

1   From Alliance of Artists Communities website, July 9, 2010.

2   The Windgate endowment will also allow the program to expand to ten students.

3   Interview with Jane Brown, October 1, 1999.

Core fellow Robyn Raines working in the book studio, 2006.
Photo by Robin Dreyer

"As a core fellow I took advantage of the collective wealth of knowledge that is Penland at any given time—all the instructors and staff and students. Coming out of that program, I had a completely altered understanding of material and process—both what I can do personally and what is possible."

Jack Mauch, 2011–2013

Opposite page:
Core fellow Leah Frost behind the glass studio, coating a cast glass piece with iron filings, 2011.
Photo by Robin Dreyer

CONVERSATIONS WITH THIRTY-TWO ARTISTS

The best way to tell the full story of Penland's core fellowship and resident artist programs is through the experience of the participating artists. To that end, thirty-two artists were invited to be interviewed for this book. At the time of the interviews (2014), there were 200 former core fellows and 138 former resident artists. In the interest of creating a representative sample, artists were selected from each decade since the beginning of the programs, and they were chosen to cover a wide range of media. The artists interviewed work variously in book arts, ceramics, glass, iron, metals, photography, letterpress printing, papermaking, textiles, wood, and mixed media, with a balance between those making primarily functional work and those making sculpture. Most of the artists have pursued full-time studio work or they have been faculty at degree-granting institutions. Many of them have had an ongoing relationship with Penland as instructors, students, or trustees.

The interviews were conducted by Deborah Morgenthal, who edited the artists' words into the form presented here. These were open-ended and loosely structured conversations; however, each of the artists was asked a common set of questions that included the following:

How did you first learn about Penland?
What were you doing before you joined the program?
What were some of the main rewards and benefits of the program?
What were some of the challenges you faced?
How did your peers in the program affect your experience at Penland?
What important changes in your work or life resulted from your time at Penland?

Reading through these conversations, some common themes develop.

Former resident artists spoke about the program as an opportunity to challenge themselves artistically and to explore transitions in their work. They also found the time useful for figuring out how to make a living, how to balance studio time with the need to run a business. They spoke about the program helping them develop professional networks and find teaching opportunities. And they appreciated that the residency expected personal responsibility and independence while fostering cooperation and collaboration.

Former core fellows were unanimous in saying that the immersive approach to learning so many craft processes was a catalyst to technical and aesthetic growth in their work. They talked about the value of being able to explore many different media and techniques and to also be able to deepen their skills in one or two. Many of them said they discovered their voice as an artist during the program. Core fellows valued the work exchange and found that the work they did for the school gave them useful skills and helped them develop discipline and focus in the studio.

Alumni of both programs talked about the value of being exposed to the variety of teaching styles that is such a strong component of Penland's workshop program. They appreciated the opportunities they were given to show their work. And over and over again, the artists spoke about the value of living in a supportive, nurturing, and creative environment where artists learn from each other; they cherished the generosity of their peers. These conversations serve not only to illuminate the significance of these two Penland programs, but also to provide insight into the many paths artists take through their lives and the deep value of the artistic community in fostering creative work.

The introduction to each conversation was written by Kathryn Gremley.

Core fellows Ronan Peterson and Benares Angeley working on the porch of the Northlight building during a 2001 workshop in encaustic painting.
Photo by Robin Dreyer

Opposite page:
A view of the Lily Loom House and the Craft House from the Penland meadow, 2012.
Photo by Robin Dreyer

"I think one of the unique things about the residency and what it has become is that, by encouraging so many artists to stay in the Penland area, the program really is effective in showing new artists how to become professional artists."

Cristina Córdova, 2002–2005

Core fellow Meghan Martin in the Penland iron studio, 2014. Photo by Robin Dreyer.

CORE FELLOWS

MEREDITH BRICKELL
CORE FELLOW, 2000–2002

Ceramic artist Meredith Brickell is best known for her handbuilt earthenware vessels: ambiguous sentinel forms suggestive of intangible, unfamiliar landscapes. Recently she has moved to creating installations that explore her interest in place, history, memory, and the visible and invisible effects of time (marks made in the earth by structures long absent, fragments of fence lines, impermanence and flux). Each plays a role in her narrative constructions. Brickell's work vibrates with implication, like fleeting shadows or the return of a memory. Her installations, such as Construct, *reshape materials to exist in the space between the familiar and the unfamiliar, the memory of an object, or the aura of a place from her past.*

Brickell presents her work in national and international exhibitions, including Santa Fe Clay (NM), the Clay Studio (Philadelphia), and the Taiwan Ceramics Biennale. She has been an artist in residence at the Guldagergård International Ceramic Research Center (Denmark), Watershed Center (ME), and Threewalls (IL). Brickell also engages in community-based projects, many of them in collaboration with Big Car collective (IN). Place, Pockets, and Possibilities: The Work of Meredith Brickell *was published in* Ceramics Monthly *in 2013. She earned an MFA in Ceramics from the University of Nebraska–Lincoln in 2005 and a Bachelor of Art and Design from North Carolina State University in 1994. She is an associate professor of art at DePauw University in Indiana.*

SENSE OF PLACE

I first heard about Penland from a college friend, Dave Wofford, who went to Penland in 1995 for a concentration and then became a core student. But until I took classes there, I didn't understand why people were so passionate about the school. After being there myself, I realized that all these people were interested in the same thing, and to have them all in the same place was unusual. It created a situation where the minority became the majority—where alternative choices became the norm. I think of Penland as a microcosm of its own.

• • •

I went to NC State in the College of Design to study graphic design. By chance, I took a pottery class at The Crafts Center on campus, and I liked it, but I didn't immediately recognize ceramics as something I wanted to pursue as a career. I was making traditional work at the wheel using stoneware fired in a reduction kiln and mimicking what other people were doing as a way to learn technical skills. Eventually I became a studio assistant at The Crafts Center and learned to load kilns and mix clay.

I also was working as a graphic designer and doing pasteup for the local newspaper. After three years of juggling three jobs, I decided to pursue clay full time. I had taken more classes and workshops locally, and I had set up a studio at an artist co-op in Raleigh called Antfarm Studios; Dave Wofford was there, too, having finished his core fellowship.

• • •

In 1998, Suze Lindsay, who had been a Penland core fellow and resident artist, taught a workshop at The Crafts Center. She sensed that I was serious and urged me to take a class at Penland. I applied to her session as a work-study student. What I learned in those two weeks blew my mind: I recognized the potential of the field as a professional life, instead of a hobby. I met so many people there who were living a creative life in so many ways—either by making art, teaching, or working in the field of craft. Penland offered me mentors and role models to help me set goals. That's the power of turning the minority into the majority: you're surrounded by people who are like you. Those anxiety-ridden questions, like how am I going to do this, fall away because you all are concerned with what motivates you to be an artist, as opposed to fearing the things that will kill or dampen creativity.

• • •

Meredith Brickell
Construct-825 Jefferson Street, 2013
Digital print: 6 x 4 inches
Nails: 5 x 3½ x ¾ inches
Purple coneflower, yellow oxeye daisies, bentonite clay
Photo by artist

Opposite page:
Photo by Michelle Given

After the session with Suze, I applied to core, but didn't get it the first try. I went back to Penland the next summer to volunteer at the benefit auction and be a studio assistant for Nick Joerling and Silvie Granatelli, potters who have taught at Penland over the years. I was accepted as a core student for 2000. At that point, I was still accumulating skills and making functional pots. Coming from a design background, not a fine arts background, the logic of functional work appealed to me. I was learning how to make objects and getting control of the materials.

After the first year as a core fellow, my interests began to move beyond functional work. In my early twenties, I was learning to cook, so making functional pots became a parallel exploration. But at Penland, they cook for you. Also, my job was dining hall manager, which de-romanticized the meal for me. I don't want to misrepresent the amazing food experience at Penland: it's a beautiful dining hall, those great tables, people eating communally, that big buffet of delicious food! But when you're responsible for cleaning it up and dragging work-study students out of bed in the morning to do their work—mealtime loses its romance.

So I started paying more attention to influences outside food and function. The rural landscape of my childhood had made a strong impression, and at Penland, I experienced its impact again. I began to think about landscape and place as the subject of my work. I was still making pots and vessels, but they weren't about food—they were containers—and the motivation was not food, it was about a certain kind of aesthetic attached to place.

• • •

Being a core student is a full-on immersion and it's quite exhausting. All summer you're running at a level of intensity that is designed for two-week increments. I got tired of having breakfast with sixty people every morning. Admittedly, I'm an introvert. I love being social, I love community, and then I need a little down time on my own. That was hard to get as a core student, and it was in opposition to the collective momentum of the place. This intensity was a challenge. I don't know if there's anything I could or would have done differently if I'd been able to prepare for this. It's just the reality of the program. The spring and fall concentrations are a different thing; they're designed for an eight-week experience. Everyone's a little more relaxed.

The first year in core both my concentrations were in clay. In the summer, I took two or three clay classes, either because I admired the work of the instructors, or because they taught at a graduate school I was interested in. The non-clay classes I took—shibori, printmaking, and metals—were low-tech and as a newcomer, I was able to jump in and play with ideas right away. I wanted to explore things I was trying in the clay studio, but in another medium. I started to see some continuous threads.

Meredith Brickell
Shed, 2014
Cut saplings, milk paint, shed
Photo by Robin Dreyer
Created at Penland School of Crafts during the 2014 core fellows work retreat.

Meredith Brickell
Palimpsest, 2011
10 x 56 x 32 inches
Plaster, soil, paint
Photo by Michelle Pemberton

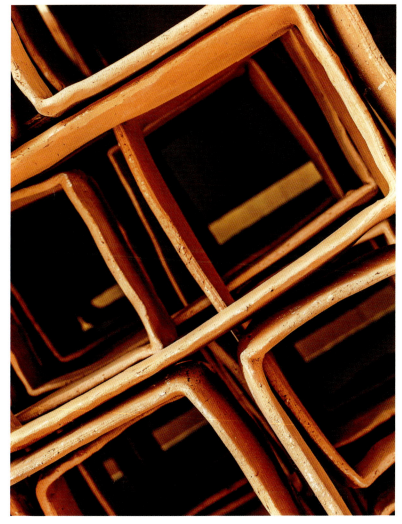

Meredith Brickell
Stack, 2012
22¼ x 30 x 25¼ inches
Watershed clay, pallet, milk paint
Photos by Michelle Pemberton

Being at Penland for two years exposed me to many approaches to working with clay. I learned to slip cast from Tom Spleth, to wood fire from Jane Shellenbarger, to hand build from Sandi Pierantozzi, to name a few important lessons. All of this helped me clarify which materials and techniques did or did not support the ideas I had in the studio. For example, I fell in love with casting forms out of porcelain, but I struggled to control my surfaces in the wood kiln, especially after discovering that I didn't want wood ash on the work. But I had to try things to know for sure. That's what I tell my own students: it's not really about figuring out what you want to do, it's about figuring out what you don't want to do. And because we never quite find that thing, we keep trying. Somehow this feels like clarity. My time at Penland was a lot about trying things. I know many of my peers took a greater variety of classes. But for me it was mostly clay, although by the time I left, I was using it very differently than when I first arrived at Penland.

Because I was thinking about graduate school, I would ask people about their experience. I was eager to have that kind of critical thinking and the time to devote to more exploration. I was working really hard to be a sponge at Penland, but we had very few moments to pause, reflect, and respond to what was happening; all this information was coming in, and I wanted time in a learning environment to digest and respond to that. Graduate school seemed like a really good opportunity for that. I eventually earned an MFA at University of Nebraska, which offered lots of focused time in the studio. Grad school was a great follow-up to being a core fellow because I was so full of information and ready to explore what to make of it. What is unique about the core fellow experience is that it's intensely educational, but not academic.

What I discovered after leaving graduate school was how much I loved participating in a learning community. After a few years working as a studio artist, I felt strongly that I wanted to contribute to something bigger than my own set of interests and agenda, and that's when I started looking into teaching. I'd done some part time and loved it. I wanted to be part of a community where conversations about ideas were a natural part of the environment.

...

When I think about the way that I work and teach ceramics, I want to give credit to Penland for how people there are cultivating a very intentional awareness of materials. I think knowledge of materials is critical and increasingly rare in contemporary practice. Studying the content of a material, including its historical implications and cultural associations, has become embedded in my studio practice. As we're all being distracted more and more by devices, we tend to forget that the physical world is still here. I love that attention to the physical nature of materials and place. And all of that stems from Penland.

CRITZ CAMPBELL
CORE FELLOW, 1994–1996

The rural southern vernacular interpreted by an urban maker can be as complex visually as it is metaphorically. Designer, wood artist, and educator Critz Campbell pulls his narrative imagery from his deep roots in Mississippi and filters it through European and industry experiences. Campbell uses low-relief marquetry for a recent series of "paintings" with precise employment of wood grain and tone. These are architecturally distilled landscapes of pitched house roofs and hyper-focused renderings of enigmatic boxes floating in perfect perspective linear fields. Campbell's series Three Feet High & Rising came in the wake of Hurricane Katrina as symbolic reflections on home and family. In Facing South, an elaborate network of observations, he records his environment and influences with evolved detachment.

Campbell earned a BFA from the School of the Art Institute of Chicago in 1990. The SAIC then designated him a post–graduate exchange student at Ar.Co (Centro de Arte e Comunicação Visual) in Lisbon. Following his core fellowship at Penland, he pursued furniture design at Parnham College (UK) before establishing B9 Design Studio. Campbell has served on the faculty of the SAIC and is currently associate professor of sculpture at Mississippi State University. His work was included in Inside Design Now *at the Cooper-Hewitt Museum (NYC),* Furniture Future Tense *at the deCordova Museum (MA),* Seven Days—Seven Nights *in the LIMN Gallery (San Francisco), and it has been shown at the International Contemporary Furniture Fair (NYC). Campbell has also received grants from the Mississippi Arts Commission and the National Endowment for the Arts.*

SERVICE AND EDUCATION

Jim Lawton, a Penland core fellow and a resident artist in ceramics, was a visiting instructor at the Art Institute of Chicago when I was getting a BFA there. He's why I took a clay concentration in low-fire work with Deb Groover at Penland in the fall of 1993. My work at the time was definitely wheel-based but pushing towards narrative. I was a scholarship student, and I enjoyed doing work for the school. About halfway through the concentration, I realized I might have a chance to be chosen as a core student, so I did a lot of carpentry for the school and did my best to impress the people who would make that decision.

I thought my core fellowship experience would be to produce my portfolio for graduate study in ceramics. But pretty soon after I joined the program, I realized I wasn't only in love with clay. At first I felt a bit guilty that I was as interested in wood as I was in ceramics. It took me a while to realize that my openness to other media was an asset. I started taking classes in many different studios—wood, papermaking, book arts. I wanted to be good at everything I tried, and it was very challenging to ask myself, Hey, can I learn this?

• • •

Living with others as a core fellow was the most challenging part of the program for me. Privacy was limited, and we were pretty isolated—no Internet, just a pay phone. You had to drive a long way to get anything or go anywhere. It turned out that the communal aspect was also the most rewarding. I had to learn how to ask for help and how to communicate and cooperate—things that when you're twenty-four you don't want to do. There was also a feeling of responsibility to the field. I felt like core was similar to being a hospital intern. Everyone saw us as the next batch of makers, paying our dues to deserve the next step in our art careers. Meanwhile we're completely exhausted and overwhelmed, and that's part of the learning process. It's very empowering to feel that you are being watched because a lot is expected from you, and you are being trained to be the next generation.

The first year I was the driver—twice a week I'd go to the airport to pick up people, and drive to Asheville to pick up supplies at the grocery stores or the printer. It was fun to be the errand boy because I could arrange my schedule

Critz Campbell
Tap, 2012
9 x 3 x 3 inches
Bleached maple, ebonized Jabota
Photo by artist

Opposite page:
Photo by Jamie Stukenberg

around those trips. The second year I was part of the weekend cooking crew. Everyone but me was very good at it, and I just followed directions. I was pretty good at making rice and bacon.

I saw the core fellowship as my job and as a service, and I felt that my artwork came second. I had to do my duties for the school and do them well in order to be at Penland and participate in all the school offered me. I felt so lucky to be able to take classes; I didn't feel stingy about getting studio time for myself. Work responsibilities came first. My next priority was to learn as much as possible. I wasn't trying to leave with a body of work (my original intention) as much as I was trying to fill my bag of experiences as much as I could. I liked learning new things. I have this attitude that if someone else can do something, I should be able to figure out how to do it, too. I tend to try to emulate someone's techniques so I can see what they do. I didn't realize how rapid-fire the summers would be. I thought I'd get deeper expertise in a variety of classes, but really I was getting little shots of a lot of things. One of my favorite classes was with ceramicist Robert Turner, who focused on a single formal issue over his forty years. I was so young that I couldn't understand how he could do that, but as I matured, I realized how amazing that was, what depth and focus he had.

• • •

During those two years at Penland, I realized I was going to figure out a way to make a life out of craft. The painter Clarence Morgan, who was on the Penland board at the time, said to me (as I was taking him to the airport) if you keep making stuff until you're thirty, you're not going to have a choice but to keep going, because no one is going to hire you to do anything else!

I remember being ready to leave the core program with great eagerness; that's my nature—I'm always ready for the next thing. So I moved home to Mississippi for a year, and then in 1999 I entered the intensive training and apprenticeship program at Parnham College in England. Then I returned to Chicago, set up a studio, and launched a small line of furniture. I licensed some designs with Crate and Barrel and created an illuminated chair called *Eudora*, which was included in the Smithsonian's Design Triennial at the Cooper Hewitt Museum in 2003.

In 2005, I moved back to Mississippi and took the furniture company with me. I was asked to teach an intro design class and later some sculpture classes at Mississippi State University. Teaching has proven to be a good fit for me as it keeps me engaged in the arts and has relieved me of the commercial pressures I faced running a business. My broad and diverse skills have worked well for me as a teacher. Because of the wide variety of processes I learned at Penland, I often tell my students that I may not know how to do what they are looking to do, but I have seen it done, so let's figure it out together.

Critz Campbell
Mother Is a Fish, 2009
36 x 72 x 22 inches
Pine, oak
Photo by artist

Critz Campbell
Eudora, 2001
36 x 31 x 31 inches
Illuminated fiberglass chair, vintage fabrics; upholstered
Photo by artist

Critz Campbell
Penland Water Tower, 2015
120 x 48 x 2 inches
Bleached maple, ebonized oak
Photo by artist

I think Penland is the ideal model for how craft ought to be learned. I don't think a university is the perfect place to learn art. The Penland studios are now so amazing. Every student I've recommended go to Penland has come back with a deeper level of commitment to making art, and they come back understanding why I, as a teacher, am the way I am about certain things. Like putting the shop back together after every class. A lot of my work ethic is based on the cycles that Penland goes through—seven sessions in a row; you're trained to make the space ready for the next class. And I also encourage students to not get locked into one area, but to go and explore and see what they can learn in different media.

• • •

When people ask me what I make, I talk about how I want my work to be very American and very Southern somehow—regardless of the media. I don't know if I have gotten there. Do you know the photo of John F. Kennedy Jr. saluting his father's casket? There's something so innocent about that image, but it also carries the weight of a historical tragedy and so many layers of meaning. If I can make work like that—accessible, but with a deeper weight—I would be very satisfied.

In the winter of 2014, I was privileged to spend four months of my sabbatical at Penland, where I created a new body of work. Having a winter and spring in the studios, exactly twenty years after I arrived as a core student, was truly a gift. It reminded me how fortunate I am to still be making work. The time allowed me to reflect on my journey and define where I want to go over the next twenty years.

• • •

Being a core student was such an important link in my career that it's hard to imagine how I would have gotten from point A to point B otherwise. I think the core fellowship and resident artist programs are the runner roots of Penland and vital for the larger organism to thrive. It's important for people to experience that "internship" of service, learning, and making. When you transition from student to professor, having put in hours and years to your craft and community, then you really are ready to teach. If you choose to do that, your understanding of how to make a life in art is so much richer.

SUSAN CHIN
CORE FELLOW, 1983–1984

"A brooch or ring emerges from my stash of materials and is coaxed and teased until it is a thing which can be cherished." Susan Chin's jewelry pieces balance on an edge between less and more, assemblages and abstractions, primitive minimalism and opulent bits of material she refers to as unobtainium. In an inherited box of tools, she first discovered her signature materials of hand-carved ebony and bone—materials she has never strayed far from. Her nebulous pods are tattooed with 18-karat gold studs or implanted with a soft growth of golden wires and gathered together with stones and fragments in a collective conversation, emerging as adornment.

After receiving her BS degree in nursing from Columbia University (NY) in 1977, Susan Chin's career path as a jeweler began with a class at the YMCA in Philadelphia, which eventually led her to Penland. In the years following the core fellowship, Chin established herself as a studio artist and began exhibiting work through galleries and at the Philadelphia Museum and Smithsonian craft shows. Since the late 1980s, her jewelry has been included in a lengthy list of national exhibitions, including Freehand Gallery (CA), Facèré Jewelry Art Gallery (WA), Aaron Faber Gallery (NYC), Mobilia Gallery (MA), and the John Michael Kohler Arts Center (WI).

Susan Chin
Crusted Circle Brooch, 2006
1¾ x 2 x ½ inches
Bone, 18-karat yellow gold, green, pink, orange, and blue sapphires,
peach moonstone; carved, drilled, fabricated
Photo by artist

Opposite page:
Photo by Ron Schwager

BALANCED PERSPECTIVE

I was always a maker of things, even when I was a child gluing rocks onto a toothpick box. My approach is still much the same—I consider how much time I have before I'll get interrupted, survey my materials, check in with what I feel like doing, and then dive in. My older sister had gone to art school, so as the youngest daughter, I chose the path that would irritate my parents the least. My mother had aimed to be a nurse, so I went to nursing school. This choice has served me well—as I transitioned to becoming a jeweler, nursing allowed me the flexibility and the financing to go back and forth to Penland. The hospice nursing I do now more than twenty years later nurtures the other parts of who I am and has given me the financial stability to take more risks with my jewelry.

I started making jewelry my second year out of college. While working as a nurse, I took a jewelry course at the YMCA in Philadelphia. I had inherited my sister's tools because she had redirected her artistic ambition toward writing fiction. Then I took night classes at what was then Philadelphia College of Art. I learned a lot, made some work, and was encouraged to visit the Philadelphia Craft Show. Many of the artists showing that year had Penland addresses and that's how I first heard about the place. In 1981, I drove there for fall concentration; Kathleen Doyle was teaching general jewelry making. Those eight weeks were a wonderful immersion into the culture of the place: Kathleen's approach to teaching; the full day and night experience of being a craftsperson; eating, breathing, and embodying the handmade, personally styled, off-the-treadmill life.

When I arrived for that first concentration, I felt intimidated. I was living in a dorm again, and it was scary not to know anyone. I'm a shy person, but I adapted within a few weeks. I was there to work and learn things and I fell in love with the whole experience. I am naturally a hardworking person, and I saw being there as an immense opportunity. Compared to working all day as a nurse and then taking night courses in jewelry, there I was at Penland, involved with jewelry all day, and often there were people in the studios with me in the middle of the night! Also, the setting is so beautiful. I was seduced by rural life and the community aspect of Penland.

• • •

I was assigned to work in the kitchen. Back then, in the days of Jane Brown, everyone in concentration had to work for the school two out of their eight weeks—no exceptions. I integrated fairly quickly. I wasn't ready to say it out loud, but secretly I hoped to be a studio artist one day, and that's why I approached the concentration with such vigor. I thought, this is my chance—I have an eight-week launch! Not having gone to college for art, I didn't understand how you might get from here to there, and I saw Penland as an alternative route to learning how to become a working studio artist.

• • •

I returned for a second Penland concentration and felt like a pro at the life there. I had some money saved up, so when Jane Brown invited me to stay on as a core student, I accepted. I enjoyed one year of the Browns' leadership before they left. Bill had so much charisma, was an artist himself, and drew a lot of talented people to the school. Jane treated us like an extension of their family, and their life seemed to be inextricable from Penland itself. They wanted us to behave in a manner that reflected the school in a positive way, to work hard, and make the school coherent with their vision.

Being at Penland as a core student was more than a fair exchange. Rarely did money change hands. We stayed in one of the houses and had full use of the studios. Having access to the studios twenty-four hours a day was a heavenly gift.

I started out the first year as the driver running errands in Asheville. You're kind of on the outskirts of the school as the driver. When that job ended, I was the dining hall manager, overseeing the work-study students. The school maintained a beautiful garden down by The Barns, and I had the privilege of making the twenty flower arrangements for the tables every Sunday. People often perceive me as this extremely calm person, reliable and serene. This is not really true, but I did okay as dining hall manager. I had to come out of my comfort zone in order to haul a few students out of bed for work in the morning to do their designated job. I was absolutely driven to get in the studio and make jewelry when I wasn't in classes, so it was really useful to work for the school because it offered me a sense of balance. Sometimes it's necessary to get away from your bench and do some simpler work.

• • •

The number and type of classes you could take was limited in my time—for example, core students didn't generally take glass classes because paying students always filled those. I know twenty-four isn't old to be choosing a second career these days, but at the time I was so directed to maximize my time at Penland that I only took classes in metals, enameling, and blacksmithing. I have some regret about not exploring other media. I could choose my bench in a jewelry class before the other students arrived, so I had a five-by-three-foot sense of place in the metals studio, even though the faces of the instructors and students kept changing.

Susan Chin
Miko Bracelet, 2013
8 x 1½ x ½ inches
Bone, sterling silver, fine silver, 18-karat yellow gold, 22-karat yellow gold, ebony, turquoise, pink cobalto calcite, orthocere fossil
Photo by artist

Susan Chin
Bone Stick Brooches, 2007
4 x ½ x ½ inches
Cow bone, 18-karat gold, 22-karat yellow gold, opals, peridot, apricot moonstone, iolite, sterling silver; cured, carved, fabricated
Photo by George Post

Susan Chin
Hoary Heart Brooch, 2005
2½ x 2 x ¾ inches
Ebony, 18-karat yellow gold, sterling silver, 22-karat yellow gold, sunstone; carved, drilled, fabricated, forged, oxidized
Photo by artist

Susan Chin
Lapis Chunks Bracelet, 2014
8 x 1½ x ½ inches
Sterling silver, 18-karat yellow gold, bone, copper/silver mokume gane, lapis lazuli, glass taxidermy eyes, freshwater pearls, jasper, agate, white onyx
Photo by artist

The galleries in Philadelphia were carrying my work back then, but with the Penland connection, I picked up more galleries. My fellow core students and I did a craft show in Charlotte, my first experience with that. We were working artists while we were core students.

When the Browns left, it felt like we had been orphaned. We didn't understand the decisions that had been made. After core, when Verne Stanford came in as director, I worked as his office assistant for a few months, but I felt that my tenure at Penland had ended. I went to work for metalsmith and former core student Paige Davis in Bakersville for a year. I lived in a rustic cabin on a sixty-acre hilltop property that I shared with a small cemetery. Twice a week I'd drive to her studio. Paige continued my education in how to make it work as a studio artist/craftsperson—what shows to do—all that. Working with her I could see firsthand how people manage this life, even if they live in a rural place. The area was rich with other craftspeople doing that very thing.

When I came back to teach at Penland twenty years later, the school felt very different. Jenny Mendes, a dear friend who was a core fellow with me, had returned for a residency and was thriving at Penland. I think both the core fellow and the resident artist programs now are much more helpful to the participants. It was onerous back then to launch your career from that distant rural environment, but now the school helps you with your CV, coaches you on how to approach galleries—it's more geared to support you professionally as well as artistically.

• • •

Now I work two days a week as a hospice nurse, an organization I have always wanted to be involved with. I was too isolated working in my studio for so many decades, and I wanted a more stable income. With my hospice work, I can still do the American Craft Council Baltimore show and include my work in a number of galleries, but I am able to focus more on one-of-a-kind jewelry, and I don't do production work anymore. I just want to make work that I would like to own.

Some people are surprised that I have combined being a professional jeweler with being a working nurse for the last few years. The work with hospice is grounding: I make a real difference in people's lives, and I like that practical and meaningful activity as a counterpoint to being alone making jewelry. My work as a nurse also gives me perspective. When I'm making jewelry, I sometimes get sucked into this worry about finishing the piece on time—but thanks to my work in hospice, I know that it's not life and death.

DANIEL ESSIG
CORE FELLOW, 1992–1994

Daniel Essig is noted for his extreme interpretation of the book form. Drawing from the work of medieval scribes and illuminators, reliquaries, and Wunderkammer—the historical cabinets of curiosities—Essig creates book-based sculptures and wood-covered books. Employing a fourth-century binding known as Ethiopian-style Coptic and pages made from retired linen fire hoses, Essig creates books that are a repository for his collected ephemera. N'Kisi Bricolage Sturgeon, for example, is a carved and painted mahogany fish with mica scales, fins of refashioned text paper from the 1800s, and rusty iron nails and diminutive books running down its backbone, trailing lines of vertebrae and detritus as if Essig conjured it from the depths of a bookmaker's watery dream.

Essig holds a BA in photography from Southern Illinois University–Carbondale. Following his core fellowship years, he attended the graduate certificate program in book studies at the University of Iowa Center for the Book. He is a 2004 recipient of a North Carolina Artist Fellowship Grant, and his work is in the permanent collection of the Renwick Gallery of the Smithsonian American Art Museum (DC), the artists' books collection at the University of Iowa Libraries, and the special collections at the University of California–Santa Cruz, McHenry Library. Eager to share his knowledge, he was a featured artist in the Penland Book of Handmade Books, *and he dedicates a significant part of each year to teaching workshops all over the world.*

Dan Essig
N'Kisi Bricolage-Sturgeon, 2009
13 x 59 x 14 inches
Mahogany, mica, nails, handmade paper,
found natural objects, tintypes,
19th-century text paper, carved and painted wood,
Ethiopian-style Coptic bindings
Photo by Walker Montgomery
Collection of the artist

BOOK-BASED SCULPTOR

I went to college at Southern Illinois University at Carbondale to study photography. Early in my time there, I stopped hanging my photographs on walls and instead mounted them in boxes and books—I wanted to invite people to interact with the images rather than just look at them. At first, I was making some pretty basic book forms, but then I visited my sister Mary in Iowa City and met a friend of hers who made wooden-covered Coptic books. The binding allows the book to open flat, which is good for mounting photographs, so I started working with that form.

Carbondale has many ties to Penland. As a photography student, I worked with Chuck Swedlund, who had taught at Penland. And my first book mentor was Frances Lloyd, a graduate student at Carbondale, who made exquisitely crafted books. Frances looked at my early books and saw they lacked craftsmanship. She had studied at Penland and suggested I take some classes there.

From my very first session at Penland, I knew this was the place for me. I was a terrible student when I was young, but I was always interested in drawing and photography and did well in those classes. It was only when I went to Penland that I realized I could make a living as an artist. That had been my dream since I was a child, but my college courses seemed to be teaching me how to be a professor. At Penland, I met so many artists who had kids, bought homes, and earned a living making art. I thought, If they can do it, I can too. I loved that so many people at Penland were working towards the same goal I was, and that they were so generous and giving.

I knew right away that I wanted to be a core student, but I was very shy. As a work-study student, I went to classes, did my chores, and then walked back to Horner where I lived and attended my workshop. I didn't talk to anyone. I threw myself into the classes and went to the slide shows, but I was too intimidated to hang out with so many people socially.

• • •

After that session, I applied to be a core student, but I was turned down because nobody knew who I was. That was when Julie Leonard came into the picture and spoke up for me: she said I could do the job of core student even though I was shy. The school told me to come back as a work-study student for another

Daniel Essig
Book of Nails II, 2003
14 x 8½ x 11 inches
Mahogany, handmade flax paper, tin, velvet, linen thread,
mica, nails, trilobite fossils, carved and painted wood,
Ethiopian-style Coptic bindings
Photo by Walker Montgomery
Collection of Smithsonian American Art Museum-Renwick Gallery

Opposite page:
Photo by Robin Dreyer

session, get more comfortable interacting with people, and then apply again to be a core student. That's what I did, and it worked out.

I arrived in the spring. At that time Tim Veness was the Penland staff member in charge of the core students, and he took good care of us that first year. He was a huge advocate for us and made sure we did things together as a group off campus. One time he rented the roller-skating rink in Burnsville for us. He believed that the workload and the classes and interacting with the public could get overwhelming, so he wanted to give us a break.

I came into the core student program with photography as my craft, but with an interest in books as well. Over the course of those two years, books became my main focus. There weren't a lot of book classes to take, so I dabbled in other techniques, which turned out to be a great thing for my work. I took woodcarving classes and learned carving and painting techniques. Even in iron classes, I was making parts for books. All those classes and instructors influenced my work—although some of what I learned at that time didn't show up until years later.

It was hard to get studio work done as a core student. I have a lot of train wrecks from that time—works that were truly terrible in form and balance, but that taught me a lot in the making—because my first priority was my work for the school. Being a core student for me was less about my own work, and more about learning new techniques and materials, working with different instructors, and meeting all the people who came to those sessions all summer.

The financial part was very difficult. We received only a small stipend the second year; on breaks I took on extra work at the school, painting buildings to make some money. My main job as a core student was dining hall manager. I was comfortable with that job. I trained people how to wash the dishes and set up the dining room. I liked it.

After those two years, I assisted Julie Leonard in her spring concentration in 1994. Then I needed a few years away from Penland to recover from the intensity of being a core student. It took me five years before I could go back to the Pines and be sure that no one would tell me the milk machine needed to be filled.

I think the greatest thing I gained as a core student was something I didn't realize until years later, and that is my love for teaching workshops. So many of the instructors I studied with taught me the gift of being willing to share knowledge. I love to teach at Penland and experience the full circle of the place, sharing with students the way instructors once shared with me. I can honestly say I enjoy teaching workshops as much as I enjoy working in my studio.

I have so much history with Penland, so when I teach there, I feel like I have lots of eyes watching me—

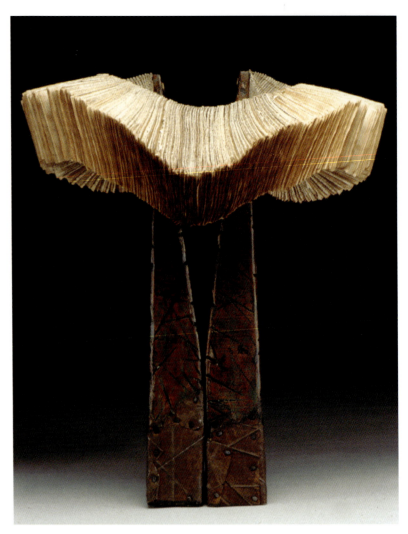

Daniel Essig
Bridge Book: In Spirit, 1996–1997
32 x 18 x 8 inches
Poplar, milk paint, tin, linen thread, 19th-century text paper;
Ethiopian-style Coptic bindings
Photo by Walker Montgomery
Oberlin College Library, Special Collections

Daniel Essig
Profezia del Cardellino, 2013
20 x 24 x 8 inches
Mahogany, Italian olive wood, Mount Vesuvius rocks, locust thorns, printer's type,
Victorian velvet, mica, nails; carved, painted, Ethiopian-style Coptic bindings
Photo by Steve Mann

Dan Essig
Detail of *N'Kisi Bricolage-Sturgeon*, 2009
13 x 59 x 14 inches
Mahogany, mica, nails, handmade paper, found natural objects, tintypes, 19th-century text paper, carved and painted wood, Ethiopian-style Coptic bindings
Photo by Walker Montgomery
Collection of the artist

those eyes are supportive, but I also feel as if I have to live up to some high expectations. I'm a scholarship student, turned core student, turned studio assistant, turned studio artist, turned instructor. I put more pressure on myself when I teach at Penland than at any other place. And I like that.

I don't have extra money I can donate to the school, so for the auction I donate the biggest and best piece of work I can. That's one way I can give back. I owe the school so much—almost every thread in my life goes back to Penland.

During my two years as a core student, I developed lifelong friendships with my fellow core students and dozens of instructors and staff members. I can mention Dolph Smith, whose work influenced me greatly, or my friendship with Dorothy Gill Barnes, whose work inspires me. There are countless other folks in between who have become friends, mentors, and mentees, and we enrich each other's lives.

I gained so much confidence being a core student. Most of my life, I was the tall shy guy who didn't really fit in. But at Penland, my confidence rose. Working with that group of core students, I had to learn to get along and engage and build relationships. We created a family of artists. We relied on each other. You pick your friends, but this group is just handed to you. You're thrown together by chance, and then these people become your closest friends for a lifetime. While there is a link between all core students, the bonds I formed with my group are deep. They are my siblings, my family.

Daniel Essig
Icon, 2012
9¼ x 7 x 2½ inches
Holly, mahogany, milk paint, handmade paper, mica, lead type; Ethiopian-style Coptic bindings
Photo by Steve Mann
Lafayette College, Skillman Library, Special Collections

ALIDA FISH
CORE FELLOW, 1971–1973

"At the heart of my artistic efforts, lies an urge that has existed since childhood: the desire to create a world of my own invention." Photographer Alida Fish is known for her still-life work using manipulated photo processes, mythic tableaus of flora and curiosities, and disquieting spectral images. In Fish's work, historical and digital processes vacillate and commingle, disregarding visual and material boundaries. Tissue: Bending was first printed on delicate paper coated with iridescent ground fish scales, then torn and reassembled with solemn intimacy. Throughout Fish's career, she has indulged the make-believe, using photography as a tool for her imagination. In her words: *"The impulse to populate and control an invented world has led to photographs of sculptures that appear to metamorphose into living flesh, plants that emerge as heroic in their struggle to exist, and curious objects that are a testament to the wonders of life on this planet."*

The Core Fellowship Program was in its formative stages when Fish began her relationship with Penland. She had earned an MA from Harvard University (MA) and a BA from Smith College (MA) before arriving at Penland, and she went on to receive her MFA from Rochester Institute of Technology (NY) in 1976. She began teaching photography at the University of the Arts (PA) in 1981, where she served as media arts department chair and interim dean of the College of Art, Media and Design. Her work is found in numerous collections, including the Philadelphia Museum of Art, George Eastman House (NY), and the Delaware Art Museum. Highly respected in her field, she has received grants from the Delaware State Arts Council and the National Endowment for the Arts, to name just two—her résumé of achievements is lengthy and well deserved.

Alida Fish
Tissue: Bending, 2013
11 x 8½ inches
Pigment print, drawing, rice paper, iridescent fish scale
Courtesy Schmidt-Dean Gallery

INTREPID IMAGE-MAKER

I have made photographs since I was a kid—my grandmother gave me a Kodak Brownie camera when I was five. I had a little darkroom kit and would climb into my closet, process the film, and make contact prints. My grandfather was a painter, as is my sister, and my mother was a sculptor. I liked tinkering with mechanical things—particularly bikes and mopeds. My family felt that if I was going to be an artist, photography, with its mechanical aspects, might make sense.

• • •

A friend of mine had been to Penland for a weaving workshop, and she thought I should check it out. Summer vacation was approaching, and I was looking for something interesting to do. So I traveled by bus from Manhattan to Penland to take a photography class. I took a three-week class with photographer True Kelly, who still lives in the Penland area. She was mostly self-taught, sort of a performance artist. She broke all the rules. At Harvard, I had received hard-core technical training in photography—so serious! We learned the Zone System—all about the precise shooting and printing methods used by Minor White and Ansel Adams. Then I came to Penland, and it was like, "Oh, let's just pour this chemical on the paper and see what happens…. Forget about f-stops and shutter speeds." It had more to do with making discoveries and finding surprising pictures. We did everything somewhat intuitively—just experimenting.

The third day, we decided to photograph at night. True recruited Rick Cronin, Penland's weekend cook, to come along to be a model. It was instant magic—we fell in love. Rick and I spent every moment together; I was either in the photo lab or with Rick. People used to refer to Penland as Magic Mountain because so many hot romances magically happened there! After the session was over, Rick and I drove to Delaware to meet his parents. I returned to Manhattan; Rick returned to Penland. Two months later, after not seeing each other, we got married at Penland out on the knoll in front of the Pines dining hall. Talk about an impetuous decision! We felt we had the same goals in life. At our wedding, Bill Brown gave me away.

• • •

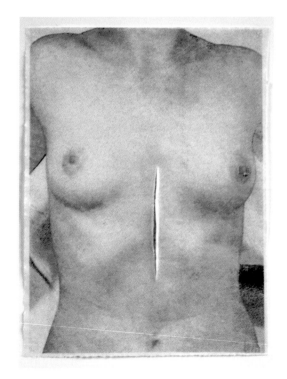

Alida Fish
Tissue: Cut Chest, 2014
11 x 8½ inches
Pigment print, drawing, rice paper, iridescent fish scale
Courtesy Schmidt-Dean Gallery

Opposite page:
Photo by John Carlano

I started to work for the school doing odd jobs: cooking on weekends, washing pots, and so on. Sometimes I changed the beds and cleaned all the rooms during the changeover between sessions. I was also the studio assistant for the photography and printmaking classes. I assisted the instructors, ordered materials, oversaw the studios, and, most importantly, participated as a student in each workshop. What I did for the school in exchange for tuition and room and board became the basis of the Core Fellowship Program. In later years, as the school expanded and became more organized, the core program was more clearly defined, and core students were assigned more manageable workloads. In my era, we were so grateful to be there that we would do pretty much whatever was asked of us—we knew we were having a remarkable experience and were being given a lot. But I do remember complaining on Wednesdays about having to get up at the crack of dawn to wash and wax the cement floors in the Lily Loom House before anyone came into the offices. We did odd jobs and filled in wherever we were needed. Sometimes, it was tough, menial work.

• • •

From that very first session with True Kelly, and after studying with many other talented instructors at Penland, I came to realize there are hundreds of ways to work with photographic materials and techniques—there is no one way, the Zone System way, the "right way." This knowledge opened up a new world of photographic image-making for me.

During my first year at Penland, I concentrated on photography. My interest turned more and more to alternative process and hand-altered work. I'm proud to say that I can put a photograph on almost any surface—I learned this at Penland. I worked with Ron Garfinkle, a ceramicist, who was one of Penland's resident artists. I photographed scantily clad models to make decals he put on his salt-fired pots. They were beautiful! I also made decals with enamels for transferring to glass, and collaborated with several people using light-sensitive emulsions to put photographs on wood and fabric. My photographic practice is securely grounded in the love of craft and handwork I acquired at Penland. Since that time, I have concentrated on playing with the believability of the photograph by making handmade images that cross into printmaking, drawing, and painting.

During those two years, I met remarkable people and learned tons. I worked with exciting contemporary photographers like Evon Streetman, John Pfahl, John Wood, Betty Hahn, and so many others. On top of that, there was a steady stream of extraordinary artists passing through the school, teaching, giving demonstrations, and making presentations on their work. There was an informality that made learning an integral part of our daily existence there. It was a life-changing experience.

• • •

Alida Fish
Water Lily, 2013
19 x 14 inches
Offset print
Courtesy Schmidt-Dean Gallery

Alida Fish
Luna Moth, 2012
8 x 10 inches
Pigment print
Courtesy Schmidt-Dean Gallery

Rick and I stayed at Penland for two years. He was offered a job as an assistant in the sculpture studio at Pratt, working in their foundry. I decided I wanted to teach on the college level and wound up going to Rochester Institute of Technology for my MFA. I chose RIT because two Penland instructors, Betty Hahn and John Pfahl, taught there and encouraged me to apply.

Six years after arriving at Penland, I was again single and needed to support myself. I had been filling in as a part-time instructor for teachers at different colleges—all those contacts came from my Penland connections. Finally, I applied for full-time employment and was hired by the Philadelphia College of Art, now the University of the Arts. I continue to maintain a close relationship with Penland, having taught seventeen summer workshops and serving on their board of trustees. I will be chair of Penland's board from November 2016 until November 2018. I've formed lifelong connections and friendships through Penland. It was at Penland that I decided to become a photographer. I credit much of the foundation of my career, the teaching and the studio work, all that feeds me, the lifestyle I've enjoyed—all of that—to my two early years at Penland.

• • •

Today, the core fellowship is a unique program. With thoughtful oversight, it acquired more structure and a positive mentoring system. Its reputation has grown dramatically, making the selection process extremely competitive. Talented individuals are accepted who are mature and focused when they arrive. The Penland community is openly proud of its core fellows. The fellows, with their enthusiasm for their program, have become some of the school's best ambassadors. I think of the core fellowship now as "the jewel in the crown" for Penland.

Top:
Alida Fish
Floating Figure, 2014
10 x 8 inches
Photographic pigment print transfer on oxidized aluminum
Courtesy Schmidt-Dean Gallery

Bottom:
Alida Fish
Winged Pod, 2014
10 x 8 inches
Photographic pigment print transfer on oxidized aluminum
Courtesy Alan Klotz Gallery

SETH GOULD
CORE FELLOW, 2011–2013 | RESIDENT ARTIST, 2015–2018

Seth Gould is a metalsmith and artist toolmaker, which is to say the nucleus of his studio practice has been the study and crafting of fine tools, implements made with equal regard for aesthetics and function. Gifted with an analytical mind and an eye for mechanical design, Gould extracted the fundamentals of lock and key, specifically a nineteenth-century three-bolt English door lock, and inverted the inner working structure, bringing beauty to functional application. Hammer, caliper, and cleaver each become intimate objects embellished with Gould's signature inlay. In what he refers to as "line drawings," Gould uses the hammer to intentionally loosen our grasp on function, imaginative steel sketches taking liberty with convention.

Gould received his BFA in metalsmithing and jewelry from Maine College of Art in 2009. After the core fellowship, he set up shop in Cleveland, Ohio, as a full-time studio artist, fabricating his sculptural work and a collection of fine bespoke tools, locks, and hardware. His work has been exhibited at the National Ornamental Metal Museum (TN), the Torpedo Factory (VA), the Houston Center for Contemporary Craft, and Greenhill Gallery (NC). Gould has been a presenter at the Society of North American Goldsmiths conference and the Furniture Society conference, and he has been an instructor or given lectures at Penland School of Crafts, Maine College of Art, University of Arkansas, and Massachusetts College of Art and Design, among others.

ARTIST AND TOOLMAKER

Growing up I always felt I was artistically inclined, and so when I finished high school, I applied to several art colleges in the Northeast. I was accepted at the Maine College of Art and thought I would be a graphic designer or an illustrator, but during the first semester of my freshman year, I took a basic metalsmithing class, and it opened up a new world for me. My grandfather, father, and uncle are all mechanics, and I think working with my hands is in my genes, but this had not been so clear until I started working with metal. I received a BFA in metalsmithing and jewelry design. It wasn't until my senior year that I became interested in forging. The college didn't have the resources for the craft, so I built a gas forge and started to teach myself.

• • •

I first heard about the core fellowship at Penland from a college friend. I applied with a portfolio of metalwork. I intended to try different media, but there was so much to learn about metalsmithing that I ended up enrolling in almost all metals and iron classes, learning new skills and working with different materials, like pewter. The one exception was a concentration in fine bookbinding, learning traditional bookbinding and box-making techniques, including leatherworking. I was able to apply those skills to make cases for some of the tools I was creating.

• • •

Not having been to Penland before, it was exciting to arrive with an open mind. My job the first year was working in the dining hall during the week and in the coffee house on the weekends. The second year I was a weekend cook. Overall, I felt able to balance the multiple demands of the program pretty well. I can't say I ever felt overwhelmed by what the school asked of me. There were times when there was a lot of studio work to get done, and my job in the dining hall may not have been on the top of my list, but I knew I was there to work for the school in exchange for all they were providing me, which was a very fair tradeoff. I think I was always able to keep it all in perspective and to recognize how incredible the opportunity was.

I think the core program works especially well for individuals who have room to grow as artists. I was more interested in developing my technical skills than receiving critique on the conceptual aspects of my work. As a core fellow, it's difficult to develop a body of work with your own voice. Between class and

Seth Gould
Planishing Hammer No. 3, 2011
32 x 32 x 1 inches
Steel, hickory
Photo by artist

Opposite page:
Photo by Suzanne Price

work, your schedule is intense. I tried to absorb as much as possible during the hectic summer, knowing that during the winter when there were no classes, I could digest and process all that information and turn out more finished work.

• • •

I feel extremely fortunate to have been a core fellow with the individuals who were there with me during my two years. We pushed each other in terms of our work and really contributed to each other's experiences. For example, Ian Henderson was relatively new to metalsmithing, so he was always picking my brain. He is such an intuitive maker and he learned fast, which pushed me to do better things. Jack Mauch and I had an easy back-and-forth competition going, making work around a playful theme. It often inspired me to make work that was more colorful and loose than anything else I had made, and I think the real value was that it showed me that I could. This was the case with each core student relationship I had. Whether I was asking advice for my own work in the wood studio, or helping a friend problem-solve in the ceramics studio, these relationships helped me grow and understand craft as a whole. Each person shaped and enhanced my time, and it was a more enriching experience because of them.

• • •

I took two classes with metalsmith Hiroko Yamada while I was at Penland. She introduced me to Japanese-style inlay and engraving, and shortly after I finished core, she invited Jack Mauch and me to travel with her in Japan for what turned out to be an incredible trip. Japheth Howard's blacksmithing class also stands out in my mind. He is an extremely knowledgeable smith with great attention to detail. My first summer class at Penland was an advanced level class with Italian blacksmith Claudio Bottero. Claudio didn't speak English, so with a translator, we were basically his apprentices for two weeks while we collectively made an intricately forged kinetic sculpture. He had a way of moving metal that I'd never seen before. Equally important was getting to spend time with all the professional smiths that were in the class. I really tried to pay attention to how each of them got where they are, and how they were making their livings as craftsmen.

• • •

During core I tried to be as in the moment as possible, aware that in the future I wanted to make metalsmithing my livelihood. Often I wondered if after core I would need to get a steady job and make my work during my time off. I wasn't interested in grad school—having spent two years learning from so many talented instructors, absorbing information, and honing my technical abilities, I felt ready to set up a shop and make a living. And that's what I did. The knowledge I gained and the relationships I developed gave me the support I needed to make this happen. I recognize how much I've grown in terms of my technical ability, but the first thing I think about is

Seth Gould
Pig Cleaver, 2013
3½ x 10 x 1 inches
Iron, tool steel, fine silver, brass, osage orange; forged, filed, inlaid, engraved
Photo by artist

Seth Gould
Scroll Lock, 2014
5 x 8 x 4¼ inches
Steel, brass, iron; forged, filed
Photo by artist

Seth Gould
Duck Press, 2015
18 x 14 x 12 inches
Steel, copper, bronze, cherry
Photo by artist

all the people I connected with. They are in my contacts list now, and that network is invaluable.

I felt respected and appreciated by the school for the role we played as core students, both in and out of the studio. The community supported us, too, during the Core Show and at benefit auctions. All of this really puts you on top of the world, which is a double-edged sword. We knew that although we were praised while core fellows, it did not mean we had it made after Penland. The core program would not be such a rich and meaningful experience if you could stay there forever. Knowing that you will have to enter the real world again, but fortified with the amazing knowledge and experience of the core program, is both scary and exciting.

• • •

Having been involved in the review process for prospective core fellows, I will never again be disappointed if I get rejected for something. I saw firsthand all the things involved in making those selections. I tell hopefuls to be very honest about their goals in the application. It's not wise to try to impress or say what you think the reviewers want to hear. You really need to think about and express why the core program is right for you at that time in your life.

• • •

I feel fortunate to return as a resident artist. I intend to design and execute more ambitious work that takes more time, research, and exploration to create. Having been part of the community as a core fellow and experienced the incredible support Penland provides, I know the residency will afford me ballast as I move from being an emerging artist to becoming a more established presence in the field.

Seth Gould
Jeweler's Saw, 2014
4 x 11½ x 1½ inches
Steel, brass, mahogany; forged, filed
Photo by artist

DOUGLAS HARLING
CORE FELLOW, 1987–1989 | RESIDENT ARTIST, 1992–1994

Goldsmith Douglas Harling is a master of granulation, the ancient technique of fusing minute granules of precious metal to create pattern and texture. His brand of pointillism exploits the luminous tones of 22-karat and 14-karat gold, the play of light across the surface, and a tactical mastery of his materials. Harling's adornments are inexplicably suspended in time: set with opulent stones, bearing titles evocative of other eras and places, and wrapped in an aesthetic suggestive of ancient cultures and codes. The brooch Alive and Dead, *with its mysterious gold calligraphy and landscape of ripe jewels, or Harling's fruit motif brooches,* Pomegranate *and* Samarkand Peach, *are unfailingly lush and belie the quiet, unpretentious persona of the maker.*

Harling lives in Kalispell, Montana, and is head of the jewelry program at Flathead Valley Community College. Before moving to Montana, he taught at Hazard Community & Technical College's Kentucky School of Craft in Hindman, Kentucky. His awards include a Southern Arts Federation/NEA Grant, a North Carolina Artist Fellowship Grant, and an American Craft Council Award of Excellence. He has taught numerous workshops across the country, exhibits internationally, and was a featured artist in the Penland Book of Jewelry: Master Classes in Jewelry Techniques. *Exhibitions include* Innovation/Tradition: Masterpieces of Southern Craft *assembled through the Southern Arts Federation,* The Nature of Craft *and* The Penland Experience *at The Mint Museum of Craft + Design (NC), and* The Art of Gold, *which toured through Exhibits USA. Harling received his MFA in metals from Southern Illinois University–Carbondale in 1992.*

Douglas Harling
800 Buddhas, Brooch, 2013
2 x 2 x ¾ inches
22-karat gold, 14-karat gold, emeralds, South Sea pearl; granulated, fabricated
Photo by Tom Davis Photography

Opposite page:
Photo by Marita Combs

BECOMING A GOLDSMITH

I grew up in Greensboro, North Carolina. I had taken jewelry classes for fun since high school, but my undergraduate degree is in biology. My dad was a veterinarian, and after college, I worked for him full time. I enjoyed it, but I was restless. I continued taking jewelry classes but soon exhausted the local options. I first heard about Penland from Paula Garrett, a metalsmith who had been a core student and had also taught there. I decided to go for the spring concentration in 1987. I took a leave of absence from my job, ran off, and joined the circus. My first class at Penland was a concentration taught by Tom McCarthy, also a former core student. All the jewelry classes I'd taken before that one were beginning classes. I don't think I'd had instructors before, other than Paula, who were totally immersed in what they did. That's really what I got from Penland the first time—here were artists immersed in their work and sharing what they knew.

After that concentration, I went back to Greensboro. A few months later I got a call from Penland, asking if I'd be interested in the core program because they had an opening. I was thrilled at the opportunity. Verne Stanford was the director and his wife, Joy, was in charge of the core program; Nita Forde was her assistant and worked closely with the core students. I had totaled my car just before core started, so my parents dropped me off with $20! That didn't matter—I was fed, housed, and I had saved a little money. Most of the year, we lived at Morgan, a house on campus with little heat. During the winter, we moved into a warmer house on the main campus. In the winter, Penland really became a community. A close-knit group of core, residents, staff, and area craftspeople lived and worked together without the influx of students. I really enjoyed getting to know the people who lived nearby. I've always been sorry I didn't buy that "shack and thirty acres" in the surrounding area.

My first core job was to work in the Penland Gallery on weekends, which was then in the old weaving cabin next to The Barns. I also did some kitchen prep. The next year, I was in charge of the coffee house/library, housed in Ridgeway Hall at the time. Joy and Nita made an effort to match individuals to a job that suited, but some positions were only available by seniority. There was the "party planner," "weekend cook," "coffee house host," "dining hall manager," and the "sheet house manager," among others. None of the positions could be described as glamorous, but I was much happier hosting in the coffee house than I would have been cooking breakfast for 150. On changeover weekends, we all scrubbed bathrooms, made beds, and shined the place up for the next session. All the core students took a great deal of pride in how they did their jobs.

The schedule of a core student was always busy, with a lot of stops and starts to your day. Summer sessions were particularly intense. Classes would continue with demos and projects whether you were present or not, so I always felt a need to catch up. The intensity of the classes and demands of the core program required coping skills. Sometimes you retreated from the school and were less involved—you had to recoup—and then the next workshop you were wide open and in full swing. You learned to pace yourself. Penland re-creates itself every session. The core students play a big role in making that happen.

• • •

As a group we were very focused on our chosen medium: I took only metals classes, the ceramics people took all ceramics courses. In the second year, there was some push for us to broaden a little bit and explore other areas. I ignored it completely! What I wanted and found at Penland was the chance to focus. That depth of understanding has served me well.

I think being there at that time in my life also opened up the possibility of making art a career. In year two, I decided to pursue an MFA in metals at the University of Southern Illinois University at Carbondale. Brent Kington and Richard Mawdsley were the metals professors there, and I met both when they taught at Penland. I became good friends with Tom McCarthy and Sarah Perkins (who had been a studio assistant for Richard when I took his class at Penland), and the three of us were graduate students at SIU together. To this day, I consider myself a "child" of two places: Penland and Carbondale, and I am incredibly thankful for both.

The core program really made a huge difference in my experience of graduate school. Core was a true work-study program: we were supposed to work hard for the school, be a part of everything, learn as much as we could about craft and art, and—a little bit like children—be seen but not heard. My growth over that period was largely personal. When I went to visit graduate schools, it was exciting because I received feedback about my work. As a core student, during my time, there was support from instructors but relatively little feedback.

My goals with graduate school were to participate in critical study and continue working in the studio in the very selfish manner that grad school affords. One of the real gifts of Penland is that it lays everything out with equal value; you'll take a workshop with someone

Douglas Harling
The Road Home, Brooch, 2013
3½ x 2 x ½ inches
22-karat gold, 14-karat gold,
black jade, rubies; granulated, fabricated
Photo by Tom Davis Photography

Douglas Harling
Everything Blooms Eventually, Brooch, 2012
2 x 2 x 1 inches
22-karat gold, sterling silver, diamonds, rubies, emeralds,
pearls; granulated, fabricated
Photo by David Ramsey

Douglas Harling
Alive and Dead, Brooch, 2009
2¾ x 1¾ x ¾ inches
22-karat gold, 14-karat gold, carved garnet, black coral, colored gemstones; granulated, fabricated
Photo by artist

who is conceptually oriented, and then one with someone who is involved with the material, and then one with someone who is more production oriented. They all have equal value. Graduate school was in part a response to the eclectic nature of taking classes at Penland as a core student—it helped me put what I had learned in order and in perspective.

• • •

The Penland residency seemed like a wonderful opportunity to get started as an independent studio artist. Also, I loved Penland—it was home. I had started working with some historical processes, including granulation, and my aim during the residency was to apply these processes and build a body of work.

Our resident artist group was its own community. We socialized and had dinners together. There were always discussions about work, materials, and concepts. It was extremely interesting to see how other people worked. I saw what it took in effort and involvement to make art. I think extraordinary objects hold our attention and create a space around them—they have presence. It's the living part of what the maker gives to a piece—the magic or alchemy in the process of being an artist. I learned that then. Or I started to learn that. After the residency, I returned to Greensboro and set up a studio. I relished all that time by myself at first, but after a year or so, I realized how important having the community of artists around really was.

• • •

As I began to get recognition for my work, I started to get invited to teach workshops, and I eventually wound up teaching at University of North Carolina–Charlotte. In graduate school, I hadn't focused on teaching, but at UNC–Charlotte, and later at other universities, I began to consider teaching the next phase of an essential journey: if you don't share what you do, you don't have a next generation doing it. In addition to teaching in universities, I've taught six workshops and a few concentrations at Penland over the past twenty years, and I really enjoyed those experiences.

I have worn many Penland hats: core, resident, instructor. My experience as a core student and a resident artist share one similarity: the smorgasbord that is Penland allows you to find your voice. Because you see all these different approaches and recognize their validity, you are able to more clearly see and be yourself.

Douglas Harling
Taotie Cup, 2008
1¾ x 3½ x 2½ inches
22-karat gold, resin with enamel; raised, granulated, fabricated
Photo by Tom Davis Photography

ANDREW HAYES
CORE FELLOW, 2007–2009 | RESIDENT ARTIST, 2014–2017

Volumes, the title of Andrew Hayes's 2014 solo exhibition at the Seager Gray Gallery (CA), is nuanced wordplay. His reference may be to a single book—as in the material Hayes uses as his point of origin—or to volume, as in mass or proportion. Both are apt descriptions of his sculptural fusion of formed steel and unbound pages. The content of the book is of little concern to Hayes, yet ironically it is the splayed text, the printed words on the page that create the fine patterns held fast by his steel casings. The works are saturated with potential motion, as taut sheaves of wafer-thin paper form eddies around and within his steel forms. Hayes's reductive approach is reverent and deeply personal—his intention is to create alternate stories from found books.

Hayes began his studies at Northern Arizona University, working toward a degree in sculpture until 2005. During a transitional period, working as an industrial welder and carving out studio time, Hayes was invited to attend the EMMA International Collaboration in Saskatchewan, Canada. This pivotal experience led him fortuitously to the Penland core fellowship, where he began exploring the intersection of steel and book arts. Solo exhibitions include Volumes *at Seager Gray Gallery (CA), the National Ornamental Metal Museum (TN), and the Lux Center for the Arts (NE). Hayes's sculptural books have been included in numerous group exhibitions throughout the country, including* Odd Volumes: Art from the Allan Chasanoff Collection *at the Yale University Art Gallery (CT) in 2014.*

ALTERED PERSPECTIVES

I heard about Penland in 2002 while I was in a sculpture program at Northern Arizona University (NAU) in Flagstaff. In the foundry class, we'd go to the iron pour in Tempe at Arizona State University once a year. I was talking to a grad student there and told her I was interested in blacksmithing, and she rattled off people whose work I should look at. She said Penland was an amazing place where a lot of these people taught, and that she was going to take a summer class there. On her advice, I applied to be a work-study student at Penland in a class called Forging, Fabricating, and Casting taught by Warren Holzman. I saved up money for the class by working at the university's recycling center, where, oddly enough, one of my jobs was to cut the pages out of books to recycle the paper.

I never imagined how much I would get from that one class at Penland. The first morning, Warren forged a ball on the end of a bar, which was something I'd never seen before. I think about that class almost every day. I was pretty intimidated by the power tools in the studio, but by the end of the class I was using the power hammer. One day, we took a field trip to sculptor Hoss Haley's studio in Asheville. His work really impressed me—it referenced the landscape in an innovative way, and his use of materials was direct and elegant.

I went back to Flagstaff, and my work changed. Both Warren and Hoss gave me a new perspective on steel by demonstrating how malleable and forgiving the material can be. The way Hoss built sheet steel forms without an internal structure or armature opened a fresh direction in how I could build new hollow constructions.

• • •

A year later, I took another summer class at Penland with John Rais, and this also expanded my understanding of forging and sheet forming. His assistant for the workshop was Andy Dohner, and that meeting changed the trajectory of my life. Andy worked his way up the ladder as an industrial welder. He then became interested in blacksmithing and dedicated himself to learning from smiths around the country. At that time, I was on the path to finish college and then go on to grad school; I hoped to teach someday. However, after meeting Andy, I realized that if I wanted to get better at welding and metalworking, I really needed to work at it. At NAU, I had a thesis show, but didn't graduate. Instead, I moved to Columbia, South Carolina, and completed a semester in the sculpture program at

Andrew Hayes
Kernel, 2013
9½ x 7 x 2 inches
Steel, book pages; fabricated
Photo by Steve Mann

Opposite page:
Photo by Robin Dreyer

the University of South Carolina. Then I started working as a welder at a hose supply warehouse. My dad was a welder for many years. I regret not spending time in his shop learning and working with him. I've wondered if going into industrial welding was a sort of rite of passage. Either way, it's nice to talk shop with my dad now.

In 2005, I decided to move to Portland, Oregon, to work as a welder, but before I headed out west I was accepted as a work-study student at Penland again. This time I took a class called Shrine-O-Rama, taught by Michael Hosaluk. It was a joyful experience. We made shrines to anything we wanted; we collaborated, and we had two superb visiting artists, Bobby Hansson and Paul Sasso.

In Portland, I found welding work in different factories and learned the trade. I'd work these jobs for a while, save money, and then quit. Then I'd make my own studio work for a while and apply for shows. Then I'd get another welding job, and it was back and forth like that. One day I got an invitation to participate in the EMMA International Collaboration, a biennial event that brings together one hundred craftspeople in different disciplines from around the world to make artwork that is auctioned off to pay for the next year's event. During that week, I got to talking about Penland's core program with two other collaborators and Penland locals, Paige Davis and Elizabeth Brim. Over the course of the week, they encouraged me to apply for the core fellowship.

So much of the success of the core program depends on chemistry—choosing people who are going to be able to live, work, and play well together. It's pretty amazing to consider how many people who went through that program are still friends with their core peers. Part of that is environmental—you're kind of secluded, living together in Morgan. Our group really jelled. This was the first year Penland accepted core fellows who had not been to Penland before as work-study students. If that hadn't happened, I wouldn't have met the love of my life, my wife—Kreh Mellick!

During my first summer I took a range of classes from wood and iron to metals and clay. In each class I tried to apply the focus of the class to my own work. But one class was different. The class was The Altered Book taught by Doug Beube. I didn't know anything about altered books, so I left all my expectations at the door. One morning Doug cut a book on the guillotine paper cutter. Watching the unbound mass of paper twist and move was so powerful. When I saw him do that, my first thought was that I could wrap metal around that cut book. Everyday in that class, I tried to see how I could accomplish that. Doug was very enthusiastic and supportive of what I was trying to do.

Andrew Hayes
Cast, 2014
13 x 17 x 3 inches
Steel and book pages
Photo by Steve Mann

Andrew Hayes
Wrest, 2013
21 x 5 x 5 inches
Steel, book pages; fabricated
Photo by Steve Mann

Andrew Hayes
Sentry, 2013
11 x 8 x 2 inches
Steel, book pages; fabricated
Photo by Steve Mann

In the fall concentration of my first year, Leslie Noell offered me an independent study to make a body of work. She arranged for me to spend two days a week working with Hoss Haley. This was a great learning opportunity, which was true about the whole core program. Those two years set me on a beautiful path, with the most supportive community surrounding me. I have been lucky enough to support myself through the sales of my artwork in galleries around the country. Making money as an artist can be a constant struggle. That's why the Penland core program is so valuable—I had the time to develop my own work while my expenses were so low.

• • •

In 2014, five years after I finished the core fellowship, I was accepted as a Penland resident artist, and in this new role, I've been pushing my body of work in directions I always wanted to explore, but had to put aside due to time constraints. I want to experiment with new ideas and materials. My ultimate goal is to leave the residency with momentum behind my work, feeling financially buoyant, and primed to push my studio practice to the next level, wherever I may land.

Being back at Penland has been an interesting transition. Initially my concern was making sure my wife, Kreh, found a suitable studio so we could both benefit from this time. Now we are both focusing on making new bodies of work for exhibitions around the country and finding ways to support ourselves. I am humbled by the group of residents I share The Barns studios with: everyone is extremely talented and kind. I know I will learn so much from this group. I am really lucky to be back.

The core fellowship definitely prepared me for the residency. My technical skills expanded and I learned how to pace myself in the studio, while allowing time for growth in personal and professional relationships. Without core I might not have known how to make it as a studio artist. By watching and interacting with the community, students, instructors, and residents, I gleaned tons of information and enjoyed so much support. *And* as a core fellow I learned a valuable Penland lesson: never show up late for lunch during the summer.

Andrew Hayes
Chock, 2013
16 x 16 x 3 inches
Steel, book pages; fabricated
Photo by Steve Mann

AMY JACOBS
CORE FELLOW, 2004–2006

There are two facets to master papermaker Amy Jacobs's studio practice. Independently she works with an intuitive process, employing methodical and meditative responses to her chosen materials. Her most recent work explores the imprint of time on cloth, revealing the visual history inherent in worn clothing and used textiles—faint images of print fabric overlaid with pulp fiber. On the other hand, Jacobs's responsibility as studio collaborator for Dieu Donné in New York City requires her to respond to another artist's vision, as interpreter and facilitator. Working with artists such as Ann Hamilton and Do-Ho Suh, she is both a conduit for ideas and an educator exploring new territory as part of a creative and experimental team.

Jacobs is currently the studio collaborator and education manager at Dieu Donné. Following her Penland fellowship, she received her MFA in Interdisciplinary Book and Paper Arts from Columbia College Chicago. She has been an instructor and assisted at a number of institutions including the University of Georgia Studies Abroad Program in Cortona, Italy; the School of the Museum of Fine Arts (Boston); the University of Louisville (KY); Longwood University (VA); East Carolina University (NC); Ox-Bow School of the Arts (MI); Haystack Mountain School of Crafts (ME); The Printmaking Center of New Jersey; and Chateau du Pin in Angers, France.

FIBERS OF CONNECTION

I grew up in Louisville, Kentucky, and had never heard of Penland. After finishing my undergraduate degree in sociology, I considered going to grad school for art therapy. One of the prerequisite elective classes I took was a textiles course that included fabric dyeing, shibori, a small papermaking component, and a little bit of embroidery. The fiber arts professor, Lida Gordon, asked me to be her assistant the following semester, and I just fell in love with textiles—the patterns, the construction, and the textures. I adored using traditional techniques in new ways. A classmate told me about Penland and Haystack, and Lida suggested I go to one of those places to further investigate textiles. I had never worked on a loom and thought how amazing it would be to learn how to make my own cloth. I applied for a fall concentration at Penland in weaving and surface design with Suzanne Gernandt in 2002. I knew I could go only if I received a newly offered full scholarship for a textile student. I took a leap of faith and was granted that opportunity.

When I showed up at Penland, I knew this was a place I felt at home. I worked in the kitchen during fall concentration and got to know some of the core fellows. They suggested I apply for the core program, but I didn't think I had a chance because I had not been making art for long. I stayed at Penland through the winter; I rented the weaving and surface design studios with two other people, and I wove and dyed fabric and yarn like crazy. I really started to understand the world of making things. I settled into the weaving studio, watching llamas and horses walking on the knoll in the snow—it was magical. I also observed how the core students were totally immersed in the world of creativity and new techniques. In spring of 2003, I was offered a work-study scholarship, and I took a quilt class. I often walked up the hill to Northlight, where there was a paper and book class going on. I was attracted to this material, this new world of making, folding, and sewing paper. Seeing that work made me realize I didn't want to go to grad school to be an art therapist: I wanted to make things. Penland seemed like the perfect place to learn, so I applied for the core program, was accepted, and started in spring 2004.

When you are a core fellow, you are surrounded by rotating casts of instructors and students, and you act as a kind of ambassador of the school. I was one of three core fellow weekend cooks both years. At first I was absolutely terrified, but I grew so much as a person, learning how to manage people and gaining the confidence to cook for so many people. I wound up loving the job. Ever

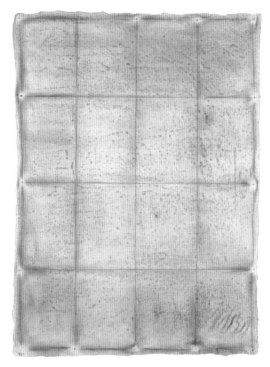

Amy Jacobs
The Poetry of Surface, 2014
30 x 22 inches
Cotton and flax paper, gesso, graphite, wax; sanded and folded
Photo by Louisa Rorschach

Opposite page:
Photo by Desiree Adams

since then, if I think I can't do something, I remember how I learned to cook and feed 150 people without poisoning anyone, and I know I can do anything.

• • •

My first class as a core fellow was papermaking, taught by Mary Hark, who was a wonderful and generous teacher. She encouraged me to follow my intuition. She used to say that there are many ways to make things. She urged me to make something a hundred different ways and in doing so, understand how I like to work. I have remained in touch with Mary, and she still inspires my work.

I also took classes in printmaking, alternative photography, metals, lost wax casting, encaustic painting, and more. I wanted to have a toolbox of different techniques and materials, although I didn't know my own aesthetic yet. As I took more classes, I learned to loosen up and trust my intuition. A similar tone started to emerge through every medium—a softness appeared across the board. I was interested in subtle patterns, themes of remembrance and forgiveness, and a sense of color and light.

In the second year, I started to focus on papermaking and book arts. For my last concentration, I proposed an independent study with Dan Essig, Carmen Grier, and Lisa Blackburn. I met at least once a week with one of them, and Leslie Noell was also a constant voice of encouragement. I had the whole of Northlight to work in. I made cyanotypes, prints, books, encaustic paintings, and a *lot* of paper—hundreds and hundreds of pieces, using stretched linen thread dipped in abaca. They were really organic, with an underlying organized structure. I ended up with these piles and piles of small pieces, and I imagined how they would look gathered together in the same place. I was turning into an installation artist.

The weaving cabin was used as a storage area at the time, crammed with looms, boxes, and dust. It was built in 1923 as a gathering place for community weavers, organized by Lucy Morgan, and it had wonderful light. I cleared out the whole place and installed the abaca pieces inside. There were about sixteen abaca and linen panels that hung from ceiling to floor, diffusing the light. It was a big experiment, but in the end it made sense. I combined all my techniques into making a place where people could come and experience a new sensation of light and space.

• • •

Audrey Niffenegger, who was teaching an aquatint class at Penland that summer, suggested I would be a good fit for graduate school at Columbia College Chicago, where I ended up pursuing an interdisciplinary book and papermaking degree. I delved deeper into the mechanical aspects and materials of book and papermaking. The studios and the people were really great. The faculty and my peers challenged me to answer fundamental questions about my practice. During the first year of grad school, I attended a Friends of Dard Hunter Conference, and met Susan Gosin,

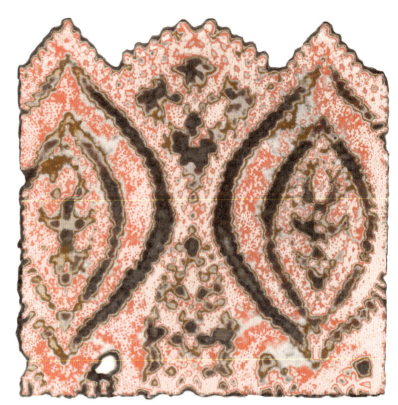

Amy Jacobs
Cathedral 1, 2013
6 x 6 inches
Pigmented linen blowout on pigmented cotton base sheet
Photo by Louisa Rorschach

Amy Jacobs
Cathedral 2, 2013
6 x 6 inches
Pigmented linen blowout on pigmented cotton base sheet
Photo by Louisa Rorschach

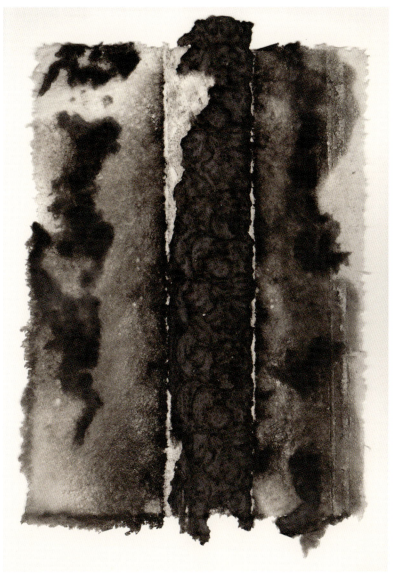

Amy Jacobs
Fragment, 2014
14 x 11 inches
Pigmented linen on abaca base sheet
Photo by Louisa Rorschach

who helped found Dieu Donné Papermill, one of the premiere papermaking facilities in the United States. Sue invited me to assist her and Mina Takahashi in a papermaking class at Haystack that summer.

After graduate school, I taught workshops across the country and in Italy and France. One of these workshops was a papermaking class at Penland with Paul Wong, the artistic director of Dieu Donné. I had sworn off assisting, but Mina called and insisted I work with Paul, who was known as a genius of papermaking and an able guru of technique and collaboration. Paul and I clicked, and I knew right away that I could work alongside him. In August 2010, I was sitting at a picnic table in front of Northlight and my phone rang. It was Kathleen Flynn, the Executive Director of Dieu Donné, and she offered me the job there as studio collaborator and education manager.

The challenges at Dieu Donné are daily and varied; we are a small staff and collaborate with amazing artists, including James Siena, Do-Ho Suh, Ursula von Rydingsvard, and Ann Hamilton. Most of the artists have never worked in handmade paper before, so it is my job to help them to understand how the material acts in terms of their own work. I also teach papermaking to kids and adults and manage a large studio of interns and equipment, do custom orders, and many other things. It is a unique place and a unique job. I have to think on my feet, stay relaxed, and change hats every day. Penland was instrumental in giving me the tools to flourish here.

At Penland, I learned the many ways there are to be an artist: you can be a studio artist, you can teach, you can help other artists. The program exceeded every expectation. Being a core fellow changed my life: the experience gave me the how-to knowledge to make things and the confidence to know that I was good at it.

Amy Jacobs
Windows, 2014
18 x 24 inches
Watermarked cotton and abaca paper, graphite, wax; embossed and folded
Photo by Louisa Rorschach

JULIE LEONARD
CORE FELLOW, 1989–1990 | RESIDENT ARTIST, 1990–1993

"Books can act on us as an icon or reliquary does, evoking a spiritual reaction, a contemplative psychic space," writes Julie Leonard, whose work in the book arts is divided between the study of historical bookbinding structures and the creation of contemporary artist books. Complex and cerebral works such as Accumulated Dreams, where Leonard incorporates acrostic text as both pattern and content, are ethereally bound, suspended, and surrounded with gestural bits of wire encased in translucent abaca fibers. An ongoing body of work makes use of old reference and botany books. Retaining vestiges of the page and word, Leonard cuts and carves the pages, drawing with negative space. This work reimagines the "old" story, layered with a new one.

Leonard received her BA in history from Vassar College (NY) in 1979 and was studying design when she discovered book arts and Penland—altering her creative path. After her time in the core fellowship and resident artist programs at Penland, Leonard established a studio in North Carolina for several years. She then continued her education at the University of Iowa Center for the Book, earning both a graduate certificate in book arts and her MFA in graphic design from UI. Leonard remained at UI as lecturer and associate professor in book arts, and she has served as visiting professor of book arts at the University of Georgia Studies Abroad Program in Cortona, Italy. Leonard has made presentations and taught workshops for the College Book Art Association biennial conference, Wells College Book Arts Center (NY), and the American Printing History Association annual conference. Her editioned and sculptural books have been shown in solo and invitational group exhibitions throughout the world.

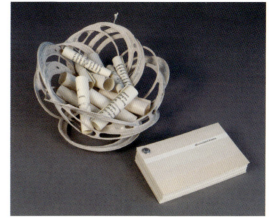

Julie Leonard
Accumulated Dreams (editioned and bound version), 2013
Book: 3 x 5 inches
Basket: 8 x 8 inches
Abaca fibers, wire armatures, handmade and machine made papers, letterpress printing from photopolymer plates, post-bound book, rolled leaves
Photo by Jill Kambs

A LIFE IN PAPER AND BOOKS

I played violin and viola through much of my young life. I was also drawn to visual arts but felt intimidated until I discovered graphic design as an entry point. Working at a small independent record label after college, I began to study graphic design and became particularly interested in book design and illustration. On completing the program, my mother, who is a potter, gave me a weeklong class at Penland for my thirtieth birthday. That was a life-changing gift. The following year I took a class with book artist Keith Smith, and in 1989 I went back to Penland with my mother for spring concentration. She took a clay class with Michael Simon and I took two workshops, one with Tini Miura and one with Joanne Schiavone.

During that concentration, two core positions opened unexpectedly. Another student, Carla Illanes, a glassblower, and I applied to fill those openings and were accepted. We had a week to fly home, rearrange our lives, and drive back to begin the program that summer.

During that year, I saw a different way of shaping my life, one that wholly resonated with me. Although my mother was a potter, she did not need to make a living at it. The lives of the craftspeople I saw at Penland and in the surrounding community were designed with an aesthetic and an ethic that seemed wholly integrated with the artwork they were making. This was utterly appealing to me.

Julia Leonard
Word, Image, Text, 1997
5 x 6 x 4 inches
Multiple dos-a-dos link stitch binding, collage, hand and machine sewing, hand-written, type-written and laser printed text
Photo by Tom Mills

Opposite page:
Photo by Barry Phipps

That summer, I was weekend cook, along with two other core students, Marion Carter and Sarah Heimann. Having had no experience cooking for 150 people, this was nerve-wracking. We had autonomy, planned the meals, ordered ingredients. If you cook, you know that it is a creative act when approached imaginatively. I learned that and the pleasure it can bring. This was a great job, too, because it concentrated the main part of my work obligations to Friday night, Saturday, and Sunday, and interfered less with time in the studios.

I took classes outside my area; in fact, I took only one book art class. The spring before I was a core fellow, I had taken two classes: one on fine binding, the other on creative and alternative book structures and processes. I knew that I was interested in both, but wanted to learn other media to bring to that work. I took classes in painting, drawing, surface design, and woodworking. It was such a privilege to have that opportunity to immerse myself in a range of media.

One particular class in drawing with Harold Kitner, who painted large murals, often of quilts, offered one of those moments one remembers as a kind of shift—a moment that allows one to move forward. His work was so powerful, beautiful, with a political message that resided in that beauty. There I was with my tiny little pads and my tiny colored pencils, making tiny detailed drawings. I apologized for not working larger, for not wanting to. He looked at my drawings and said, "Big is hip right now. But it won't always be and you don't have to do that. Do what you need to do, what your soul is telling you to make." Now it sounds hokey, but at the time it was the best thing anyone could have said. It was the first time I got a push towards myself, rather than feeling an external "should" in art making. When I think about the way I teach, I realize that almost all of my thinking on teaching, my approach, comes from people at Penland, artists like Paulus Berensohn, Christina Shmigel, and others who know how to draw out an individual, working to find what that person hopes to accomplish with the work and helping her get there.

I chose not to do a second year as a core fellow. I had been in school right before coming to Penland and with that and the classes I'd been taking at Penland, I felt ready to move into a situation where I could focus on working independently and developing a career. Instead, I applied for the Penland residency to build upon my core experience.

It was, in some ways, a difficult transition. I had no experience setting up a studio or knowing much about how to go about making a living with the work. I had a hard time getting started, building a rhythm in the studio. I probably spent as much time trying to work out how to be a professional artist, how to make it work financially, as I did focusing on the kind of work I was making. For example, during my first year as a resident artist, I was accepted into two competitive craft shows, but had little clue how to proceed. I needed a booth display; I needed a way to transport that and my work; I had no idea how to light a booth—on and on. But I got so much help from other residents and local craftspeople: they shared their experiences and loaned me the lights. In fact, Nita Forde lent me her entire booth setup for my first show. That generosity was stunning to me. If I had to pick one thing Penland—the place itself and the people—does so beautifully, then and now, it is to create an environment that bolsters your ability to get to where you want to be with your work and your professional life. It's a unique combination of independence and support. The expectation is that you are going to do this yourself, but you are doing it in the context of so much shared knowledge and experience.

• • •

Julie Leonard
Accumulated Dreams, 2013
Hanging: 24 x 24 x 60 inches
Abaca fibers, wire armatures, handmade and machine made papers, letterpress printing from photopolymer plates
Photo by Jill Kambs

Julie Leonard
Detail of *Accumulated Dreams*, 2013
Hanging: 24 x 24 x 60 inches
Abaca fibers, wire armatures, handmade and machine made papers, letterpress printing from photopolymer plates
Photo by Jill Kambs

The book arts community in Penland and the area was quite small at that time, and I wanted more exposure to the field: to trade and fine binding, edition binding for fine press printers, artist bookwork, conservation, and repair. So after the residency and a few years living in the area, I moved to Iowa City in 1997 and enrolled in the newly established Graduate Certificate at the University of Iowa Center for the Book. Book artist Dan Essig, another former core student, had gone out the year before to work with papermaker Tim Barrett. My second year, I was accepted into the MFA program at the (UI) School of Art, and in 2001 I earned an MFA in Studio Art and a Graduate Certificate in Book Studies and Arts. I stayed on to teach at the Center for the Book and the design area in the School of Art.

• • •

During my time at Penland, I was a core fellow, a resident artist, and a studio coordinator for the book, paper, and drawing studios. At the end of my residency, I moved to a cabin in nearby Celo for four years, during which I taught a spring concentration and worked in the public schools as a visiting artist. After moving to Iowa, I served on the Penland board of trustees for eight years.

I suspect that without my time at Penland, my path would not have unfolded in the same way. So much of what I absorbed while I was there—the way I think about making work, the kind of work I make and why, how I teach, how I think about art making and its place in culture and in our society—this is all marked by my Penland years. I carry those impressions and ideas with me. Although I was in the Core Fellowship Program for only one season, it was that experience that opened up a world. I don't segment my connection to Penland into those various roles, but rather, they form a whole and very significant part of my life that still continues.

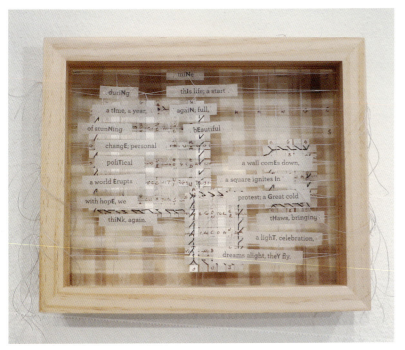

Julie Leonard
Changes, 2014
8 x 10 x 2 inches
Papers, ink, thread, handmade paper; woven, sewn, handwritten, printed
Photo by Julie Leonard

SARAH LOERTSCHER
CORE FELLOW, 2005–2007

Jeweler Sarah Loertscher credits the landscape of her youth—Midwest plains with expansive skies and industrial silos—as the wellspring of her minimalist metalwork. "These immense objects impressed upon me the feeling that structure itself is beauty, and the bare bones of a form are the often the beautiful parts," Loertscher explains. Her work has continually explored these forms, paring away the extraneous to leave a precise skeletal structure in silver or gold. Loertscher mimics crystalline formations in pieces such as Structure Necklace #13, building with line to suggest mass. Loertscher's visual acuity and uncompromising attention to craftsmanship are fundamental to her refined jewelry.

Loertscher was raised in Indiana and attended Ball State University (IN), receiving a BFA in metalsmithing in 2003. After apprenticing as a jeweler for several years, she made her way to Penland and the core fellowship. Directly after leaving Penland, Loertscher established her studio in Seattle, where she began teaching at Pratt Fine Arts Center (WA) and creating a diverse and thriving jewelry business. Opportunities to work alongside the fashion industry resulted in collaborative projects with clothing designers Mila Hermanovski and Angel Sanchez. Faucet manufacturer Moen featured Loertscher's interpretation of their products in a multimedia advertising campaign. Her work is sold at galleries throughout the United States, including LIGHT Art + Design (NC), the Museum of Contemporary Craft Gallery Store (OR), the Walker Art Center's Walker Stop (MN), and the Seattle Art Museum Shop (WA).

REPETITION AND GEOMETRY

I first became aware of Penland in 2001, as a metals student at Ball State University. My professor, Patricia Nelson, enthusiastically encouraged me to get there any way I could. The following summer, Penland awarded me a work-study scholarship to attend a metals class taught by Kiwon Wang. Penland recommends arriving before sunset to avoid getting lost in the mountains, and I pulled onto Conley Ridge Road as the sun was setting. I was utterly confused about where to go so I sat in my car and called my mom. She said, "You made it to Penland, so you can do *anything* now." She was referring to me having completed my first long-distance trip, but her words would come back to me repeatedly: I had no idea the impact my arrival at Penland would have on my life.

Those two weeks introduced me to a new way of learning—immersing myself in the medium of metals forced me to make technical and aesthetic leaps that would have taken months in my college schedule. I came back from Penland excited by what I witnessed: "Did you know they make *sheet solder*? And you can set stones in *tubes*?" The exposure to new ways of metalsmithing was just the tip of the iceberg. At Penland I met other makers in other media. I learned about glassblowing and that people wove fabric on looms. Perhaps most important of all, I learned that people could make a living making things. I had also met some core fellows, and knew I wanted to be one of them someday. That first summer blew the doors wide open for me, and I saw the possibility of creating a living through craft.

After graduation from Ball State, I worked in a retail jewelry store at their front desk, taking in repairs, helping with sales, and eventually working at the bench doing light repairs and stone setting. I applied to the Core Fellowship Program, but my initial application was denied. This was a quiet time for me creatively. I focused on gaining skills and efficiency, but rarely made my own work. I felt grateful to be at the bench, but I was disconnected from making personally meaningful objects.

After a year and a half, I needed to make a change. I applied for a work-study scholarship for Penland's 2004 fall concentration with Lisa Fidler, intending to reset my course. At first, my confidence was low and I had no clear sense of navigation. Spending the next two months at the bench sharpened my creative

Sarah Loertscher
Mariapilar, 2014
1¼ x 1 x ¾ inches
18-karat yellow gold, Colombian emerald; scored, bent, soldered
Photo by Eliott Peacock

Opposite page:
Photo by Eliott Peacock

drive, and most notably, reaffirmed my desire to return to Penland as a core fellow. I reapplied, and on December 13th (my birthday!) I got the phone call: I was in.

The first year challenged me on many levels. I had never been thrust so outside my comfort zone. I had never been in the spotlight or managed people. I had to confront my insecurities (*all* of them—artistic, technical, personal) and my newly discovered social anxiety. I had a rough spring concentration, struggling to manage the ebb and flow of people coming through my life and home. Although I was uncomfortable, I owe most of my resilience today to that first year. I learned I could handle much more than I thought, socially and emotionally. I began to learn balance. I learned to show up to the studio everyday.

Artistically, Penland's greatest gift was that I was exposed to a plethora of makers, students and instructors alike. Each person brought a new way of working, thinking, and problem solving. The opportunity to see so many brilliant minds solve problems had a huge impact on my making; it was a concrete way to learn that there are a thousand solutions to every problem.

• • •

My second year began with the most pivotal class I took at Penland—printmaking with Susan Goethel Campbell. The class was more than building skills and learning technique. Susan encouraged me to shift my focus to the process, not the end product. This took the pressure off making, and I began to pay attention to what I enjoyed doing. I realized I felt grounded in process, rules, and repetition—both the repetition of labor (hammering a hundred perfect marks into a plate, inking a hundred screens) and the end result of that labor—seeing a hundred objects that all looked related. I made work that was simply an experience or process I enjoyed, and in the end, that's what made it important and wholly my own.

Susan's class also set the tone for summer. I became aware of my aesthetic; my need for building blocks made it easier to bounce from class to class. Whether it was printmaking, metals, or glass, I would use a triangle as my starting point. This allowed me to get to work quickly, without the emotional labor of "what should I make?" This is still how I work today.

• • •

After Penland, I knew I wanted to create work to sell and knew I was lacking the skills to do so. I was new to the ins and outs of production work, and I was told the best way to learn the business was to assist a working artist. Through friends, I wound up living and working in Seattle, assisting jeweler Lulu Smith. I helped with her production line and studio upkeep, and began to learn how small manufacturing works. Being immersed in a studio practice taught me the basics: shipping and receiving, photography, suppliers, pricing, web presence–and how to make jewelry efficiently. Jewelers John and Frances Smersh also had a huge impact in my growth as a professional.

Sarah Loertscher
Mila, 2014
¾ x 1 x ½ inches
Palladium, gray diamond; lost wax cast, soldered
Photo by Eliott Peacock

Sarah Loertscher
Structure Bracelet #2, 2012
2¾ x 4 x 2 inches
Sterling silver; scored, bent, soldered, oxidized
Photo by Eliott Peacock

Sarah Loertscher
Structure Necklace #13, 2013
8 x 9 x 3 inches
Stainless steel, sterling silver; scored and bent, soldered
Photo by Eliott Peacock

I assisted in the production of their jewelry, while also working at their design store. Both Lulu and the Smershes were open with every aspect of their business—successes and failures—and I learned from their experience.

While working for Lulu, Pratt Fine Arts Center hired me as a studio monitor, a work-study position. Pratt connected me to other working artists and offered me my first teaching job in 2007. I was shy about teaching, but determined to share the knowledge I had accumulated in the same way it had been freely shared with me.

• • •

In 2012 I was invited to design and fabricate jewelry to accompany LA-based apparel designer Mila Hermanovski's fall/winter runway shows. This opportunity shifted my jewelry into a large-scale, more sculptural realm, and this work began to attract the attention of media, stores, and other designers. In 2013, Angel Sanchez, a NYC-based designer, invited me to show with him at New York Fashion Week, and we collaborated on three more subsequent collections, which challenged me to work in new arenas and with new materials. Later that year, Moen, a US-based faucet company, invited me to collaborate on an advertising campaign, in which they commissioned jewelry designers to make necklaces, based on the company's faucets. The fashion and design worlds work on tight, intense deadlines, and my two-week classes at Penland had exposed me to creating work under tight time constraints.

At Penland I also learned to be fearless in saying yes to opportunities, even if the outcome is not clear. Jumping headfirst into new sales arenas has proved to be rewarding: collaborating with designers, photographers, and corporations has greatly impacted the trajectory of my career.

In spring 2014, I taught a Penland concentration in metals, my first teaching experience at the school. It was an honor to come full circle through the roles I've held there—work-study, volunteer, employee, core fellow, studio assistant, and then instructor. My experience as a core fellow deeply impacted my life. It intimately introduced me to a community of makers, reinforced the value of teaching and sharing and the rewards of saying yes, and helped me discover how and why I make things.

Returning to this focused place of making reminded me how deeply I am rooted in those mountains and studios. At the heart of it all, amongst the busyness, I am a single link in a long chain, passing knowledge down to another generation of makers.

Sarah Loertscher
Lattice Earrings, 2013
3 x ¾ x ¾ inches
Brass, powder coat, 18-karat vermeil, stainless steel; stitched, assembled
Photo by Eliott Peacock

JACK MAUCH
CORE FELLOW, 2011–2013

Dynamics of form, functionality, and efficiency of process are tenets in Jack Mauch's cross-disciplinary studio work. His facility with multiple materials—predominantly wood and metal—is evident in both his functional and sculptural work. His marked aesthetic is a paring down of elements to evoke a reference to nature or the human form—a table leg with a subtle tarsal spur, or the curve of the hand on a pocketknife. He is a critical thinker, an analyst of both material and design. The work he produced during the core fellowship indicates a comprehensive exploration of the techniques within his reach at Penland.

Mauch received a BFA with a focus in ceramics from Maine College of Art in 2006. From 2008 through 2010 he worked as an exhibition designer and fabricator for the Harvard Graduate School of Design (MA) before arriving at Penland as a core fellow. Since leaving the core program, Mauch participated in the Center for Furniture Craftsmanship Studio Fellowship Program (ME) and has established a studio practice in Allston, Massachusetts.

VEHICLE FOR CREATIVITY

The first elective class I took at Maine College of Art was wheel throwing, and I fell in love. That was the moment when I became aware that making things could be a magical experience. I studied ceramics all four years. I also got into woodworking, and for one year double majored in furniture design and ceramics. Ceramics is inherently a mysterious and miraculous process, far more than woodworking. With woodworking, you make a plan and the process happens slowly in front of your eyes. It's nothing like the incredible transformation that happens on the wheel, when you take a lump of clay—a formless ball of potential—and turn it into something in a matter of minutes.

I was passionate about making pottery, but in my senior year I started to get affected by the kind of work I thought I should be making, what's valued at art school, and I began making work that was ambiguously functional … somewhat sculptural. I definitely strayed away from what I originally fell in love with.

• • •

In college, I was required to take a shop class as an introduction to tools and machines to be able to use the shop safely. We made a picture frame, a box, and a spoon. I remember sanding my carved spoon meticulously and presenting it to the instructor, thinking I was done, but he pointed out a rasp mark. I couldn't really see the flaw until that moment. Developing the ability to see deeper and deeper into the nuances of my work has been a huge part of my experience as a craftsman, and especially relates to my experience at Penland. This spoon was the first time I realized it's not just technique that improves with practice—it's also my ability to perceive the object I'm making. So I sanded out the mark.

When I learned that Penland was such an integral part of the studio crafts movement, I applied for a work-study scholarship for a wood-firing class with Jack Troy and Chuck Hindes in the summer of 2004. I couldn't believe I was actually studying with these legends, and I thought Penland was the most magical place on earth. I'm sure I drove the core fellow leading my changeover team nuts by pestering her with questions about the program. I decided then that I was going to be a core fellow.

I sent Penland eight photos of my pots, two photos of chairs, and one of a cabinet. In my application I wrote I wanted to reconnect with my ceramics practice and try to develop an "aesthetic voice" as a ceramic artist. I also wrote that I wanted to develop more woodworking technique and learn some metalsmithing. When I started as a core fellow I was signed up mostly for ceramics workshops, but over the course of a month I dropped them all for woodworking classes. I felt guilty about this, like I should be studying ceramics, and that woodworking or

Jack Mauch
Black Table, 2012
27 x 17 x 17 inches
Poplar, oak, maple, milk paint; carved, painted, veneered, iron-stained, varnished
Photo by artist

Opposite page:
Photo by Jesse Beecher

metalworking were just fun distractions, but the opportunity to learn new skills was too enticing.

My first year I was dining hall manager—definitely a hard job. To be honest, I liked that I had a hard job. I took it seriously and tried to do well. What I didn't do as well was balance that work with the rest of my life as a core fellow.

I also found it challenging to live in such a close community. Core fellows are an integral part of the school, and I struggled with how I fit in. The fact that my core peers that first year were the sweetest bunch of people I've ever known actually made my social anxiety even worse. I was stunned that there could be nine talented individuals in a selective program with virtually no ego or malicious competition—only the friendly competition of being inspired by each other and wanting to raise the bar higher. I'm the youngest of five children, and there were times when my siblings and I would pile up somewhere, on a bed or the couch. This would happen at Penland, too—we'd all just be in a pile somewhere. It really was like being with family, and I'm not just being romantic. I also felt insecure and alienated a lot of the time, even though I loved everyone and knew I was loved, supported, and accepted. I still am deeply connected to these core fellows, and expect they will always be a part of me and influence the work I make.

Seth Gould had the biggest impact on me, mainly because we have many shared interests, and I admire him so much as a craftsman and a person. We had a goofy back and forth with sausage-themed work; it was fun to go to "show and tell" with a new piece and try to show each other up, or just joke about it. It's also wonderful to now be able to process life after Penland with Seth as we start our careers.

• • •

In my second year, I continued to study woodworking and metalworking, and explored some other media as well. I took advantage of the collective wealth of knowledge that is Penland at any given time—all the instructors and staff and students. Coming out of that program, I had a completely altered understanding of material and process—both what I can do personally and what is possible. Because I was working in different media, I found it hard to talk to people about what I did, what the point of my work was. I felt like I wouldn't be understood or taken seriously if I couldn't identify with a single medium.

I've finally accepted that for me the core program was about broadly exploring material and process. In fact, it's the only program I know of in which I could do this. I'm happy I used my time in this way. At some point I stopped drawing hard lines between different media and studios. I realized that a lot of crafts involve similar processes and tools. You cut things. You stick them together. You hit them. I began to see how limited people are by what they know. I watched even skilled instructors work in a way that was really inefficient just because they were using the technology that was

Jack Mauch
Salt Spoons, 2011
2½ x 1 x 1 inches
Pewter; cast, carved, patinated
Photo by artist

Jack Mauch
Detail of *Arrowood Table*, 2014
24 x 18 x 18 inches
Walnut, walnut burl; dissected, reassembled, carved, veneered, stained, varnished
Photo by artist

Jack Mauch
Tavern Mug, 2012
11 x 5 x 5 inches
Pewter; cast, carved, fabricated
Photo by artist

Jack Mauch
Pocket Knife, 2012
Open: ¾ x ½ x 4 inches
O1 steel, brass, ebony, sterling silver;
fabricated, heat-treated
Photo by artist

familiar to them, when maybe there was a tool in another studio that would accomplish the same thing faster and more accurately. By the end of my time as a core fellow, I never did a woodworking project in which I didn't at some point travel to the metals or iron studio, and vice versa.

This lack of limits could be overwhelming—especially in winter, when I had access to all the studios. I'd arrive on campus in the morning and have to choose, not just which project to work on, but also which building to work in. Different instructors certainly influenced my aesthetic, but I also strove for continuity in my design—regardless of the media I was working in. When I look at the work I made at Penland, there is an aesthetic thread that carries through—an emphasis on curves and volume, in particular. I give great thought to the contour line of the object I'm making, the big form, not the ornamentation. I think this derived from looking at pots on the wheel sideways, because you're looking at the silhouette, the contour—you don't look down on it or it's just a circle. And when you're throwing a pot on the wheel, you have incredible sensitivity to the shape, which you can change, literally, as fast as you can think. What I internalized from that was sensitivity to line.

In part, I defined my successes as a core fellow by the level of praise I received and whether I was perceived as a competent maker. Also by whether I could make a piece that had no discernible flaws. I felt that recognition was the goal, and I just needed to be shown in galleries, have articles written about me, create a body of work that was instantly identifiable as mine and I'd be doing fine. The truth is, right now, I'm seeing that my desire for recognition is an insidious temptation that blocks the passion for creativity I had when I was making pots in college. I am starting to realize that a lot of the impetus for the work I've been making recently is just so it will be accepted and look coherent in relationship to what I've already made. This seems like a dangerous thought process and is no longer my goal or what I'm interested in.

I believe so strongly in art and its power to connect people to the incredible depth of human experience. I hope the making of it can connect you as much as the consumption. I'm at a transitional moment when I'm realizing there are creative possibilities beyond my imagination and I need to be open to making work that will fail and be rejected.

My sister introduced me to the idea of the Daemon, that there is another entity responsible for creativity and we're just a vehicle. It's such a great concept because it allows you to feel less responsibility for the success or failure of the work and freer in making it. Because of Penland and all I learned there, if I can let myself be more affected by the process and not the outcome, I can be a powerful vehicle. I just I don't know yet what the work will be.

RONAN PETERSON
CORE FELLOW, 2000–2002

Ronan Peterson grew up in the rural mountains of North Carolina, his childhood filled with woodland fantasies, superheroes, imaginary aliens, lush forests, and cicadas. As an adult, he unites both the natural and fantastical in his ceramic vessels, which display an artistic narrative of the forest floor, ripe with texture and color. Eccentric pots with exaggerated details and cheeky references to plant morphology are functional tableware nonetheless. Grubby Stump Box, Green Shroom Flasket, Peanut Moon Platter, *and* Seed Plate *are exuberant examples of a fruitful imagination. Peterson is also a studious and impassioned potter with affection for glaze chemistry and a reverence for the historical maestros of clay. Despite a penchant for arthropods and puns, Peterson's work has depth and complexity in tandem with his humor.*

Peterson attended the University of North Carolina–Chapel Hill and in 1996 received a BA in anthropology, with a minor in folklore. Peterson's work is included in the permanent collection of the North Carolina Pottery Center in Seagrove, North Carolina. Primarily working and exhibiting as a studio artist, he also teaches workshops throughout the country at venues that include Penland School of Crafts, Arrowmont School of Arts and Crafts (TN), Mudfire Studio (Atlanta), and The Kiln Studio (AL).

INFLUENCE OF NATURE

I grew up in a very small mountain town near Penland. My childhood was spent playing outdoors, camping, and exploring. I was very drawn to the cycles of nature, especially the lives of insects. I remember being fascinated by the way cicadas shed their skins. I didn't know much about Penland School of Crafts. The first time I went up the mountain to Penland was with a 4-H club, when we caught bugs in the field where the llamas used to graze. In high school, I visited the school and felt more open to the place: it seemed like there were kindred people there. Eventually I got married up at Penland and my parents and family came. I think local people are more accepting of the school now, too.

• • •

I didn't explore art until I graduated from college. At UNC–Chapel Hill, I got a BA in anthropology in 1996, with a minor in folklore. I went to a high school with only 1,300 students, so going to a university with 26,000 students was a huge change. It was good and it was rough. I signed up for art classes, but I never took them because I was terrified of critique. The only art course I took was a modern art survey class.

I studied Appalachian history, including handicrafts and material culture. I got a couple of articles published, one about my grandfather, who hunted for ginseng, and one about an ax-handle maker in Spruce Pine. This interest in handicrafts led me to take a ceramic hand-building class at John C. Campbell Folk School after college. The folklore field started to feel limiting, and when I took that first ceramics class, I was wide open. I fell in love with clay, and that's what I've been working with ever since.

• • •

After college, I set myself up to learn more about clay, and started working for potters Steven Forbes-deSoule and David Voorhees. In 1999, they pushed me towards Penland's spring concentration in wood and soda firing, taught by former core fellow McKenzie Smith. I attended as a work-study student. It was a huge vote of confidence for them to urge me to study at Penland. Although I was pretty integral to what Steven and David were doing, I was still a beginner. During concentration, I fell in love with Penland. The other students were an incredible part of the experience. It was the first time I felt comfortable around a group of people. I was so shy and didn't know how to interact with people. At Penland, we had a common interest, and we could just geek out on clay.

Ronan Peterson
Round Stump Teapot, 2015
10 x 10 x 6 inches
Red earthenware, slips, terra sigillata, glazes, woven metal handle
Photo by Kathryn Gremley

Opposite page:
Photo by Kara Ikenberry

Also, I could see what the core students were doing for the school. I was able to get the weekend cook work-study position and I worked closely with three core students. Kara Ikenberry was my boss in the kitchen. She was focusing on blacksmithing, and we got along well. (We later married in 2002.) As a work-study student, that cooking shift was the best because you had the whole week to yourself in the studio. I was very focused: I was there to make pots. I had fun, but I was working hard on what I was learning and doing the best I could at the kitchen work.

• • •

At that time, a lot of my work had cartoon drawings of bugs on it. I was encouraged to stop doing this. At first, this was hard for me to accept: I was selling quite a bit of those pots. Kathryn Gremley suggested that the work was one-note and needed to develop and mature. She was right. Roaches on cups—it's a novelty up to a point, but the audience is limited. Now I enjoy my work more because I've broadened it, even though I still have some "bugginess" in it. The emphasis is on the natural world seen super close up—cell division, growth and decay, how things inflate and deflate, and the textures and colors taken from nature. My work has an animated look. I get much inspiration from looking at painters like Phillip Guston and Matisse, who worked with such great color and patterning.

• • •

After that concentration, I worked in the kitchen the summer and fall of 1999, took Kathy King's clay class as a work-study student, and rented a studio on campus that winter. I had applied to the core program that fall and was very nervous because I wasn't very sure of my technical and aesthetic skills. But I believed this was the next step for me as a ceramic artist–potter and felt really lucky when I was accepted into the program.

At first, I had a really hard time balancing class time, work in the kitchen, and my relationship with Kara. After the first concentration as a core fellow, I had a better sense of how to pace myself. It takes a while to understand the rhythms of the school and what is expected.

• • •

Although my focus was ceramics during my core years, I took other classes—blacksmithing, painting and drawing, jewelry making, bookmaking. I didn't have an art background, so I felt like I was catching up. I think I tried every medium except for glass. Bookmaking with Barbara Mauriello was hands-down my favorite class. She was a great teacher, the students were phenomenal, and the process was completely foreign to me.

• • •

The hardest and most exhausting aspect of core was the continual social interaction during the summer. Being a shy introvert, the constant flow of students and visitors was challenging. I was living off

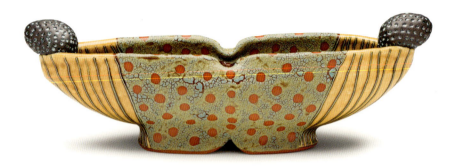

Ronan Peterson
Yonic Double Seed Server, 2015
7 x 21 x 7 inches
Red earthenware, slips, terra sigilatta, glazes
Photo by David Ramsey

Ronan Peterson
Green Shroom Flasket, 2014
9 x 6 x 3 inches
Red earthenware; wheel thrown, altered, layered slips, terra sigilatta, glazes, wax resist patterning; electric fired, cone 03
Photo by Fancy Rondo Prod.

Ronan Peterson
Peanut Moon Platter, 2013
5 x 18 x 18 inches
Red earthenware; wheel thrown, altered, layered slips, terra sigilatta, glazes; soda-fired, cone 03
Photo by Kathryn Gremley

Ronan Peterson
Tribud Vase, 2013
8 x 10 x 4 inches
Red earthenware; wheel thrown, altered, layered slips, terra sigilatta, glazes, wax resist patterning; electric fired, cone 03
Photo by Fancy Rondo Prod.

campus with Kara and our house was a great escape from the flurry of excited people. As I drove on Conley Ridge Road toward the school, I could feel the energy of the place, and I would actually get light-headed. The resident artists have the cushion of not being in classes, and people come to visit them. But the core fellows are the face of the school. We're the go-to people. The core experience was invaluable, but I could not go back now and do it again!

• • •

The other big adjustment for me was to trust that I was accepted by other artists and that my ceramic work was valued. I learned studio practice from my core peers. For example, I didn't really have good workflow, and Meredith Brickell was especially good at planning and working efficiently in the studio. Gradually, I developed my own studio practice. I filled in some holes in my art background by taking classes in different media. By talking with other core students, I learned a lot about painting and sculpture. Their confidence in what they were doing helped me, too, because I could see they were on their way, and it made me less scared to imagine that life. I could see myself earning a living by selling pots and enjoying it. Technically, the core program gave me the ability to be a professional studio potter.

• • •

After my two years as a core fellow, Kathryn Gremley hired me to work in the Penland Gallery. It was helpful to see all these professional artists who were working at such a high standard. I considered applying to be a resident artist, but Kara was ready to leave the area, so we moved to Chapel Hill. I effectively set up the studio life I would have had at Penland as a resident artist. I regret that I didn't have that constant exposure to aesthetic ideas and other artists, but it was time to do something different and new.

In addition to making pots, I started teaching ceramics classes at night. I got braver and found I liked teaching. I've also taught a couple of times at Penland, and those were great experiences.

The stars aligned for me to go to Penland, first as a work-study student and then as a core fellow. I wasn't very far along in clay when I was working in the kitchen that first time. I've had many blessed occurrences in my life, and being a core fellow was one of them. I have tried to make the most of my experience and investment in core, as well as Penland's investment in me.

LINDA FOARD ROBERTS
CORE FELLOW, 1982–1983

Studies of the Anatomy of Time, *a title Linda Foard Roberts has used to wrap her entire body of photographic work, suggests a poignant and percipient view through the artist's lens. Working mainly with large format black-and-white images, Roberts's photos read as poetic distillations of insightful moments. The narrative is captured seamlessly in* A Measure of Time, both thirteen years old, *in which youth is caught unguarded and the wind moves past the viewer. Roberts is a storyteller or scribe of life's passages, and though her images are filled with a personal tenor, they compel us to find bits of ourselves in her photographs.*

Roberts earned an MFA from Arizona State University in 1990, and a BFA from Virginia Intermont College in 1982. Her work is in the permanent collections of the North Carolina Museum of Art, San Diego's Museum of Photographic Arts (CA), the Gregg Museum of Art and Design (NC), and the Mint Museum (NC). Her photographs were shown in Shoot'n Southern: Women Photographers, Past and Present *at the Mobile Museum of Art (AL), and at Sol del Rio Gallery (Guatemala City) in the* American Photo 30 *exhibition.* Father's Day, *from her series* Belongings, *was awarded second place for the Julia Margaret Cameron Award for Fine Art and was exhibited at the Palais de Glace (Argentina). From 1990 to 1995, she was the executive director of The Light Factory Photographic Arts Center (NC); she is a 2008 recipient of a North Carolina Visual Artist Fellowship.*

Linda Foard Roberts
Mercy from the series *Grounded*, 2006
36 x 28 inches
Gelatin silver photograph,
5 x 7-inch negative

Opposite page:
Photo by Deborah Triplett

COLLECTIVE ARTISTRY

I was a photography student at Virginia Intermont College, when my professor Jay Phyfer invited me to meet Ben Simmons, the keeper of Penland's photography program at the time. Ben encouraged me to be a core student and he put in a good word for me. He also gave me responsibilities running the photography facilities for the summer. I was fortunate to become a core student through his recommendation because other core students were chosen from previous Penland work-study students.

Penland provided me the opportunity to continue doing my own art within a community of supportive artists, teachers, and art enthusiasts from all over the world. This foundation of support was invaluable to me at a very important time in my career. The experience greatly contributed to what I'm doing now—I continue to create art, which is an integral part of my life. The amazing sense of community at Penland and its creative support system enabled everyone to be nurtured and feed off each other.

I took only photography classes while I was a core student, but I gathered inspiration by wandering through other studios to see what students in other disciplines were studying. The early photographic work I created at Penland focused on portraits of women. I was looking for myself in the imagery. I was in my twenties and trying to figure out who I was. My models would come from all the different disciplines offered at Penland, and we would collaborate on the imagery. It was a good time for me to explore my work without traditional pressures.

• • •

My core student job was to be the school driver and photography technician. I was the first female in this position. The driver is the person who runs errands and picks people up from the airport in Asheville. I remember, one time, I had to pick up Fran Merritt, the founder of Haystack Mountain School of Crafts. At first, I couldn't find him at the airport because I was looking for a woman—and he couldn't find me because he was expecting a man. We finally got it figured out and had a good laugh about it.

I took my job as driver very seriously: I meticulously cleaned the cars for Bill Brown, who was very thankful. Other jobs as a core student included the changeovers between sessions, where I learned to make the beds using hospital corners. Another favorite core job was helping to cook the Sunday brunch. The food was always amazing. The granola and homemade yogurt were a favorite. I immensely enjoyed the work as well as the time spent with the other core students. I was so grateful to be part of this community. We were creative people, supporting each other, working hard together for Penland. What could be better than that?

I was also in charge of the parties that were held at Bill and Jane Brown's home. Before every two-week session, all the students and instructors were invited to the Browns for a party. Marvin Jensen helped me pick the music—Motown and rock and roll and lots of Aretha Franklin. During the party, the core students would move all the furniture out of the living room and stack it in another room so we had adequate room to dance. These parties were fabulous. And to this day, I love to entertain.

• • •

I was grateful for my time at Penland, where every day was a day to create art. Having new instructors and students every two weeks for the sole purpose of creating art was amazing. I enjoyed taking classes with the many talented photography instructors, including Alida Fish, Dan Bailey, Ben Simmons, and John Menapace. The students came from all over, with varying levels of experience in photography, and we were all bonded by our love of the photographic image.

While at Penland I was able to trade my work for the work of other artists. These trades made me feel fortunate for the friendships and validated as an artist. And I remember when I was first asked to submit work to Penland's annual benefit auction. I felt gratitude and a new sense of being valued for my work. I came away from Penland feeling such respect for the sense of community that the school creates. There isn't another place on earth like it.

After I'd spent a summer and a fall at Penland, Bill Brown recommended me to be one of two summer assistants to the director at Haystack for the following summer. When I was offered the job, I said yes. I believe that you have to say yes to the things that come your way, or they stop coming. At the end of the summer, I came back to Penland as a core student for the fall and winter sessions.

• • •

When I became a core student, I put graduate school on hold. Later, I went to graduate school at Arizona State, where I worked for Northlight, the university gallery. When I graduated, I became the executive director of The Light Factory Photographic Arts Center in Charlotte, North Carolina. In that capacity, I used many skills I learned at Penland and helped nurture a community of photographers, students, and art enthusiasts. We were a hub of creativity. While I was director, I met Jean McLaughlin, who was at that time the visual arts director at the North Carolina Arts Council. In that role, she helped guide me in the grant-making process for The Light Factory.

Linda Foard Roberts
A Measure of Time, both thirteen years old, 2014
36 x 30 inches
Gelatin silver photograph,
8 x 10-inch negative

Linda Foard Roberts
Ashes, from the series *Passage*, 2000
28 x 36 inches
Gelatin silver photograph,
4 x 5-inch negative

I still use 4 x 5, 5 x 7, and 8 x 10 cameras and film. I don't think it really matters whether you use film or digital technology to create your work; I think either medium is just a vehicle for saying what you are trying to express. It's all about your voice and what you are trying to communicate with your work.

• • •

I was six or seven months pregnant with my daughter, who is now sixteen, when I took my last Penland class. I've stayed in touch with the school and taken my children there to visit. I am looking forward to when they are old enough to take classes. Now I focus on creating my own work and taking care of my children. I savor all the moments with them, and that is one of the things that my work is about—recording the passing of time and holding onto moments in life and cherishing them.

If I had not been a core student, I'm not sure my life would have taken the same path. I feel so fortunate and so grateful to have had this experience. The core program is an incredibly generous opportunity for the school to offer. When I tell people what my alma mater is, it's Penland. That's where I truly went to school, and where my heart is.

Linda Foard Roberts
97 Years in Candles, for Grandmother, from the series *Simple Truths,* 2009
28 x 36 inches
Gelatin silver photograph, 5 x 7-inch negative

Linda Foard Roberts
Fifteen, 2014
36 x 28 inches
Gelatin silver photograph,
8 x 10-inch negative

CORE FELLOW CONVERSATIONS 109

HOLLY WALKER
CORE FELLOW, 1979–1981

Holly Walker's pots are hand built—a process of pinching up each layer of rolled coil to build the form. Pinching is a slow, rhythmic process that allows the artist time to envision a piece while working. Walker values the directness of touch with pinching and the quality of light on the resulting dimpled surface, intending for the speed, pulse, and tempo of making to be revealed in the finished pot. Walker approaches the outer surface of a pot as a painter—brushing colored slips over the raw terra-cotta surface in abstracted organic images built from transparent layers that reveal and visually retain the entirety of the process. Walker manipulates the robust forms, deftly altering the ratio of utility and concept.

Walker's education began as a painter; she received her BFA from Ohio University in 1974. There were sixteen years of experience in the arts, including her core fellowship years, before she received her MFA in ceramics from Louisiana State University. From 1990 until 1995 she was the executive director of the Watershed Center for Ceramic Arts (ME). Walker served as Penland School's outreach coordinator for several years before returning to her studio full time. Her résumé includes an extensive and far-ranging list of teaching engagements, including Nova Scotia College of Art and Design, Northern Clay Center (MN), Dartmouth College (NH), and Penland.

Holly Walker
Good Humor Jar, 2012
11 x 9 x 12 inches
Terracotta; hand-pressed slab, pinched coils, painted slips, glazes; electric fired, cone 04
Photo by Michael Sacca
Private collection of Gretchen Keyworth, director emerita of Fuller Craft Museum

Opposite page:
Photo by Michael Sacca

DIRECTNESS OF TOUCH

After graduating from college with a BFA in painting, I followed my brother, who was a chef, to Nantucket. I was living with a photographer and my wheel was set up in the darkroom. So I learned to throw pots with the lights out. I really learned to sense the material.

Pretty quickly, I realized I could use more instruction. An acquaintance knew of Penland and recommended it. I came to the school for the first time in 1978 as a work-study student to take a fall concentration in throwing and high-fire, taught by Jon Ellenbogen and Becky Plummer. I worked in the dining hall; I remember happily rolling silverware in napkins! I didn't want to leave. So in the winter I rented a little red house around the corner with a classmate. I worked for Jon and Becky in their newly built studio on Conley Ridge Road. Then I asked Jane Brown if I could be a core student and she "interviewed" me. I think she rewarded me with a core student spot because I was so intent and persistent about staying at Penland. I was an involved concentration student and also made myself useful and available as a scholarship student. I have always been responsible and hardworking—it's my nature—and I imagine Jane Brown recognized that.

...

I was a weekend cook. I had a little planning to do during the week to order the food, but mostly it was a Saturday and Sunday job. At that time, the kitchen cabinets hung down from the ceiling in a way that blocked my view of people's faces, so I got to know them by their midsections! I loved my job. I always had an interest in cooking, so both parts of my life were being fueled: working in the kitchen and creating in the studio. Because I'd been out of school a few years and had worked at jobs like waitressing to support myself, I was so appreciative that I could simplify my life and not worry about money. The trade part—that we could work for opportunity—was ideal for me.

I worked in clay the whole time I was a core student. For the instructors, having core students in their classes meant they could get some help with setup or finding supplies. We knew the classrooms because we were in them all the time. Being a core student meant learning to work with other people; having demands made on me; setting deadlines; getting the school ready for the next sessions; always interacting with people. It was a lesson in community living.

...

The first time I went to graduate school, I went to the University of Iowa, to study with Chuck Hindes, who had taught a wood-firing class at Penland. I was hooked on that technique, which was the focus of Iowa's program. Pretty quickly I realized I wasn't ready for a graduate program and that I had chosen the wrong place. I'd had such a well-rounded experience at Penland that I realized I wanted a more diverse approach, like I'd had as a core student. So after one year at Iowa, I went to the Archie Bray Foundation and studied there over the summer. Then I moved to the NYC area and set up a clay studio in my apartment. For five years I made slab-built forms and decorated them with majolica. Back to painting!

Then I found the right graduate program: Louisiana State University. I wanted an MFA so teaching could be a possibility. My main goal was just to keep learning, but teaching could allow me to have meaningful work. I started to explore what the role of a teacher meant. From my time at Penland, I recognized that teaching is much more than just skill development, and that students need to feel they've come to their decision making on their own. I saw my role as a teacher as being able to see what students want from their experience, and to just guide them in the way that makes the most sense to them personally.

After graduate school, I was hired to be the executive director at Watershed Center for the Ceramic Arts in Maine, where I started the Artists Invite Artists program. After five years, I started to miss Penland and that community of artists. In 1997, I convinced my husband, Geof, to move to the area. Ken Botnick, who was the director then, hired me to head up the new outreach program, bringing kids from the community to Penland for different enrichment experiences. I was the coordinator and Meg Peterson ran the educational component. Thanks in large part to Meg, we made that program work, and it became valuable to the school and the community.

It was a challenging job, and after three years I needed a change. So I stepped into a position at the Penland Gallery with Kathryn Gremley, which gave me time in my studio. When I turned fifty, I wanted more of that, so I gave notice. My last day in the gallery, I took my watch off, and thought, that's it: I'm just going to be a potter.

We moved to Vermont for a number of reasons, and it's been a good life. I have a studio right behind my house. I teach when the opportunity arises, which is a way for me to experience community.

When I teach at Penland now, the thing that strikes me about the core fellows is that they are apt to take classes in all areas. I don't get the sense when I teach a clay class that a core student is necessarily making pots as part of his or her trajectory. It's a different focus now, not good or bad. The school has grown so much since the '70s. So has its programming, which is a good thing. The mix of ages in the classes promotes the notion that you learn throughout your

Holly Walker
Palette: Intersections, 2015
15 x 8½ x 2½ inches
Terracotta, hand-pressed slab, pinched coils, painted slips, glazes; electric fired; cone 04.
Photo by Michael Sacca

Holly Walker
Elliptical Bowl, 2014
6½ x 4¼ x 13¾ inches
Red earthenware; pinched coils, hand-pressed slab; slips, glazes; electric-fired
Photo by Michael Sacca

lifetime. And the growing community of craftspeople and artists in the area really enriches what happens at the school. I think that the thing you lose as the school gets bigger is the sense of intimacy that I experienced; having fewer people on campus meant that each one of us played a bigger role. We knew most of the people who were around. A few of us would sit in local potter Cynthia Bringle's hot tub to warm up in the winter, and she would open her home for holiday meals for those of us who couldn't get away. I understand she still holds a Christmas Eve potluck to this day.

...

I know that as a core student I learned my dedication to my craft. I also learned to take more direction for my life, to make important decisions wisely. I learned the importance of community—we all had to pitch in to get the school ready for the next session. We represented the school—we were our own community and part of the larger one. Having role models nearby was also very important—the residents and artists working in the area—Paulus Berensohn, Jon Ellenbogen, Becky Plummer, Jane Hatcher, Cynthia Bringle—and so many others. Watching them create a life in crafts was thrilling. And knowing the impact of community on their lives had a big effect on me, too.

When I look at the work I made when I was a core fellow, I see the same simplicity yet quirkiness of form that still resonates with me. I also see in the more decorative early pieces my love of color and painting, which has become even more important to me in recent years. That early work has a certain elegance and casualness I've always put together. The experience I'm having while I'm working is what's important to me still. I know I'm going to have a product at the end, and that's fine, but the part that's really exciting for me is the actual work and stretching my imagination with each piece. That's what I honor the most.

Top:
Holly Walker
Mazurka, 2014
5 feet x 5 feet x 2 inches
Red earthenware; hand-pressed slab; slips, glazes; electric fired
Photo by Michael Sacca

Bottom:
Holly Walker
Step Jar, 2006
21 x 10 inches
Terracotta; hand-pressed slab, pinched coils, painted slips, glazes; electric fired, cone 04
Photo by Tom Mills

DAVE WOFFORD
CORE FELLOW, 1995–1996

The term atelier *seems most applicable in a studio where technical antiquities blend effortlessly with the digital age. Book and letterpress artist Dave Wofford approaches literary and graphic projects as artist, designer, and technician—often collaborating with writers to produce well-designed, hand-printed materials. A collective mind-set has been present in his studio environment as well; he has worked in or created collaborative spaces throughout his career. Critical to his artisanal philosophies is the belief in the value of intimate, tactile artifacts—the worthwhile pursuit of aesthetic beauty in the everyday object. Wofford's portfolio of fine press books reflects his ruminative sensibilities—soulful details such as paper made from old Confederate flags for a book of sonnets or a hand-printed bookmark for* Maji Moto, *included to complete the experience of reading the book. Wofford is an accomplished graphic designer with a varied and impressive roster of clientele, including Duke University Press (NC), the Full Frame Documentary Film Festival (NC), and novelist Allan Gurganus.*

Wofford is the proprietor of Horse & Buggy Press, a graphic design and letterpress printing studio, established in 1996 and housed in the Bull City Arts Collaborative in Durham, North Carolina. Horse & Buggy Press has collaborated with writers, visual artists, and historians on a range of award-winning book productions, including Maji Moto: Dispatches from a Drought, *featuring photos and essays by Fulbright fellow Courtney Fitzpatrick. Wofford's fine press books are included in the rare-book rooms of the New York Public Library, the British Library, the Library of Paris, and the Vatican. He is a 1994 graduate of the North Carolina State University College of Design.*

ARTISANAL PRINTER

I started out as an architecture student at North Carolina State University. In my second year I switched to the design and art department, which allowed students to chart their own course across all five departments to get a broad-based education. I really responded to this approach. I came across a flyer for a work-study opportunity at Penland, and my instructor, who taught typography, encouraged me to apply. So my first Penland experience was a photography/mixed media/sculpture class the summer of 1992, taught by Dana Moore and Tony Shipp. I went to Penland three summers in a row as a work-study student, taking workshops in drawing, photography, and printmaking.

Toward the end of college, I stumbled upon a Vandercook letterpress in the basement of the design school. I monkeyed around with it late at night. What I was doing was pretty crude, but I learned enough to produce a résumé that I used to apply for Penland's fall concentration in book arts in 1994. I learned so much during those two months from the instructor and the other students. I really wanted to stay on at Penland after the concentration. The role of core students and the opportunity to take classes appealed to me, so I applied to the program. I worked for the school over the winter, before my core student time officially started in March.

...

During the year I spent as a core student, I unexpectedly became interested in bookbinding and papermaking, especially papermaking because it was such a physical activity. I got really into what Paulus Berensohn, who used to give the talks at the beginning of sessions, said about meditation through repetition. When I pulled sheets of paper or used the letterpress, I used my body in a meditative way that I enjoyed. I made a bunch of journals and sketchbooks, and I was able to sell a few of them. I also sold a few letterpress books I made, collaborating with others. I made a book called *The Penland Coffee House* that included recipes from the coffee house, a few poems others wrote, and some of my drawings. I wanted to make things that were collaborative and had meaningful content.

Dave Wofford
Sound of Singles 7 inch, 2005
7 x 7 inches
18-pt chipboard; letterpress printed in three colors; edition of 300
Photo by artist

Opposite page:
Photo by Raymond Goodman

Another book I made utilized photographic imagery printed on handmade paper with Liquid Light emulsion. It was the Holy Grail to me at the time—making the paper, setting the type, putting my images down, and publishing my words with those of others. The writing was about not trusting society's "givens" and what you've been told, but investigating the world for yourself and forming your own opinion, looking out into the world, and challenging everything, including your own opinions.

• • •

Early on during core, I realized I was interested in collaborations and literary-focused projects. I wanted to make books that "regular" people would buy (as opposed to working to create things to appeal to collectors and special collection librarians). A lot of my inspiration at Penland came from metal workers and potters, because I saw them combining their body and their mind to make things designed to be used over and over and touched every day—a bottle opener or a mug—ordinary objects that are special because of their design, and because they invite people to be aware of the ritualistic moments every day when they use them.

• • •

My first winter as a core student, I distributed type in the letterpress studio, did a little design work for Penland, and worked with Meg Peterson on a educational book. I liked that work, but it isolated me from my core mates. I was happier when that work ended and I got to be in the kitchen with Critz Campbell, Leslie Noell, and Jana Harper. We were weekend cooks. I like the ritual of food preparation: it's like making a book—planning and prepping, and then cooking and cleaning up. I took a lot of pride in what I did and worked hard to make the food delicious so that people would look forward to coming to the dining room. It's one of the ways Penland takes care of people—providing great food and the chance to enjoy it with other people at those beautiful round tables. Cooking was also exhausting—eleven-hour shifts on weekends, two days in a row. But being twenty-two, I thought I could do it all—go to Saturday night dances, traipse through the woods on full-moon nights, work all those hours, and take five classes in a row. I burned out in session four!

Looking back, eighteen years later, I wish I'd stayed another year and taken workshops that were more experimental and exploratory and outside my focus. But at the time, I was all gung-ho to set up my own letterpress studio. And also I was totally broke. First-year core students didn't get a stipend when I was there. I remember trying to get $20 out of the ATM in Asheville one day and I didn't have it—that was the moment I realized I needed to find a job.

In March of 1996, I went back to Raleigh. Ray Duffey was a friend finishing up at design school, and he was interested in letterpress printing too. While I was still at Penland, we bought our first press. Ray had joined an artist cooperative called Antfarm in Raleigh. I con-

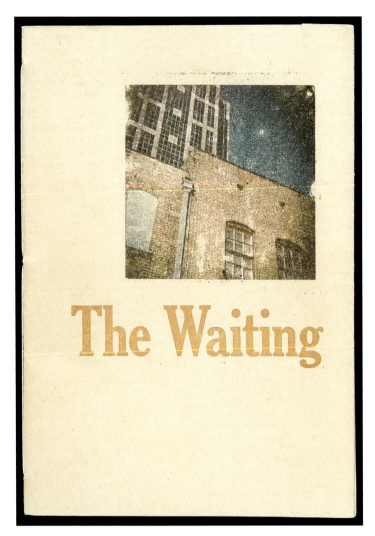

Dave Wofford
The Waiting (book cover), 1997
Poems and prose by Stephen Gibson
10½ x 7½ inches, 36 pages
Color Xerox transfer from Diana camera photograph by Dave Wofford; hand-set letterpress type, hand-sewn binding
Photo by artist

Dave Wofford
Ms. Films Festival Poster, 2004
9 x 11½ inches
18-pt chipboard; letterpress printed in four colors; edition of 200
Photo by artist

Dave Wofford
Maji Moto: Dispatches from a Drought (title spread), 2012
Photographs and text by Courtney Fitzpatrick
12 x 9 inches, 88 pages
Fine press book; letterpress and Indigo printing,
hand-bound by Craig Jenson of Book Lab II; edition of 170
Photo by artist

vinced the other members to make a place for me. Ray and I set up Horse & Buggy Press there and started doing our first projects. I focused on book projects in between the more lucrative wedding announcement projects. It was a challenge at first, and I still worked in kitchens to support myself in the early years. When Ray left to pursue music and woodworking, I continued Horse & Buggy Press on my own.

The biggest benefit of my time as a core student was being exposed to a variety of people from all walks of life doing a variety of work for many different reasons. There were professional craftspeople, who were masters of their craft, as well as beginners in a craft new to them, and then hobbyists who were amazingly talented but do this on the side, not to make a living. I loved that mix, and I loved rubbing elbows with people working in other media. I'll never forget talking with Bill Daley, the ceramicist, every morning at breakfast. Those conversations were as nourishing as what I was learning in my classes.

I wanted the experience of the core program more than grad school, where I figured I'd have the opportunity to make a larger body of work, but I wouldn't be exposed to as many people and different philosophies. Also, I had no interest in increasing my debt with grad school. I loved going to slide nights at Penland, where session instructors and studio assistants showed images of their work and discussed their philosophies. Amos Kennedy's and Hoss Haley's slide talks were particularly memorable and eye-opening for me. Even if I wasn't interested in their media, I enjoyed hearing people talk about why they made work and what their goals were. For me the whole craft thing was pretty new, coming from a design school. Penland exposed me to so much and provided a way to intensively study a medium I had just discovered at the end of college. I was hoping during my time as a core student to learn enough to feel confident enough to set up my own studio back in my hometown, and that's what I did. Penland was an awakening for me, not just in terms of book arts, but also in shaping my life.

Dave Wofford
Farmers' Market Broadside, 2003
20 x 14 inches
Kenaf/cotton 100-lb cover stock, illustration by Josef Beery;
letterpress printed in five colors; edition of 500
Photo by artist

Resident artists at The Barns, 1995.
Left to right: Joe Nielander, Suze Lindsay,
J. Doster, Toby, Carmen Grier, Terry Gess
Photo by Dana Moore

RESIDENT ARTISTS

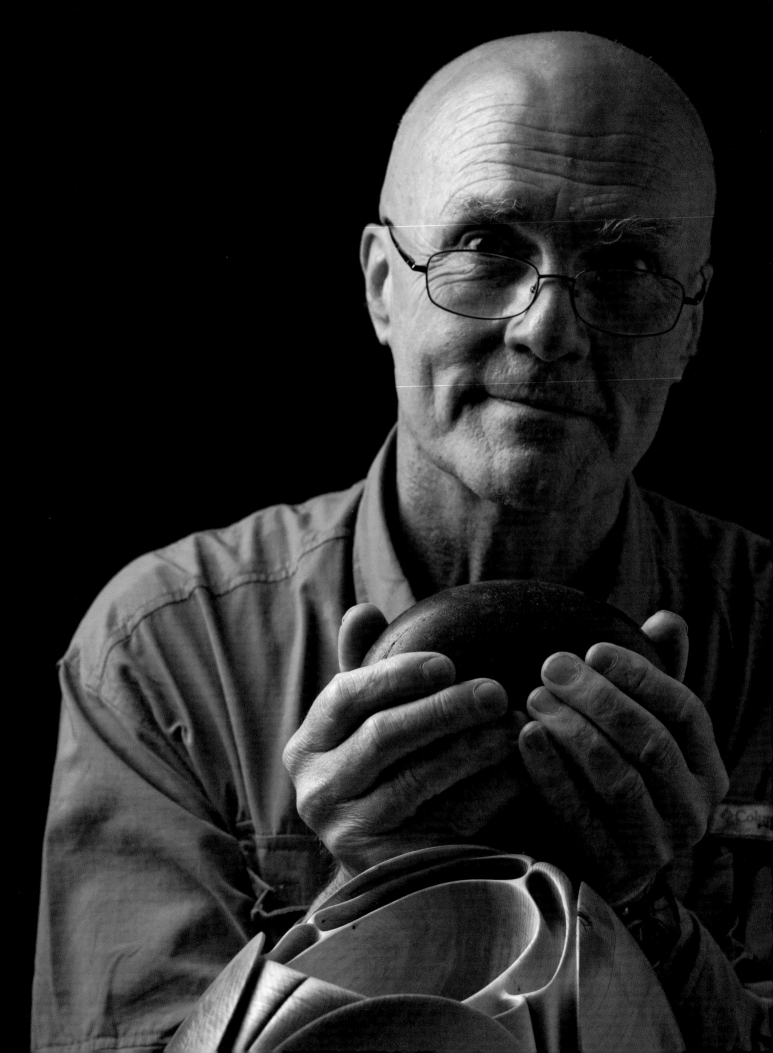

PETER ADAMS

RESIDENT ARTIST, 1979–1984

Sculptor Peter Adams defines himself as a "deep ecologist" to reflect his passionate commitment to protect earth's resources and coexist in harmony with nature. Adams's writings on his blog, Life on the Edge, *give voice to an elemental existence where there is no space between life and the artist's life's work. Adams has worked in wood throughout his artistic life, coaxing waves out of the grain and burnishing surfaces with countless hours of handwork. For Adams, the act of making is fundamental, as he works to release the form from its material restraint. He is equal parts philosopher and craftsman, producing works that quietly resonate with environmental, social, and political action.*

Adams received a BA degree from Harvard University (MA) in 1968 before joining the Peace Corps and heading to Korea. He returned to earn an MA from Antioch University (OH) in 1981. After his years as a Penland resident artist, Peter made his home in Australia, first working as a lecturer in design at the University of Tasmania in Hobart, and later as a studio artist and steward of one hundred acres of land he named Windgrove, where he has established an artists' center for retreat and sanctuary. Adams has received a National Endowment for the Arts Fellowship (1985) and an Australian Council Fellowship (1993). His work is in the permanent collections of the Museum of Fine Arts, Boston, and the Powerhouse Museum in Sydney, Australia.

AGENT OF CHANGE

I was headed back to Anchorage, when I decided to stop in Madison, Wisconsin, because I heard that the university had a furniture program. That's when I met Skip Johnson, who started the wood program there. It was late May and the school was closed, but he saw me walking around and asked if he could help. I told him what I wanted to learn and that I lived in Alaska. He invited me to his home for three days. That's the kind of openhearted man Skip was. He suggested I come back the following year, spend one year in the wood program, and also audit classes in sculpture and drawing for free. Skip had been the first resident artist in wood at Penland, so he suggested that I might be interested in going there sometime.

• • •

The summer of '76, I organized a road trip with some buddies and stopped by Penland just to visit and didn't leave—I took a course every session that summer. Penland was building a new glass studio and they needed help. I volunteered, and stayed through fall concentration. That's when I met Bill Brown's son, Bill Jr., who told me his dad wanted me to stay on through the winter. I got a place to live, and I had access to the wood shop as my studio. That was a very formative winter for me. I stayed, worked in the studio, and built the dining room table for FOPS[1] as a way to say thanks to Bill Brown Sr. for letting me stay for the winter.

• • •

In 1979, I returned to Penland and asked Bill Sr. if I could be a resident artist. He said yes, but I needed to fix up a house to stay, so I did a lot of work on Barely-a-House and lived there. I was probably one of the longest serving residents—not because of my outstanding artistic abilities but because I involved myself in a lot of activities. Making my furniture was just one aspect of my time there. Along with my good friends and fellow residents, Debra Frasier and Dan Bailey, I helped launch the Fourth of July parade. We were inseparable. Debra had great ideas, Dan went along, and I was the stand-up guy. We were behind a lot of the theatrics, the movie making, and the puppetry during that time.

Peter Adams
Buddha's Beads, at Windgrove's Roaring Beach overlook, 2009
19¾ x 2¾ x 2¾ feet
Blue gum; carved
Photo by artist

Peter Adams
Birth of Beauty, 2008
8¼ x 61½ x 9¾ inches
Huon pine, myrtle; carved
Photo by Peter Whyte

Opposite page:
Photo by Peter Whyte

Peter Adams
Ovum d'Aphrodite, 2011
8¾ x 27½ x 20¾ inches
Huon pine, stone; carved
Photo by Peter Whyte

Peter Adams
Detail of *Ovum d'Aphrodite,* 2011
8¾ x 27½ x 20¾ inches
Huon pine, stone; carved
Photo by Peter Whyte

Peter Adams
Dehiscence, 2012
15¾ x 7 x 18¾ inches
Huon pine, stone; carved
Photo by Peter Whyte

For me, Bill Brown's vision *is* Penland, and he is what drew me there and kept me there. He could see if a person had a strong artistic muse. The main attraction for me back then was the diversity of creative thinking; it was really wonderful to be a part of. Another important aspect of being at Penland was the personal relationships I developed with Debra Frasier, Paulus Berensohn, and so many others. Paulus would talk about how the handmade object had meaning—which was also what I learned from indigenous people in Alaska. The idea that you have to find out what's behind the making has stayed with me my whole life. As Rumi would say, I'm interested in finding "the star inside the pot."

To me being an artist means to be responsible beyond personal self. I can be pretty judgmental about that. I learned this from Paulus—the notion that art is not achievement, art is behavior. Reciprocity. Gratitude. Forgiveness. Being an agent of change. Making a difference. The message is that despite our pathologies, we can still do some good.

• • •

During the seventh year I was teaching in Tasmania, my house burned down. Somebody set fire to a forest near me and four houses burned to the ground. In thirty minutes, everything I owned, all my work, all of it, was gone. So I got a clean slate. I see my life as a series of blank slates; going to Harvard, Korea, Alaska, Penland, Tasmania were a series of blank slates. After the fire, I bought some land, moved a bus onto the property and lived there until I built my house in 2001. The result is Windgrove, my own version of Penland. This is my way of giving back, by re-creating something a little bit similar out here. I offer a tiny residency that I call the Refugee-in-Residence program. It's my attempt to offer a "refuge" for people seeking a place of support, rest, and inspiration for a couple of months. Those years at Penland worked that way for me. I bring workshops here; they're not always about art, but about leadership, sustainability, and personal development.

It's pretty isolated at Windgrove, although there is a creative community nearby. On the property, you feel nurtured by nature and get the chance to take your personal and professional life deeper into dialogue with the sacredness of this earth. The rural location of Penland deeply affected my experience. I need that connection to nature. I think we all do. In the city, you can't open up in the same way. Being in the country allows you to put your feet onto the earth, and there's a language you find there that allows you to tap into your creative and personal growth.

1   Friends of Penland School House, now called Heavens Above

Opposite page:
Peter Adams
Windgrove, 1991–present
100 acres, coastal Tasmania
Aerial drone panorama of installations at Windgrove.
Top to bottom of image: *Wombat Circle, Debra's Friendship Circle* (three concentric circles of trees), installation by Jenny Dewhurst for *Sculpture by the Sea—Tasmania 2001* (circle of trees with blue swirl), and *The Gaia Walk,* leading to Sunset Point. A series of benches, entitled *Seating for Dialogue,* are placed throughout the property.
Photo by Dan Bailey

ADELA AKERS
RESIDENT ARTIST, 1968–1970

The work of Adela Akers presents the contrast between ordered formalities and animate materials—the linear nature of the loom juxtaposed against the unruly nature of woven horsehair, the resilience of metal, and the force of the artist's vision. Akers has made a lifetime's work of merging mathematical sequencing with an unselfconscious process. The surfaces of her woven constructions embrace the linear discipline of warp and weft and still defy and effortlessly ignore the plane of the cloth. Exploring and continually reinventing the use of disparate materials such as linen, horsehair, and metal foil, Akers has absorbed and redefined her understanding of cultural textiles and created timeless works.

Akers has lived a multifarious and creatively rich life. She was born in Santiago de Compostela, Spain, grew up in Cuba, and graduated from the University of Havana with a degree in pharmacy. She went on to study at both the School of the Art Institute of Chicago and Cranbrook Academy of Art (MI). Her work resides in the permanent collections of the Renwick Gallery of the Smithsonian American Art Museum (DC), the Metropolitan Museum of Art (NYC), and the Museum of Arts and Design (NYC). She is professor emeritus from the Tyler School of Art of Temple University in Philadelphia, where she taught from 1972 until 1995. She has received many awards for her lifetime achievements, including a College of Fellows award from the American Craft Council and a Pollock-Krasner Foundation Grant, both in 2008. Since her retirement, her home and studio are located in Guerneville, California.

AT HOME IN THE WORLD

My undergraduate degree from Havana University prepared me to be a pharmacist, but art was always important to me, and my parents encouraged me to do what I felt strongly about. They had great confidence that I could figure it out. So I applied to the Art Institute of Chicago while I was still in Cuba in 1957. I thought I would become a dress designer. When I arrived in Chicago I spoke very little English, so school was challenging. The first year I studied drawing and design, but then I discovered weaving, and that's what I studied, along with ceramics, in the second year. I was drawn to the immediacy of clay, but I loved handling thread and using the loom.

I went to Cranbrook Academy of Art in 1960 because I felt it would help me become an artist. In 1962, my work was accepted for the first time into a big show in New York, called *Young Americans 1962* at the American Craft Museum, which is now the Museum of Art and Design. It was my first national exhibition. In 1965 I was offered the opportunity to go to Peru for four months to work with Alliance for Progress.[1] This was during the Kennedy years. I was living and working in a village in the Andes, helping Peace Corps volunteers assist local weavers to market their handmade items. That was a rewarding experience.

...

When I returned to Chicago, Joyce Chown, a weaver from Canada I met at Cranbrook, came to visit. While she was there, I got a phone call from Penland, asking me to teach a session. I didn't know much about Penland at all, but Joyce told me it was a great place, and she talked about the residency program. I wasn't sure what I was going to do next, and I thought, well, I'm a city girl, and I don't know if I want to live in the country, but I can try this for two weeks. So I agreed to teach a session in beginner's weaving.

I fell in love with the place. I asked Bill Brown about the Resident Artist Program, and he said he'd love to have me and to let him know when I'd like to come. The details were a bit vague, but he said I wouldn't have to worry about finances: the school would help with expenses, and I'd pay the school back when I could. I had gotten a small Cintas Foundation Fellowship, which was good because I felt I couldn't embark on a new plan without knowing I could pay for the residency. I went back to Chicago, packed my clothes, my portable sewing

Adela Akers
Basket, 2012
16½ x 17 x ¾ inches
Linen, horsehair, paint, metal foil; hand-woven, stitched, sewn
Photo by Bob Stender

Adela Akers
Winter Gold, 2011
11¾ x 28½ x ¾ inches
Linen, horsehair, paint, metal foil; hand-woven, stitched, sewn
Photo by Bob Stender

Opposite page:
Photo by Bob Stender

Adela Akers
Gold Rust, 2013
23¾ x 13 x ¾ inches
Linen, horsehair, paint, metal foil; hand-woven, stitched, sewn
Photo by Bob Stender

Adela Akers
Circles in the Square, 2010
19¾ x 19¾ x ¾ inches
Linen, horsehair, paint; hand-woven, sewn
Photo by Bob Stender

Opposite Page:
Adela Akers
Gold Inside, 2008
17¾ x 15 x ¾ inches
Linen, horsehair, paint, metal foil; hand-woven, stitched, sewn
Photo by Bob Stender

machine, and some yarn and threads. Then I called Bill, and he said, "Just fill it up with gas, and come." That was the contract.

• • •

I was the first resident fiber artist at Penland. I didn't even know how important weaving was to the school until after I was there a while. I didn't know much about the South either, but I had a supportive community from the very first day. I became such good friends with other residents, including Mark and Jane Peiser, and artists who lived in the area. After my residency, I came back to Penland for many years at Thanksgiving and Christmas—the people and the place became part of my continuity. It felt like coming home.

• • •

At the end of the first year of my residency, The Barns were renovated so we could work there all year round. I had my own separate studio upstairs—it was beautiful and very quiet. The only bad thing was that my studio was above the potters, and sometimes dust would rise through the wood floor into my studio!

I remember standing in the studio and thinking, I'm going to have all this height—the ceiling in The Barns was very high. So I started working larger: eight and ten feet tall. I hung one piece from the ceiling. This was an exciting opportunity. I worked so many hours every day. We all did. Many days were difficult, but I continued to use the time well. I was making work for myself, not to please everybody. I was making these big black-and-white shields. One time, the artist Lenore Tawney[2] came to visit my studio, but I wasn't there; I learned later that she was impressed with my work. That was very encouraging. Those two years at Penland gave me the freedom and the time and the space to develop my work in new directions.

• • •

During the residency, I was always sending my work to shows, and I was getting invited to be in exhibits. I was in a show called *Objects: USA* in Winston-Salem in 1969, curated by the art dealer Lee Nordness. My piece was one of many that were donated in the 1970s to what is now the Museum of Art and Design. This gave me a big step up in the art world.

After two years, I knew I wanted to go back north. I moved to New Jersey and then to Philadelphia because I got a teaching job at Tyler School of Art at Temple University. I came back to Penland when Bill got an NEA grant in 1971 for the "Nifty 50"—imagine 50 Penland instructors and past residents spending two weeks at the school—such a wonderful experience and so much fun!

• • •

I come from a family of survivors. My parents lost everything in the Spanish Civil War, and then they lost everything in Cuba. We started all over when we moved to the US. I saw how it was possible to do that—to have the strength to begin again. All the places I studied art were important to my work. Because of the timing in my life, Penland stands out as being the most important. It was a home, a place to work and a community, with all that support, emotional and financial. And we weren't competing with each other; we were supportive of what we each were trying to accomplish.

The program changed my life. During those two years at Penland, I was independent: I learned to be on my own and to have confidence that I could make work that pleased me. The residency gave me the time to develop the strength to know that I could do it—be an artist. There is strength you can draw from those mountains.

1   The Alliance for Progress (Alianza para el Progreso), initiated by President John F. Kennedy in 1961, aimed to establish economic cooperation between the United States and Latin America.

2   Lenore Tawney (1907–2007) was a pioneering American artist whose innovative woven work helped to shape the course of twentieth-century fiber art. Her connection to Penland began in 1954 with a tapestry workshop taught by Finnish weaver, Martta Taipale, and continued throughout her long life. Tawney considered her 1954 experience at Penland to be a turning point in her career. In recognition of this association, the Lenore G. Tawney Foundation endowed a scholarship at Penland in 2004.

STANLEY MACE ANDERSEN
RESIDENT ARTIST, 1979–1983

Stanley Andersen is a studio potter—he has devoted a life's work to producing functional earthenware meant for daily use: utilitarian tableware. Wheel-thrown, sturdy, domestic forms are the canvas for a vibrant palette of exuberant brushwork. Using the historical Italian technique of maiolica, painting with stains and oxides over an opaque white surface, Andersen creates distinctive and expressive work. The thought of an assured hand moving quickly and directly over thousands of pots may contradict the complexity and thoughtfulness of his work. The rim of the plate is the correct rim; the handle of the mug, the right fit—here is the balance of workmanship and artistry.

Roots in Iowa farmland, followed by work on a cross-country pipeline construction crew, prefaced college years at the University of Iowa, where Andersen received his BA in philosophy and sociology and, later, an MA in library science. A period of employment at Columbia University Law Library (NYC) was followed by a long sojourn in Europe and a return to Iowa where he began working in clay. He received an MFA in ceramics from Rhode Island School of Design in 1978, just prior to arriving at Penland. He has lived and worked in Mitchell County, North Carolina, ever since.

PHILOSOPHER POTTER

After high school in Iowa, I worked as a farmhand and on cross-country pipeline construction for two years before I decided in 1963 to give college a try. I fell in love with learning. I graduated from the University of Iowa in 1967 with degrees in both sociology and philosophy and had every intention of pursuing a scholar's life. I was accepted to graduate school in philosophy at Iowa, and promptly set off on a six-month motorcycle trip from Turkey to the Balkans, through Europe to Morocco.

When I returned to Iowa City to begin graduate school, I discovered that the life of a scholar no longer held the appeal it once had, and it was clear to me that I had a strong need for physical as well as mental activity. I dropped out of school in 1968 and moved with Karen, my future wife, to New York City, where I worked as the circulation desk supervisor at the Columbia Law Library and Karen worked in publishing. After two years of working and saving, we went to Europe for ten months. Then we moved to Iowa City, where I enrolled in graduate school in library science with a view to becoming a reference librarian.

• • •

It was then, at the age of thirty, that I began working in clay, taking classes at the craft center in the student union. Before long, clay became central to my life. One day I accosted Chuck Hindes, the head of the University of Iowa ceramics department, and asked if he'd be willing to let me work informally in the clay studio; he kindly agreed. From then on I spent every spare moment in the clay studio. Chuck suggested I look into the MFA program at Rhode Island School of Design (RISD), run by Norm Schulman. And that's what I did, graduating in 1978.

I knew I didn't want to teach. I wanted to be a full-time studio potter. Norm told me about the residencies at Penland. In his view, the residencies were set up for people like me, just out of school, people needing breathing space and time, affordable rent, and a nourishing environment.

• • •

Norm and his wife, Gloria, had a home in Penland, and they invited me to stay with them, look around, and meet the Browns. So in the fall of '78, I did. I met Bill and Jane. I spent most of the day walking around campus, meeting the residents at The Barns, and talking to Cynthia Bringle. I thought the place looked pretty good. At the end of the day, I went to Bill and said I'd really like to come down here, this looks like a good deal. And Bill just gave me this blank look and

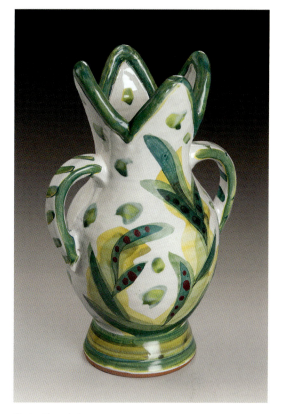

Stanley Mace Andersen
Vase, 2014
12 x 8½ x 6 inches
Earthenware; wheel thrown, assembled, oxidation fired, cone 03; maiolica technique
Photo by Mary Vogel

Opposite page:
Photo by Robin Dreyer

said, "Well, you can't do that. We don't know who you are. You've never taken a class here, and you know, this is a small community. I'm sorry, but we just don't do that."

I asked what I could do to introduce myself a little better. Bill said I could come down and be a studio assistant in one of the clay classes that summer. Don Reitz was going to build a salt-kiln during a two-week session and he needed help. So that's what I did. In addition to working on the kiln, I washed pots and pans after lunch every day. I didn't sleep much. There was a lot of pressure to get the kiln built, and we did and fired it a couple of times. It was incredible. There was a tremendous sense of energy on campus, exhilarating and exhausting at the same time. Those two weeks were an excellent introduction to life at Penland. At the end of the session I found Bill and Jane at the Pines, and I said, well, what do you think? Bill said, about what? I said, well, could I come down and be a resident? He said, of course!

• • •

When Karen and I moved to Penland, there were still original local folks living around the school. Cordie Tipton lived just down the road from us. When she found out I was from Iowa, she called Karen and said, "Now, you have Stan come down here. I've got some chickens I want him to take care of. You can have all the eggs, but if once a day he'd feed them and put some water out, I'd appreciate it."

There were some town folks who were suspicious of the hippie artists at Penland, but there were others who worked at the school, like cook Pearl Grindstaff, who was part of the Penland family. The maintenance staff took care of Cordie, too, fixing broken pipes, etc. The school was so small then. It was a different time.

After I fed the chickens in the morning, I'd head for The Barns. I was delighted with the size of my studio space, the biggest I'd ever had. I worked long hours. It was a really important and positive period. Except for the brief period of potting in my cramped basement, I'd never before been able to devote all my time to making pots.

• • •

I fit in pretty well with the other Penland artist residents, even though, at thirty-seven, I was the oldest. Karen and I were very quickly swept up in the life of the school, a more communal experience than either of us had had before, and one that neither of us would have imagined enjoying quite as much as we did.

I set up my studio in The Barns and continued to work out some of the technical difficulties involved in maiolica. I had just been accepted into the Philadelphia Craft Show, so that was auspicious. Those three years were really important to me artistically and professionally. I was building a production line of maiolica dinnerware with repeatable forms, and I was developing my painting style. The work back then was very spare, very few colors. I was taking this

Stanley Mace Andersen
Longnecked Vase, 2012
14 x 7 x 8 inches
Earthenware; wheel thrown, assembled;
oxidation fired, cone 03; maiolica technique
Photo by Mary Vogel

Stanley Mace Andersen
Gumbo Bowl, 2013
4½ x 8 x 5½ inches
Earthenware; wheel thrown, assembled;
oxidation fired, cone 03; maiolica technique
Photo by Mary Vogel

Stanley Mace Andersen
Pitchers, 2013
10 x 7½ x 5½ inches
Earthenware; wheel thrown, assembled;
oxidation fired, cone 03; maiolica technique
Photo by Mary Vogel

work to shows and fairs, putting it out into the world. During the course of my residency, I established relationships with a number of galleries and other outlets. By the time I left Penland, I had built the foundation of my career. I believed I was actually going to be able to make a living doing what I loved.

• • •

One of the interesting things about the Penland residency was there wasn't that kind of tension, suspicion, and competition I felt at graduate school. Being a resident meant you were at another stage in your profession, and there was a lot of interaction with the other resident potters and artists, and we gave each other tips and shared information. The program was great for someone like me, who came out of the rarified atmosphere of RISD and had to learn to deal with students and visitors in the summer who showed up at The Barns. I learned a lot about how to talk about my work. The public's response to my work became an important part of how I experience being a potter.

• • •

Though Karen and I hadn't originally intended to settle in North Carolina, in the end that's exactly what we did. We bought an old farm about fifteen minutes from the school. I built a studio and settled into the life of a full-time studio potter. It has been satisfying to be surrounded, not only by old friends we've known since 1979, but by the gentle yet constant influx of new artists, new friends, drawn to the area in the past thirty-five years by the presence of Penland.

Stanley Mace Andersen
Tureen and Plate, 2010
11½ x 10 x 10 inches
Earthenware; wheel thrown, assembled;
oxidation fired, cone 03; maiolica technique
Photo by Mary Vogel

JUNICHIRO BABA

RESIDENT ARTIST, 1998–2000

The Memory of Shadows, an exquisite series devoted to Junichiro Baba's fascination with light, mass, and the balance between man-made structures and nature, spans nearly twenty years. Baba grew up in Tokyo surrounded by urban geometries; the play of light and shadow and natural versus artificial environments is key to understanding his material choices. Devoid of color, the cast glass acts as a conduit for absorbed light, shifting the light to shadows before being caught against the cast-concrete elements. Light is the critical material in Baba's work, as he creates three-dimensional drawings with clear glass cane or cast vessel forms to contain it.

Baba began his glass studies in his native Japan at the Tokyo Glass Art Institute before traveling to the United States to receive his MFA from Rochester Institute of Technology (NY) in 1996. After completing the residency at Penland, he began a trans-Pacific teaching career as a glass instructor at Appalachian State University (NC), Meisei University of Art and Design (Tokyo), and Joshibi University of Art and Design (Japan). He also teaches private classes in his Tokyo studio. He maintains his artistic and personal connections to North Carolina by having a seasonal home near Penland.

CONDUIT FOR IDEAS

After I graduated from Rochester Institute of Technology (RIT), I was accepted into the fellowship program at the Creative Glass Center of America at Wheaton Arts in New Jersey, where I met Kenny Carder. He was also a fellow at the Creative Glass Center and had been a resident artist at Penland. That's how I learned about the school. At RIT, I was drawn to glass as my medium, but I minored in ceramics and metals. I really liked those materials, too, because we used heat to change their form.

My main goal when I applied for the Penland residency was to show my work to the public as much as I could—to see how my work "works" in society. I am the kind of person who wants to collect ideas, make something, and bring that to the public. I want to minimize my own personal expression. I just want to pass along the ideas. I visualize something, and then I make, for example, a sphere of glass to sit on a table. When people see it and feel peaceful, that feels best for me.

• • •

I was born in Tokyo. I grew up among concrete structures. There was so much that was square, that showed mass—so much steel, reflecting glass, mirrors. The buildings were very geometric and man-made. But even with all that, I could feel the force of nature, which is there, showing up in the little grasses and moss that grow between the concrete. Living in the shadows of the building, we can still feel the rays of sunlight, and the light makes beautiful shadows, too. That's what I look for, and then I convert the languages of the scenes into my pieces.

I make forms with glass that express weight and scale, movement and stillness, and that invite light to pass through. Glass is a manufactured material, but when glass melts, it flows into the mold with gravity, and that's a force of nature. We can feel the force of nature in the processes of the materials, and I can visualize that geometry and put that form into my work.

Truly, I didn't do much while I was a resident except work in the studio. I sold some of my pieces during that time through the Penland Gallery and Blue Spiral in Asheville. I have never made pieces just for the sake of selling them. That's just a waste of time to me. I just wanted to make the pieces and show them. If people like them, they buy them. The most important thing to me is the visualizing and creating for myself, not the selling.

• • •

Junichiro Baba
The Memory of Shadows, 2012
19 x 15½ x 5 inches
Glass; cast
Photo by artist

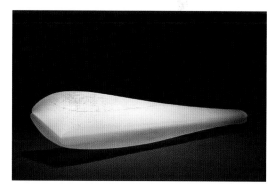

Junichiro Baba
The Memory of Shadows, 2009
8 x 46 x 9 inches
Glass; cast
Photo by artist

Opposite page:
Photo by artist

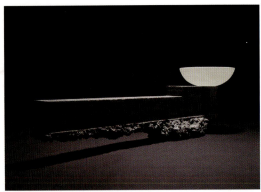

Junichiro Baba
The Memory of Shadows, 2010
12 x 48 x 15 inches
Glass, concrete; cast
Photo by artist

There were six other resident artists when I was at Penland. I liked them all, and still have a friendship with many of them. Hoss Haley is a good friend. I really enjoy seeing him work. He uses concrete and iron and makes these heavy, big pieces. I can feel the weight of them, and I want that weight in my own work. He also appreciates the materials he works with. His techniques show his ideas clearly. I really appreciate that. He makes a lot of simple forms, and what he feels about his materials is very similar in some ways to how I work. I wanted to learn how to forge, so I took an iron class while I was a resident. That influenced my work and how I use other materials with the glass.

• • •

Every year I feel much more responsible to bring my ideas to society. I have a studio in Tokyo in which I make artworks, and I also teach private classes there. If people want to know how to work with glass, I am happy to help them learn how to realize their dreams. That's very creative to me and important, and it feels like the same motivation as making my own art—to be able to pass on this knowledge to other people.

I don't feel that I'm teaching—I am just passing knowledge along. I am providing freedom to the students to find out for themselves. I usually ask the students questions: Why this? What are they trying to do? If their work is good, I ask more questions! I just want to give them the opportunity to think about what they are doing.

At Penland, the students who came to my studio mentioned that my place was peaceful. They needed a space to be quiet, in peace. My studio at Penland was very different from Penland's teaching studio where loud rock and roll music was usually playing. They were also interested in how I make my pieces because I usually carve clay as a mold material. It's a slow process. I appreciate the process, more than what the piece looks like in the final form. To me it is very important to be in peace when you make the mold or are carving. I might have influenced students in that way.

• • •

I think of Penland as my second home, although it is 10,000 miles from Tokyo. Nothing follows me from where I live in Japan. Everything at Penland is different—the forms of the trees, the clouds, breeze, rocks, grass, the people. That difference makes my mind clear. Here I feel like I'm in the middle of my dreams at midnight. So much contrast makes this place special to me. I feel totally new, like a baby, and that's so precious.

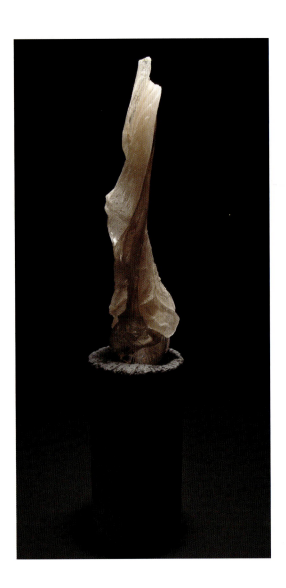

Junichiro Baba
The Memory of Shadows, 2012
37 x 6 x 6 inches
Glass, concrete; sand cast
Photo by artist

Opposite page:
Junichiro Baba
The Memory of Shadows, 2012
19 x 8½ x 4¼ inches
Glass, concrete; sand cast
Photo by artist

VIVIAN BEER

RESIDENT ARTIST, 2005–2008

Vivian Beer is a furniture maker, yet her materials and vision are from decidedly nondomestic sources. Automotive paint surfaces on voluptuous steel fabrications, concrete over steel armature, masculine and feminine, cool and fierce, craft and design under tension—these are the elements at play in the work. Beer deconstructs the functional aspects of furniture, retaining necessities and seamlessly morphing the planes and surfaces to redefine the function. The spaces in between appear to be as critical as the steel or concrete mass itself, considered and deliberate design choices. Beer counterbalances her industrial lean by consciously referencing the human element in her furniture.

Beer earned her BFA from Maine College of Art in 2000 and her MFA from Cranbrook Academy of Art (MI) in 2004. In addition to the Penland residency, she has been a Windgate artist in residence at SUNY Purchase (NY), a resident artist at San Diego State University, and a research fellow at the Smithsonian Air and Space Museum (DC). Her work is included in the collections of the Renwick Gallery of the Smithsonian American Art Museum (DC), the National Ornamental Metal Museum (TN), and the Museum of Fine Arts, Boston. Beer's work was included in 40 under 40: Craft Futures, *the 40th anniversary exhibition at the Renwick Gallery of the Smithsonian American Art Museum in 2012 and in* Furniture Divas: Recent Work by Contemporary Makers, *at the Fuller Craft Museum (MA) in 2012. Supported by the John D. Mineck Furniture Fellowship, Beer traveled the country during 2014 in a mobile studio, searching for inspiration and collaboration. In March 2016 she was the winner of Ellen's Design Challenge on HGTV.*

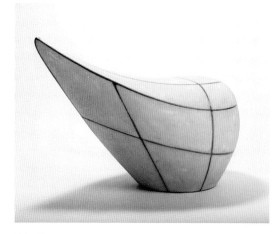

Vivian Beer
Rain Drop, 2011
25 x 25 x 39 inches
Patinated steel and cement with pure pigment
Photo by Alison Swiatocha

Opposite page:
Photo by Alison Swiatocha

INNOVATIVE DESIGNER

After I graduated from college with a degree in sculpture, I worked as an architectural blacksmith. Although I loved blacksmithing, the work limited what I wanted to say artistically and as a designer. My goal became finding another career where I could work with metal and expand my design vocabulary.

I chose to get a master's degree in metals at Cranbrook, not to become a teacher, but to be a professional designer and entrepreneur. The school has a great industrial design program as well as metals program. And, they emphasize the decorative arts history of metalworking. I got to be around people working at a very high level intellectually.

• • •

In 2003, I went to Penland as a work-study student to take a furniture design class in the wood shop with Peter Pierobon. It was the summer after my first year of graduate school. While I was there, resident artist Marc Maiorana suggested I apply for the residency. I was uncertain, but being at the school and talking with Marc gave me a chance to see what the residency was all about. I decided to apply with work that showed my interest in furniture making. I saw the program as a way for me to try out the artistic voice I had developed and was ready to put into action. The residency is meant to give you a chance to make a change in your career; sometimes that means at the beginning of a career, and sometimes midcareer. For me, I wanted to make a living off my own designs.

• • •

A lot of life happened in the year between applying and getting that phone call from program director Dana Moore. I was working full time as a manager in a metals studio in Florida. When I got the "yes" call, I was very excited. Even so, it's hard to walk away from a real job and go where you're not sure you can make enough money to buy food. I took a big risk in going to Penland. On the plus side, Penland is so supportive, and the rent is very low. I believed I could risk it all artistically and not freeze or starve to death. Still, I had to build out my shop and buy equipment. I had just enough equipment to start—a welder, an air compressor, a grinder, and some hand tools.

At first, I was intimidated. I worried about how I would thrive as a self-employed artist in the middle of the woods. I also felt very witnessed—because your studio is open to the public at Penland. I was dropped into this community where everyone knows each other and no one knows you, and they are watching you and the work you do. It took a lot of confidence for me to just stay in my studio and send a postcard with my work to galleries and to everyone I knew—that's what I did the first four months. I was hunting down galleries, sending proposals to publications. Rather than being prolific in the work itself, I did this major PR push. That was hard because people asked, so what are you doing? I was afraid I was promoting work that no one was ever going to see. I figured I'm never going to be able to sell my work if no one knows about me and I'm in the middle of nowhere. I didn't realize then how many people were going to come to me. I didn't appreciate then the visibility of being at Penland with 200 people coming to my studio every two weeks.

• • •

Finally I got so bored doing the marketing that I needed to make something! A few months of not making had become torture. I think those first months were also about procrastination. It was scary to be in a situation where I could make whatever I wanted. Then I kicked it into gear and I was a monster! Years two and three were so productive that I stopped having a social life. It got intense. That may be part of the cycle of self-motivation, but I learned how to push really hard. This was different from doing work for a critique in grad school; it was more like training for a marathon. The residency is like a pressure cooker—you have three years and only three years. I knew I wasn't going to stay and start a life in the Penland area. My thoughts were, if you can't make it happen in three years, then you're going to get a real job. It wasn't like life as usual; I put my all into those years. I was really focused.

• • •

It was very helpful to see people living the lifestyle of full-time artists at Penland. I was able to witness firsthand what that looked like. It's a different residency for every person; some spent more time up on the hill being social and making connections. Some turned out a production line. And others, like David Chatt, were there to learn a completely new material. Jenny Mendes and her husband were like roadies doing the craft shows. Anne Lemanski was more like me—doing time-consuming work and going after a few galleries. Cristina Córdova was showing her sculptures at SOFA.

I started getting into galleries after a year and a half. In year two, I was working with Bill Zimmer, owner of the William Zimmer Gallery in Mendocino, California, and going to SOFA and Art Palm Beach. One year I packed up this moving truck with my artwork and work from other Penland residents to take to SOFA Chicago. I must have had $300,000 worth of work in

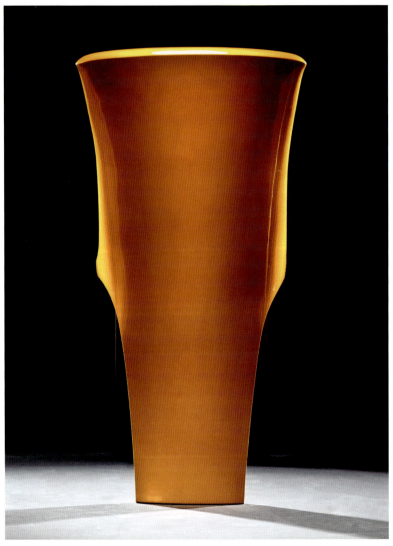

Vivian Beer
Anchored Candy no. 6, 2014
60 x 21 x 42 inches
Steel, automotive paint; cold hydraulic press formed, fabricated
Photos by Kenneth Ek

Vivian Beer
Ruffle Chair, 2008
25 x 22 x 28 inches
Steel, automotive paint; formed, fabricated
Photo by artist

the truck—everyone chipped in to rent it, and I drove it all the way to Chicago.

•••

During open houses at Penland, I didn't have anything to sell. I didn't want to make one hundred bottle openers. I felt that if I had to do that, then I would be wasting my time. I'm lucky in that I've always had a large technical skill set, and when I couldn't buy food, I'd go help build stuff. Anne Lemanski's builder partner, Matt, would hire me to work with him; I'd help him pour a house foundation or put shingles on a roof. I helped Cristina on some of her big pieces that involved metalwork. This was a better option for me than coming up with a production item.

•••

The Resident Artist Program was a hard dismount because the economy crashed the year I left. But by then, I'd made enough work to show for a year, without making new pieces. The relationships with galleries that I'd been fostering began to pay off. I had my first solo show—*A Colorful Tide*—at the 1912 Gallery in Emory, Virginia. After two years of resettling in Manchester, New Hampshire, I had my shop and was starting to rev up for production. The last few years have been my busiest, most productive—absolutely glimmering—and each year has been better.

It was an honor to be a Penland resident artist, and I'm proud of what I did with the time. The residency is not a pedigree, and not everyone would want it. In many ways, it's like a gun to your head. That's the thing that's great and hard about it.

Vivian Beer
Forth Bench, 2011
48 x 96 x 48 inches
Stainless steel, concrete, ferro-cement; formed, fabricated
Photo by Alison Swiatocha

CRISTINA CÓRDOVA
RESIDENT ARTIST, 2002–2005

Visualizing emotion and conjuring a physical form to contain it, sculptor Cristina Córdova taps complex sources of personal expression and technical ability. Córdova's sculptures are poetry embodied in human forms, infused with potent gestures and a guarded gaze—introspective narratives concerned with personal and cultural history. There is a field of vision surrounding the work, an unavoidable engagement and spiritual directness that are unflinchingly honest. Córdova often places her figures in mythic landscapes, accompanied by subjective creatures as if on a quest. The use of material is equally transcendent, showing minimal regard for technical limits and the conventions of accepted ceramic properties. Córdova works intuitively, processing the ingrained influences of her culture, environment, and education, yet she is able to convey universal concepts in her work.

Córdova completed her BA at the University of Puerto Rico in 1998, before earning an MFA in ceramics from Alfred University (NY) in 2002. She has received numerous grants and awards, including the North Carolina Arts Council Fellowship, a Virginia A. Groot Foundation Recognition Grant, a USA Artist Fellowship, and several International Association of Art Critics of Puerto Rico awards. In 2012, Córdova was included in 40 under 40: Craft Futures, the 40th anniversary exhibition at the Renwick Gallery of the Smithsonian American Art Museum (DC). Her work is in the permanent collections of the Renwick Gallery, the Colección Acosta de San Juan Puerto Rico, the Mint Museum of Craft + Design (NC), and the Museum of Contemporary Art (Puerto Rico).

DEDICATED MAKER

When I finished undergraduate school in art in Puerto Rico, I had fallen in love with clay. My educational options in my country were limited, so I scheduled a variety of ceramics courses at craft schools in the United States. One of these was a pinching workshop taught by Paulus Berensohn and Jimmy Clark at the Touchstone Center for Crafts near Pittsburgh. Paulus, with his long Penland relationship, talked about the school like it was Shangri-la. The pinching workshop was wonderful. I had never done work like this before. I was already in love with the material, but I wasn't mature in terms of my concepts or technique. I had dabbled in the figure, but I could have easily been swayed to do anything else, so long as it was exploring clay.

In 2002, I was finishing graduate school at Alfred University in New York. My husband Pablo Soto, who was in the glass program, comes from a family of makers. His grandmother was familiar with Penland and spoke highly of it as a community. She suggested we look into the residency program. There were several students in graduate school who told me about Penland, too, and thought it would suit us well as a creative family; we had recently had our first baby. So I called the school to see if I could apply for the residency, and the people I spoke with told me again and again that they highly recommend we come visit. I took this to mean that our chances of acceptance would be better—I don't know if that was exactly what they were saying, but that's how I took it. So we scrambled and scheduled a quick trip there. We stayed with potter Cynthia Bringle. I'd never met her, and I was totally intimidated by her at first. Little did I know that she would become a dear friend. But that first encounter—with her crisp answers—was intimidating.

•••

We were very excited about coming to Penland as a family. But when I shared my excitement with my professors, they were a little mystified. Some had never heard of Penland, and others had no sense of the program, or how it would reflect on me career-wise. I think the notion for many of them was that after you finished graduate school, you got a teaching job and started to go up the tenure ladder. Most of my peers had chosen to do that. So when I came to Penland, some of my peers and advisors thought that I didn't fully understand what I was getting

Cristina Córdova
Temporal, temporal, allá viene el temporal ("The storm, the storm, the storm is coming," from Puerto Rican folksong), 2014
26 x 17 x 10 inches
Ceramic, metal; hand built
Photo by artist

Cristina Córdova
VACA, 2013
14 x 9 x 10 inches
Ceramic; hand built
Photo by artist

Opposite page:
Photo by Robin Dreyer

into. But I trusted the fact that people we loved, who loved us, had told us to look into Penland.

Early on in my life, I identified myself as a maker, as opposed to somebody who could split her life between academia and time in the studio making work. In graduate school I felt we'd been in this bubble, and afterwards there was no mediation between that world and the real world. Not only materially—Pablo and I had no budget in place and no network of support—but also emotionally; we were uprooting ourselves from a place we'd been for so long, and we weren't certain we'd find that flow again. That's what I was looking for when I applied to Penland to be a resident artist. Also, being married to a maker, I was looking for a place that could accommodate him as well. Fortunately, when we arrived at the school, Pablo started working right away with Greg Fidler, a glass artist and second-year resident who became a dear friend and mentor.

...

We arrived at Penland to begin my residency right before auction weekend, and I was told to put my work out in The Barns. I had brought two pieces from my thesis show and some sketches. We had just packed up and moved to this unknown, rural, quiet place, and all of a sudden the floodgates opened, and all these people came through Penland to see my work. At the auction, I had one of my first insights about Penland—here's this place, rural and seemingly remote, that is in fact an organism that stretches itself in different ways far beyond its actual location and definition. It organizes people, activities, and discourse about the world of contemporary craft, and its tentacles reach all over the country and, to some degree, abroad. And these various dynamics are not visible when you first see what appears to be a craft school in the mountains.

In the bubble of graduate school, our work was inspected and talked about critically. But, honestly, the commercial part of art was kind of taboo to discuss. So I came to Penland having been put through that wringer, and felt this place was wonderful in its quietness, but I also worried that it was too remote. And suddenly at that auction I got hit with the whole side of people purchasing art: how much is this and how much is that? This jump-started a whole new aspect of art education for me, one that had to do with the commerce of work.

The other major insight my first year as a resident was getting used to the variations in rhythm from auction to fall to winter to summer again. My year started with a bang at auction—I sold most of what I had put out. Then fall and winter set in, and that was rough. It was so drastic. My studio wasn't set up yet. I had to fund all my equipment. It takes time to get all that together—you accumulate it as you go. I was working toward a show at the end of winter, and I remember that being one of the hardest times in my life. I was in this limbo: not fully understanding where I was and how to play my cards in relationship to the

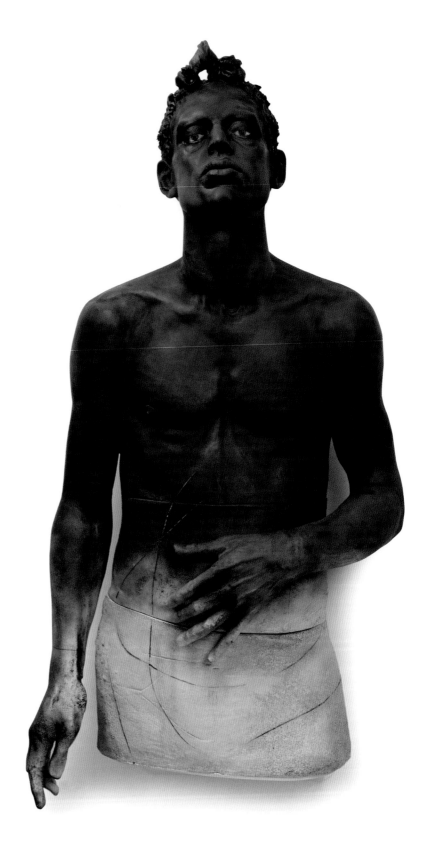

Cristina Córdova
*Autorretrato como hombre en la noche
(Self-Portrait Like a Man at Night)*, 2013
60 inches tall
Ceramic; hand built
Photo by Robin Dreyer

opportunity. And I had a tremendous amount of work to do, so I felt I couldn't really reach out to people. I also felt disconnected from graduate school and that life. And I had a husband and a baby. From our house, I would walk in the cold to the studio every day, and I called that my Walk of Fire. I would psyche myself up to such a degree that I would be like a tornado when I got to the studio. I remember that very well!

...

I was so unsure how to make the residency work—shape a life making work and selling it. On the other hand, I saw Cynthia Bringle and others making their lives as makers, so I knew it could be done. You see the evidence that it's doable, but between point A and point B—especially in the beginning—you have to take a big gulp and just go for it.

But it worked out. And soon after that, Penland became this amazing source of support for me. I remember in crunch times, needing one hundred grams of whatever, and being able to go to someone and ask if I can buy it, and have this other artist be so helpful. So there was emotional support. From a commercial standpoint, the support was there, too: my gallery found me through the school. Teaching opportunities came, too, and collectors—all those threads wind back to Penland. I think one of the unique things about the residency and what it has become is that, by encouraging so many artists to stay in the Penland area, the program really is effective in showing new artists how to become professional artists. And the school's reputation draws many different types of buyers and art supporters to come here, because they are interested in seeing what artists are doing. There are pockets like this in other areas of the country, but this region is really strong. And it's all because of the school, and in particular, the residency program.

Cristina Córdova
Colonia (Colony), 2014
52 x 17 x 10 inches
Ceramic, metal; hand built
Photo by Steve Mann

STEPHEN DEE EDWARDS
RESIDENT ARTIST, 1980–1983

A childhood on the California coast influenced Stephen Dee Edwards's early work in glass: blown glass taking on the organic tonalities of the Pacific. Complex and technically virtuosic, Edwards's physalia and tripod forms transformed glass into watery ocean dwellers. Turning to cast glass in the late 1990s, Edwards continued to abstract both human and animal forms reductively: large format, monochromatic distillations of color and texture. Title references to landscape and architecture reveal his current muse in works that employ both his skill and the material qualities of cast glass to narrate the subject.

Stephen Dee Edwards received his BA from San Jose State University (CA) in 1978, and continued his education at Illinois State University, receiving his MFA in 1980, just prior to arriving at Penland. He moved from Western North Carolina to take a teaching position at Alfred University (NY), where he taught for twenty-two years until retiring in 2010 and returning to his studio practice. His work can be found in over thirty public collections, including the Renwick Gallery of the Smithsonian American Art Museum (DC), The Hokkaido Museum of Modern Art (Japan), and the Corning Museum of Glass (NY). He is a former president of the Glass Art Society.

TUNED TO CONNECTIONS

Back in the old days of the Penland residency, it seemed like it was a handshake and a dinner conversation with Bill Brown that got you a spot. I was Rob Levin's studio assistant. His residency at Penland had just ended, and he said, "Do you want to be the next glass resident artist?" and I said, "Let's do it!" We went and talked to Bill, and I was in. Back then the residency was a unique apprenticeship. The school backed you in everything. You paid $75 rent total for housing and studio. Penland had charge accounts at places like the lumberyard and the propane company; you had a folder in the office with your account charges, and you were expected to pay back the school. If you couldn't pay it back right away, the school paid your propane bill for a few months. Making a living as an artist is tough, and the Penland residency eased you into the field.

• • •

The original Penland glass studio was pretty rough. The windows didn't have glass, so we just put plastic over them; everything froze in the winter. My first week as a resident, I walked into this empty studio. There were gas connections coming out of the wall, but other than that, you had to build your own equipment. This turned out to be a blessing because I built the studio to my needs, and when I left, people helped me move all my equipment in several trucks two mountains over. In the glass world at that time, Penland residents and students didn't leave—they moved right into the community, which felt like an extension of the school. Many of the residents started their careers, built their studios, and then stayed in the area.

My work has always been a continuum. As a resident artist at Penland, my goal was to continue to work with sea forms and imagery, and build a body of work I could sell. I learned how to make my own colors at Penland, and that's been a big advantage to me over the years. During the '80s, things were moving so fast in glass. In my last year as a resident, I applied for and got an NEA grant, which gave me the opportunity to open my studio in nearby Green Mountain when I left the program.

• • •

When I was a resident artist, we were expected to show slides of our work to students at the beginning of each session and to talk to them when they came down to the studios. That was our only responsibility. Bill Brown and the rest of the administration had a hands-off policy towards the residents. They wanted us to concentrate on our work and not have to mess with the public too much. They let the public come down once in a while, but otherwise we were protected.

Stephen Dee Edwards
Blue Swallow Tail, 2006
85 x 48 x 16 inches
Hot cast glass, steel
Photo by artist

Opposite page:
Photo by Stephen Dee Edwards

Making a living was very challenging then. I didn't have any contacts. Right after grad school, I went to New York City to try to sell my work and everyone turned me down. "Where have you shown before in New York?" they all asked. I was completely deflated. Then I came to Penland and found this super supportive glass community. The essence of the contemporary glass movement really comes from Penland because of the artists who were there—Harvey Littleton, Fritz Dreisbach, Mark Peiser, Rob Levin, Billy Bernstein. It was a terrifically welcoming and helpful community. We would exchange everything from packing materials to technical and conceptual ideas. I was going out into the world, but I wasn't alone. I had this instant support system that was so beneficial.

All the residents were 100 percent in—trying to make a living from their work. And it happened pretty fast. Within the first couple of months of being there, all of a sudden I had people interested in my work. People would come to the area to see Harvey Littleton's studio, then visit Penland School and find their way to the resident studios—and suddenly I had international curators walking into my shop. It all started for me there. It was unbelievable. Many of my commissions over the years have been directly related to contacts I made while at Penland as a resident artist.

• • •

Artists are rugged individuals, so we residents all held pretty close to what we did. The cross-pollination was more on a human level than an art level. I saw individuals affect one another in terms of how they lived their lives, rather than how they made their work.

By nature, artists are experimental, and that was the idea behind the residency program—to take some of the financial pressures off, so you could stretch your wings and fly, and not have to worry as much about having to sell work. There was no way you could fail! That was a tremendous comfort to an artist. Mutual support was key, experimentation was encouraged, and success wasn't measured by how many shows you had, but more by how you were getting along in your life.

The residency program was not like getting an MFA, where there is so much stuff that is expected outside of your studio work: taking art history classes, art seminars, critiques. In grad school, someone is checking on you and your work every day, and you have to measure up—there is a standard and a yardstick. The Resident Artist Program at Penland was more isolated, hermetic. You had to help yourself with no oversight; you had to reach out for feedback.

• • •

Success can be judged by the money you make or by the satisfaction of being your own boss. I've seen a lot of humble potters that are way happier than CEOs. They really believe in making simple things that people can hold in their hands and use. Other artists make wildly conceptual things that the one percent is willing to pay a lot of money to purchase.

Stephen Dee Edwards
Red Whale Tail, 1999
24 x 42 x 4 inches
Hot cast glass, steel
Photo by artist

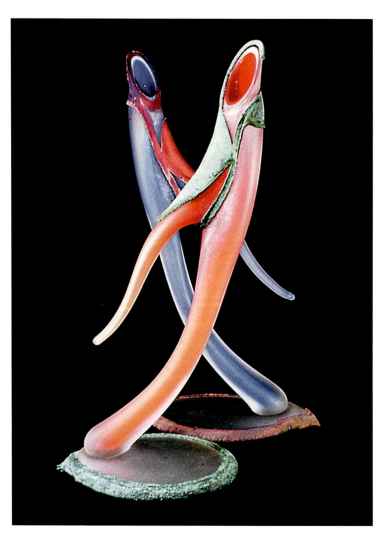

Stephen Dee Edwards
Amphibians, 1988
24 x 16 x 16 inches
Blown glass; sandblasted, acid etched, electroplated copper, patina
Photo by artist

And then there's everyone in between. Penland's residency program supports the whole spectrum—from people who do intense handwork and make a living at it, to people who do outrageously ethereal pieces that have no functionality at all. Penland puts an equal value on each of those. It's beautiful.

・・・

I love teaching. I taught at Penland once right after the residency in 1989, and then I taught there again in 2013. It was wonderful to teach at Penland again after a thirty-year gap: everything had changed and everything had remained the same!

I enjoy hearing from students who are still working with glass. It's important to me to pass on what I've learned; glass is handwork that has been passed down for centuries from one person to another. I like being part of that. My job as a teacher is also to give students a leg up. Penland people from the old days often call me up for recommendations for jobs, teaching positions, and shows. I absolutely feel a responsibility to help them out. I've been so lucky.

Being an educator has facilitated my life as an artist. I'm fortunate in that, aside from my time at Penland, I never had to make a living off my work. So the goal for the past twenty-two years has been to make enough money from my art to support the expenses of running my studio. I do make an effort to sell my work. I enjoy sharing the happiness that the work brings me. I'm still energized by making glass. I wake up at 5:00 a.m., excited about the work I'm going to do.

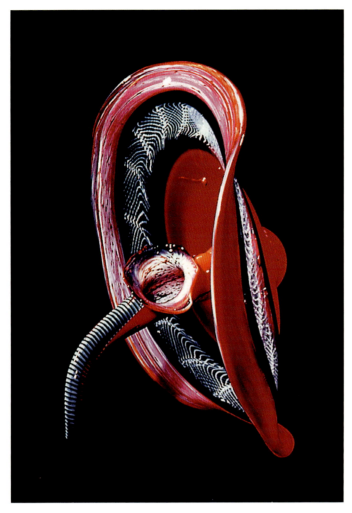

Stephen Dee Edwards
Red Physalia, 1980
16 x 16 x 16 inches
Blown glass, sandblasted
Photo by artist

Stephen Dee Edwards
Betty's Glasses, 2012
4 x 15 x 14 feet
Hot cast glass, steel
Photo by artist

RESIDENT CONVERSATION 147

SUSIE GANCH
RESIDENT ARTIST, 1999–2002

Throughout her career, artist and activist Susie Ganch has challenged our perceptions of beauty. As a studio artist, Ganch's metal work is on the margin between jewelry and sculpture, a marriage of fine craftsmanship and alternative materials. The works in her exhibition Tied *used the collective detritus of consumerism—coffee cup lids, plastic bags—accumulated waste deftly redefined as art and adornment. Ganch positions the viewer as both jury and offender, reframing beauty in the light of ethics. Her work through community-centered collaborative arts projects and education is a form of reciprocity—repurposing unwanted jewelry or fueling critical dialogue with the fundamental intention of action and consequence.*

Ganch is currently associate professor and head of the metals program at Virginia Commonwealth University. Tied, *her 2014 solo exhibition at the Visual Arts Center of Richmond (VA), included two galleries of Ganch's independent work, and one gallery devoted to the collaborative project, Radical Jewelry Makeover. Ganch is the director of the Radical Jewelry Makeover, an outreach program of the nonprofit Ethical Metalsmiths. Ganch received her BS in geology from the University of Wisconsin–Madison and continued on to receive her MFA in metals from UW in 1997. She is a recipient of the Virginia Museum of Fine Arts Fellowship, the Theresa Pollak Prize for Excellence in the Arts, a Virginia Commission for the Arts Grant, and multiple VCU faculty research grants. In 2014, Ganch's work was represented by Sienna Patti Contemporary at PULSE Contemporary Art Fair in Miami Beach, Florida.*

Susie Ganch
Falling in Love: 1999, 2011–2013
Mixed media, collected detritus, steel
12 x 62 x 12 inches
Photo by David Hunter Hale
Collection of Sienna Patti Contemporary

Opposite page:
Photo by Terry Brown

PURPOSEFUL ARTISTRY

I distinctly remember how Penland came into my life in 1996. I was in graduate school at the University of Wisconsin–Madison, pursuing a masters of fine arts in metalsmithing and jewelry under the mentorship of Fred Fenster. He asked me to go with him to Penland to be his studio assistant for a one-week pewter-smithing class in the summer. I didn't know what Penland was, although Fred talked about the school all the time. He had been teaching there for years.

We came up the mountain road late at night and there was the meadow, illuminated by the moon. Some young men were playing Frisbee in the field. I already knew this place was not of this world. The next morning the sun was out and I saw the mountains—it was pretty magical. The first day was surreal—the wonderful food in the Pines, the picnic tables, and volleyball. Everyone seemed to know each other and to not really care about a new person (like me). I felt like an outsider—a voyeur in a closed community—but I was so enchanted. By the next day, people weren't looking through me anymore. It was like, oh, you're still here? Who are you then? When I lived there, I remember looking through people, too, if I didn't think they would be around for long, because it's kind of like getting your heart broken every two weeks. You could fall in love with a new person or group of people, and then the session would end and they were gone. So, the people who live at Penland have a little bit of a protective shell.

• • •

That first week at Penland was pivotal. Fred's class was in the lower metals studio, and in upper metals, Kate Wagle was teaching. One day at lunch, Kate told me she wanted to recommend me to Marcia Macdonald as her studio assistant for spring concentration. I agreed: I had no plans after I graduated in December. Marcia called me a few weeks later and invited me to do this. So, on the one hand, I felt like a complete outsider, but I also saw how the door was opening and Penland was organically pulling me in. Everything snowballed from there. I was Marcia's assistant for eight weeks, and she became super influential and a great friend to me. She helped me figure out that I wanted to be a resident artist.

• • •

In 1997, after concentration, Geraldine Plato, who was assistant director at Penland then, invited me to be the assistant manager of the coffee house, so I stayed and got to see the residents working. Hoss Haley had just started that winter as a resident, and I got to know him and watch him work. He was called a midcareer artist and was coming in to change his work and have time to evolve. In my application, as an emerging artist, I stated that I had a threefold goal: to teach, to make my work, and to learn how to have gallery representation and sell my work. When I was accepted as a resident I felt like I was the baby of the group, being fresh out of grad school. I was really mentored by the other residents. I mirrored their work ethic and asked them questions; for example, about how to file taxes and develop a production line.

• • •

The biggest challenge for me the first year as a resident artist was making money. That first winter, I made $28.75! I had to figure out how to be disciplined about making work and how to market it or sell it. Unlike grad school, no one was going to come into the studio and give me a critique and push my work in any direction. It was all on me. I had to be my best and worst critic, my best and worst advocate. I had to have the most conviction about what I was doing. Theoretically, you learn that in grad school but then when you're switching into trusting yourself and practicing that, it is a big transition. I know that memory softens everything, and in hindsight, I think, oh, that first year wasn't so challenging. But I do remember having a hard time sometimes even leaving my apartment across from The Barns. I'd look out the door and think, "I don't know if I can go out there today."

There was plenty of support, however. The first gallery I reached out to was the Penland Gallery. Kathryn Gremley gently guided me through so many things—pricing, how many pieces in a series to do. I had never made production work before and I was just figuring that out. Then other galleries opened their doors to my work, including my one of-a-kind pieces. The galleries in North Carolina and throughout the region really respect Penland, so there's a built-up trust about the residents and their work, and doors did open.

• • •

During my three years as a resident, I learned many things about myself—what I enjoyed making and why, and what was important to me as a studio artist. My projects grew more intricate, technically demanding, and took longer to make. By the time I completed a piece, I felt like I'd had a whole relationship with it, from the beginning stages in my head to drawing and experimenting, and finally to finishing. The process was so satisfying and intimate. Outwardly, the pieces were never narrative, but the ideas embedded in the designs and decisions were clear to me because of that constant conversation with what I was making. Looking back on that time, I really grew into the artist I am now because of the relationship I developed with my work and studio. Without the unencumbered

Susie Ganch
Pile: Starbucks on Robinson, April–December 2012, 2013
84 x 120 x 12 inches
Mixed media, collected detritus
Photo by David Hunter Hale
Private collection

Susie Ganch
Detail of *Pile: Starbucks on Robinson, April–December 2012*, 2013
84 x 120 x 12 inches
Mixed media, collected detritus
Photo by David Hunter Hale
Private collection

studio time that Penland offered me, I'm not sure I would have given myself the permission to explore work in this way.

• • •

During my residency, Fred asked me to teach a five-week metals class every summer at UW. The main problem with this schedule was that I would get back to Penland in August and have to scramble for the benefit auction, and I know that I missed a lot of stuff in the summer. But I couldn't help it. I really wanted to learn how to teach, and I would never let Fred down.

When I was at the end of my residency, Dana Moore asked me to make a presentation to Penland's board of trustees about my experience, and I remember saying that my time at Penland really defined me. When I was done with my residency, I was not moving to San Francisco to take a job in a coffee shop and do my art on the side. I was an artist. That was my profession. I make art. I need a studio and I need to make my work. I think I would have arrived there eventually, but because of when I entered the residency—right after grad school—it really shaped me. I was also gifted with the other resident artists who were there; I shaped myself by mirroring them, and by the end, I was an artist.

I teach my students that they are not in art school simply to get an education and then become a coffee barista. No, they're going to be *artists* who (like everyone else) make money—even if they do that by making coffee. I also try to teach them that what they're learning is a viable, marketable skill: along with selling their own work, they could do jewelry repair or work for another artist. Other teachers may think that's telling students to sell out, but my goal is for them to be in the studio. I never forgot my sales that first winter at Penland: $28.75.

Top:
Susie Ganch
Detail of *Drag* (object), 2013
132 x 36 x 36 inches
Mixed media, steel
Photo by Terry Brown
Sienna Patti Contemporary

Bottom:
Susie Ganch
Drag, 2012
34 x 52 inches (unframed)
Giclée print
Sienna Patti Contemporary

HOSS HALEY
RESIDENT ARTIST, 1997–2000

Hoss Haley's work is informed by decades spent exploring the intersection of humans, machines, industrial materials, and pure form in artwork such as Daedalus, from 2000, a fabricated iron and steel figure with elaborate wings powered by a crank imbedded in its back, or his Coil series with elegant fluid gestures created from COR-TEN steel. A fusion of intellectual dissection, material proficiency, fearlessness, and curiosity fuels Haley's monumental and innovative works. Scrapyard waste begat The White Series; conversely, a landscape of deconstructed glacial boulders was the seed for Erratics.

Hoss Haley began working with machining and steel fabrication as a child, under the influence of Kansas family-farming traditions. Apprenticing as an architectural blacksmith in the Southwest led him eventually to Penland, first as an instructor before returning as a resident artist. During the residency he intentionally moved his work away from functional blacksmithing and toward the pure sculptural forms for which he is now well known. Embracing scale for the public arts sector, Haley has completed projects for the Pack Square Conservancy (NC), Charlotte Area Transit System and Mecklenburg County (NC), as well as privately commissioned large-scale steel sculptures. Museum collections include the Mint Museum of Craft + Design (NC), John Michael Kohler Arts Center (WI), and the Charlotte Douglas Airport FBO Terminal (NC).

SCULPTING WITH METAL

I learned metalworking growing up on a farm in Kansas. I was the fourth child in my family, the one expected to stay and take over the farm, but I really loved being in the shop and making things. As a teenager and in my early twenties, I had a couple of really good commissions. One time, a farm newspaper wanted a big wheat sculpture, and someone said, "That Haley kid north of town does metalwork." Fresh out of high school, I had BS-ed my way into this commission that is still standing, for better or worse. But I knew that if I stayed in Kansas, I would just keep making wheat and cow sculptures. So I climbed off the combine one summer day after the wheat harvest was finished and told my dad I was leaving. I think he always thought I'd come back.

• • •

I went to Santa Fe to apprentice with Tom Joyce, a very talented blacksmith, and I stayed for six years to learn and work. By 1991, I had my own studio and was making mostly vessels, because it was something I could do on weekends and sell in a gallery. Then I was invited to show my work at a California conference, and the young man who was also showing slides of his work was Rick Smith. He was a resident artist and the iron studio coordinator at Penland. We hit it off and he recommended that I teach at Penland, which I did in '93 and again in '95. Then in '97, I returned to teach a concentration. A lot of us back then had learned the trade and skills of blacksmithing, but weren't interested in doing "traditional" blacksmithing, and we were trying other ways to go. But because we were steeped in craft, it made sense that what we made had a function. Gradually, the pieces I was making were no longer functional, because the required time and the materials made them too expensive. But the pressure was on to make work that would sell.

So when the chance to apply to the Penland residency came my way, I jumped at it. Not having had a formal art education, I'd never made work just for the sake of creating. Making things was always a means to an end. I was either working for somebody or working to make money to live. I never had the luxury of making just to see what happens, which is ideally what happens in school. So that was my intention in applying to the residency. My other intention was to push the boundaries of my blacksmithing work. The artist residency exceeded my expectations in both respects—it was a phenomenal experience.

• • •

Hoss Haley
Erratic Union No. 2, 2012
111 x 50 x 34 inches
COR-TEN steel
Photo by artist

Hoss Haley
White Ripple, 2013
89 x 149 inches
Repurposed washing machines
Image © Mint Museum of Art, Inc.
Collection of The Mint Museum, Charlotte, North Carolina

Opposite page:
Photo by Max Cooper

Hoss Haley
Potential, 2000
36 inches in diameter
Steel
Photo by artist

My years with Tom Joyce were invaluable, but being Tom's other set of hands for so long meant I struggled afterwards to find my own voice. That's what made the Penland residency so difficult at first. I was trying new things, some of which didn't work. In the first year of the residency, I explored figurative work but felt frustrated with that direction. I eventually came to see that what formed my aesthetics was growing up on the plains of Kansas. When I realized that, I felt like I had something to grab onto in terms of my own expression as a maker.

During my residency at Penland, I felt I needed to back away from blacksmithing as a way of working and explore other methods. That left me feeling somewhat isolated from the blacksmithing community. But I had learned all sorts of metalwork before I learned blacksmithing, and it seemed kind of crazy not to tap into all of that. Recently I was invited by the Metal Museum in Memphis to be featured as a Master Metalsmith. I was honored, and it felt rewarding to be recognized for the work I was making on my own path.

• • •

I had a few galleries representing me during my residency, so I was selling work. Being a resident definitely opened doors. One year at the Penland auction, I kind of killed it. The large sculpture I made sold for a lot of money. It was totally surreal. In those three years as a resident, I had one great year, one mediocre year, and one year where I sold one thing. So I learned how that goes. Somehow it averages out. I wish I could share some big insights about the art market, but my experience then and over the past dozen years is that sales are totally random. Success is fleeting, so enjoy it while you have it.

• • •

Hoss Haley
Pack Square Fountain, 2009
42 inches x 20 feet in diameter
Bronze, granite
Photo by Ken Pitts Studio

After the residency, I set up a studio in Asheville. When the opportunity to bid on the fountain in Asheville's Pack Square came up, I went for it, even though I had never built a fountain. That's another Kansas thing—like with the wheat sculpture—I thought, I can figure this out. I was awarded the commission, and that job was on a par with the time I spent as a resident artist as far as pushing myself. I remember standing in a room with architects and engineers and feeling like the kid at the table. I sweated every detail, because I couldn't afford for it not to work. And it did. That, in a nutshell, was what the Penland residency did for me: I went there as a blacksmith and left with the skills to be a sculptor, a fountain maker, you name it. I developed the confidence to work with metal in some pretty amazing and innovative ways.

• • •

I feel a deep obligation to Penland. I stayed after my residency to help design the new iron studio and build its furnaces. My vision was that the studio should be flexible enough to accommodate traditional blacksmithing classes as well as casting, fabrication, etc. I felt it was important that the studio honor the deep history of metalworking while providing access to the most current technologies available.

My dad is finally getting used to the fact that I'm not coming home. He's very proud of me. I visited him recently—he's retired but lives on the home place. He still talks about the day I left. As hard as it was to leave, I have never second-guessed that choice.

Opposite page:
Hoss Haley
Tessellation No. 1, 2013
106 x 52 x 26 inches
Repurposed washing machines
Photo by Steve Mann

JAMES LAWTON
RESIDENT ARTIST, 1983–1985 | CORE FELLOW, 1977–1978

James Lawton's sinuous sculptural teapots were for many years the vehicle for his narratives. Sketches of falling objects, garments, and furniture served an illustrated function against the actual functional forms of the pots. Eventually he shifted to calligraphic mark-making and then to forms based on the shapes of the letters—what the artist refers to as "making the interior of the pots relevant." This "vowel and consonant project" fully integrates the surfaces and forms of the vessels. Valuing the duality of a lifetime as educator-artist, Lawton's work is unselfconsciously cerebral, a partnership of pot and thesis.

Lawton earned a BS degree in constructive design at Florida State University in 1976 and an MFA in ceramics at Louisiana State University in 1980. His teaching credentials include four years at the School of the Art Institute of Chicago before heading to the University of Massachusetts–Dartmouth, where he is currently professor of ceramics at the College of Visual & Performing Arts. Lawton's work is in the collection of the Renwick Gallery of the Smithsonian American Art Museum (DC), the Victoria and Albert Museum (London), the Los Angeles County Museum of Art (CA); the Mint Museum of Craft + Design (NC), the Museum of Ceramic Art, (NY) and the Icheon World Ceramic Center (Korea). He has received two NEA visual arts fellowships.

POISE IN THE POT

I started college in 1972 knowing I wanted to be in the fine arts. I found my way through a typically circuitous path to the Department of Constructive Design at Florida State University. My metals teacher was the enamelist Bill Harper, and he was insistent that I get some studio experience outside of the university. He saw me wanting more than college could give me. Harper helped me get to Penland. In the summer of 1975, I was a scholarship student in a ceramics session taught by Mike and Sandy Simon. They invited potters from the area to teach cameos. It was quite the super-session! Perhaps at that time in my life I was ready for anything, but this was a turning point. I was inducted into Penland that summer as a pot washer and potter. When I returned to college in the fall, everything had changed.

• • •

After graduating from college, I got a winter job in Florida and made enough money to return to Penland for spring concentration in 1977 with Byron Temple. This was a completely different experience from the Simons' workshop. Byron was one of Bernard Leach's apprentices. I was fresh out of college, undisciplined, and I believe he saw me as real trouble. Byron essentially put the class through his whole catalog of pots—the first two weeks we did hundreds and hundreds of cylinders; week three we got to put handles on. I was chafing at the bit—and I think I represented to him the worst of American education. So when I asked to stay on as a studio assistant, he wouldn't support me. This kid doesn't listen, how can I recommend him? I came to realize years later that Byron's influence upon me was one of the most formative in my studio life. He brought discipline to my way of making, which had been erratic and impulsive, and he gave me a sense of design, balance, and poise in the pot—a training in form.

• • •

Actually, not being accepted as a studio assistant turned out to be an opportunity, because I applied in 1977 to be a Penland core student instead. Jane Brown knew me from my scholarship work and told Bill to take a chance on me. I took an equal number of clay and metals/enameling classes while I was a core student. I was figuring out the impact of Byron's influence, along with sixteen years of schooling. Angela Fina was the instructor for the '78 to '79 fall and spring concentrations. I could not have asked for a better mentor. Angela was every bit as tough as Byron, but her approach was radically different. Over the winter we worked side by side in the glaze room. To this day I measure studio progress by the spurt of growth I experienced that year. My winter job for the

James Lawton
Faceted Teapot, 2014
7 x 12 x 5 inches
Stoneware, slips; thrown, cut, altered; wood and soda fired
Photo by artist

James Lawton
Cantilever Vase with 2 Spouts, 2014
11 x 10 x 5 inches
Stoneware, slips; thrown, cut, altered; wood and soda fired
Photo by artist

Opposite page:
Photo by Laura Ryan

James Lawton
Teapot with Ribs, 2012
7 x 12 x 6 inches
Porcelaneous stoneware; thrown, cut, altered; wood fired
Photo by artist
Collection of John Mosler

James Lawton
Corrugated Panel with Spots, 2011
42 x 21 x 2 inches
Stoneware; press-molded, glazed with oxide spots;
reduction fired, cone 10
Photo by artist

Opposite page:
James Lawton
L-Shaped Form with Spouts, 2014
14 x 8 x 4½ inches
Stoneware, flashing strips; thrown, cut,
altered, wood and soda fired
Photo by Evelin Saul
Collection of International
Ceramic Research Center at Guldagergård

school was fixing pipes under the skillful direction of Harold Jones and Charlie Stevenson, who dispensed their wisdom about plumbing and life. My summer job was as a weekend cook; sometimes I set up lunch during the week with Pearl Grindstaff and Doris Young, two other people I greatly admired.

You didn't need much money back then, and I relied on end-of-session sales to get by. Bobby Kadis, a Penland board member from Raleigh, bought a piece of mine during one of those sales. When I taught at Penland in 2012, Bobby enrolled in my class and brought that piece to show-and-tell! I understood even then, that if you put your heart into something, believe in it—reward will follow. My family taught me this: hard work is its own value; recognition is wonderful but is not the point of doing something well.

• • •

Joe Bova taught one of the sessions and we hit it off. He was keen on my going to Louisiana State University for grad school, which I did almost directly from the core program. After grad school I wanted to go straight back to Penland as a resident artist, but I didn't get that opportunity until three years later in 1983. While waiting for news from Penland, I lived on Deer Isle, Maine, from May to October, working as an assistant to the director at Haystack, and in the winter months I migrated to Florida, where I established my first studio. It was there my professional life began. The fact that I had to wait to become a Penland resident was significant. I had gained a sense of myself as a working artist.

• • •

I was in the last group of resident artists Bill Brown selected. We arrived in early September 1983, and by October, the board had asked him to step down as director. Honestly, the two years I was there were tumultuous. Most of us wondered if the program was going to continue. I focused on my work, doing what I came to do.

I had been captured by the idea of joining the residency from practically the first moment I stepped on campus. So many of my mentors—Cynthia Bringle, Bill Brouillard, David Keator (to name a few) had been residents. I wanted the time to develop my work in the company of other artists. My goal was to solidify a mature body and practice of postgraduate work. When I arrived for the residency, I was making altered pots with painted imagery. Though much of this direction was initiated between grad school and arriving back at Penland, the residency gave me time to cut loose and take risks. This was not university!

My other goals were to establish relationships with dealers and be an active member of the Penland community. I was beginning to find my own work habits, what I needed to thrive, how to meet my own deadlines to get the work out. These insights came from a number of sources, including my peers in the residency. I was beginning to sell work, so money wasn't a looming issue. But learning the ropes of working with galleries and meeting deadlines was challenging. Knowing I alone was responsible for advancing my career was a heartening and exciting prospect.

• • •

I look to both of these experiences—being a core student and a resident artist—as watershed periods in my development. Even though these periods were separated by several years, I think of them as a linked pair of experiences. I also think that as a resident I had an impact on the core students as a mentor; I'd say it was a mutual appreciation society.

I've since forgotten exactly how many footsteps there are between the upper Farmhouse where I lived as a resident and The Barns studio. But something about that distance is an ideal, representing the need for reflection coming and going from the studio. This has stayed with me. Also, the importance of maintaining forward momentum in the shop no matter how crazy and distracting the world outside is helped immensely when I went into college teaching full time. And, when that world breaks open in possibility fringed with the unknown, I often think of myself as a core student again.

ANNE LEMANSKI
RESIDENT ARTIST, 2004–2007

It begins with the endoskeleton, a welded copper-rod armature and Anne Lemanski's mastery of visualizing planes and spaces before they exist. Line becomes surface as the material "skin," often culled and created from her diverse collection of vintage papers, is meticulously sewn to the form. There is movement back and forth between form and narrative, pattern and politics, skill and humor, aesthetics and irreverence. Lemanski seeks complexity for both the artist and the viewer—fabricating her Animalia as exquisite sculptures delivering messages, engaging, provoking, or giving solace. Assemblage is inherent to Lemanski's work, increasingly so in her series of large-format prints derived from a series of original hand-cut collages—stream-of-consciousness patterns juxtaposing innumerable personal icons.

Lemanski received a BFA from the College for Creative Studies in Detroit in 1992. For twelve years she was associated with the creative retreat center Ox-Bow in Saugatuck, Michigan, as staff and artist in residence. Her work has been included in nationally regarded exhibitions such as 0 to 60: The Experience of Time through Contemporary Art *at the North Carolina Museum of Art,* Animal Nature *at the John Michael Kohler Arts Center (WI), and* Possibilities: Rising Stars of Contemporary Craft in North Carolina *at the Mint Museum of Craft + Design (NC). She was the recipient of a North Carolina Arts Council Fellowship in 2010, and in 2015, she was a Windgate artist in residence at the McColl Center for Art + Innovation (NC). Her sculptures have been purchased for the collections of several museums, including the North Carolina Museum of Art.*

MASTERING INDEPENDENCE

I grew up in Ubly, Michigan, a village of about 900 people. Ever since I was little, art has been what I wanted to do, but I didn't see much of that modeled around me, even when my mom and I moved to Frankenmuth, Michigan, a town of 3,500. I started college at Michigan State in graphic design, but after a year, I transferred to the College for Creative Studies in Detroit, because I wanted to focus on fine art, and the school offered undergraduates their own studio. For my last three college credits, I went to Ox-Bow Summer School of Art on a working fellowship. I graduated from college in 1992 and stayed at Ox-Bow that summer. In fact, I went there every summer in some capacity for twelve years. Ox-Bow is similar to Penland, but much smaller and more rustic. It was the place that made me realize what was out there in terms of art opportunities.

• • •

I moved to Chicago in 1997. First I worked as the registrar for Ox-Bow, which had its offices in the city. Then I got hired to run a frame shop. I'd work ten-hour days there, and then, on my day off, I'd work in my studio. I was making a few armature sculptures and selling them in the frame shop. I was beginning to imagine making art full time. Meanwhile, the framing business was growing, and there was talk of a second shop. That was the bridge: am I going to be a framer for the rest of my life and give up my artwork? I didn't want to go to grad school. I had no desire to teach, which seemed like the only reason I'd go to grad school. I really wanted time to focus on my work. So I started looking at residencies. I was drawn to Penland's program because it was longer than most—three years is unheard of!

• • •

One Sunday night there was a voicemail message from Dana Moore at Penland saying I'd made it to the final ten, but the committee was concerned because I'd never been to the school. They wanted me to visit. I was so excited. I hadn't told my boss I was looking around, so on Monday I went into work and spilled the beans. He was bummed about potentially losing me, but totally supportive.

When I arrived at Penland, the setting was, of course, beautiful. I met the other residents, spent the night, and then I flew home. Soon, I got a call from Dana,

Anne Lemanski
Mexican Prairie Dog, 2010
13 x 7¾ x 10 inches
Inkjet print on paper, copper-rod armature; hand stitched
Photo by Steve Mann
Imperial Centre for the Arts Permanent Collection

Anne Lemanski
Coyote, 2010
25 x 49 x 11 inches
Mexican serapes, copper-rod armature; hand stitched
Photo by Steve Mann
Private collection

Opposite page:
Photo by Dana Moore

Anne Lemanski
A Century of Hair, 1900–1990, 2007
Variable dimensions
Mixed media, copper-rod armatures,
wood stands; hand stitched
Photo by Steve Mann

Anne Lemanski
Pigeon, 2015
42½ x 54½ x 1¾ inches
Archival pigment print mounted to wood panel
Photo by artist

Opposite Page:
Anne Lemanski
Swenkwekwe (detail), 2009
26 x 13 x 17 inches
Inkjet print on paper, leather, copper-rod armature; hand stitched
Photo by Steve Mann
North Carolina Museum of Art Permanent Collection

saying I got the residency. By then, I wanted it so bad. It started in September of 2004. I knew I'd need some money, so I threw myself a fundraiser. It was pre-Kickstarter! I raised enough money to pay for moving expenses and rent for the first year.

• • •

I've been self-supporting most of my life. I made art—a piece here and there—but mostly I had worked different jobs to pay the bills. To come into the situation at Penland where I did not have a nine-to-five job and was confronted with making art full time—I had never considered what that meant. It took me about six months to get my feet under me—mentally, emotionally, and physically. The reason I wanted the residency was to focus on my work, so I struggled with whether to change gears and come up with something more production line that I could sell out of my studio, or to focus on what I was doing and was passionate about. And that's what I decided to do—continue to make sculpture, even though the building process was slow and the potential for sales was somewhat limited. To bring in some money on a regular basis, I made little earrings and folded paper bracelets that I sold at the resident open houses that we held each session. I loved the open-door studio concept at Penland. I thought buses of people would come through, but it wasn't like that. It was not disruptive at all. Visitors were engaged with what I was doing, and I got a sense of my work from how the public reacted.

• • •

When I entered the residency, my work was similar to what I do now: I was making armatures and stitching stuff over them. During the residency, my work took a leap in scale and I had the opportunity to build my skills. Putting together these armatures was challenging. They got more and more complicated. I also started a new series called *A Century of Hair, 1900–1990*. I created an iconic hairdo relevant to women for each decade of the twentieth century. If I hadn't had the residency, there is no way I would have taken on a project of that scope. Taking two years to work on an idea is luxurious.

• • •

I am a huge advocate of Penland's Resident Artist Program. The biggest thing I tell people is you have to be realistic about your financial situation. If you're stressed out just trying to pay the bills, the program may not be the right fit. I felt so lucky to be there. I had gone so long without making a lot of artwork, that when this chance to do that came along, I really appreciated it. If you're in that right frame of mind and know the direction you want to go in, it's an incredible opportunity. I'm making my work full time today because of the residency. It introduced me to a whole new group of peers and collectors who still support me today.

Knowing what I do now, I could have gone in thirty different directions in the field of art, because I have so many interests. Being a studio artist is not easy. People in other professions often think being a full-time artist is a cakewalk, and we live in some la-la land. Being an artist is a real commitment.

I'm a one woman show—it is my responsibility to make the work, have it photographed, get it out there, keep up a website, apply for grants, stay on top of correspondence with collectors, galleries, and curators—the list goes on and on—and then I pray the work sells! It took me a long time to get to this point, and I'm not willing to stop.

MARC MAIORANA
RESIDENT ARTIST, 2002–2005

To work with iron in a spartan and ascetic fashion requires courage. Rather than the addition of some trademark technique or design element, it is the absence of the extraneous in Marc Maiorana's work that is his methodology. Surfaces are pristine, with little suggestion that a heavy tool or a formidable machine played any part in forming the steel. The courage is that of exposure—the vulnerability of immaculate design. The interplay of line, mass, and fragility form the core of the sculptures. Maiorana's work negotiates the arena where function and design intersect, creating modern utilitarian items for the home with deliberate and restrained emphasis on utility.

Maiorana is a studio artist and the proprietor of Iron Design Company. He received his BFA in metalsmithing from Southern Illinois University–Carbondale (SIU–C) in 2001, just prior to his residency at Penland. Maiorana has exhibited at the National Ornamental Metal Museum (TN), Kentucky Museum of Art (KY), and the Mobile Museum of Art (AL), and was included in 40 under 40: Craft Futures at the Smithsonian American Art Museum's Renwick Gallery in 2012. Maiorana's work has been published in five books of contemporary metalwork published by Schiffer, and featured in Audi, American Craft, Gourmet, Dwell, Food & Wine, *the* Washington Post, *and the* New York Times.

Marc Maiorana
Firewood Holder, 2010
12 x 32 x 9 inches
Steel; formed, fabricated
Photo by artist

MELDING FUNCTION AND DESIGN

My father introduced me to blacksmithing, and when you have the blacksmithing bug, there are only a few dedicated schools to study forging. This is how I wound up at SIU–C. That's where I learned about Penland from my good friend Steve Yusko, who was scheduled to teach a concentration course there and asked me to be his assistant. I took a semester off from school to do that. I was Steve's right-hand man, working hard in the old Penland iron studio, with its dirt floor and smoky coal forges and funny little dark back rooms. The two months were a whirlwind. I started making forged hand bells during concentration, utilizing some of the pipe forge-welding and patination techniques he demonstrated.

・・・

After graduation from SIU–C, I taught 3-D design at Marywood University in Scranton, Pennsylvania, in 2002. I remember thinking, "I'm making my work on the side, I'm having exhibitions, and I'm making commissions successfully. I know I'm young, but I'm going to send Penland a resident artist application because I'm ready to focus on my work full time." I wasn't sure I was ready, but was I ready to try. The resident program is designed for young artists to transition to full-time making, or for existing artists who are making a large shift in their work. I was teaching, having exhibitions, making custom commissions, and I wanted to keep the ball rolling. I felt the residency program was a way to do that. I never had the urge to go to grad school. I believed in my hands and in the excitement the work was generating, and so I applied for the residency. I jumped in.

I applied to Penland with a body of work that was mostly sculpture. During the course of my studies at SIU–C, I had pivoted towards sculpture, pushing and pulling steel around to reflect the tectonic movements I was interested in. From what I remember, my application to be a resident artist included some of these works. I think I wrote in my application that I would go larger with some of the sculpture. Oddly enough, when I left the residency, I wound up doing more functional work and less sculpture.

・・・

I arrived at Penland in spring of 2002 without much stuff; I had more motivation than equipment. I remember seeing the empty studio and living space, and feeling overwhelmed. Right away, I tried to tweak the studio to make it my own and be ready for metalwork. The housing part was secondary. This was the first time I had a studio of my own.

Marc Maiorana
Penland Grand Railing, 2006
36 x 10 x 300 inches
Steel; formed, fabricated
Photo by artist
Collection of Penland School of Crafts

Opposite page:
Photo by Leah Prater

Marc Maiorana
Center Piece, 2013
14 x 14 x 9 inches
Stainless steel; formed, fabricated
Photo by artist

Marc Maiorana
Renwick Gate, 2011
62 x 48 x 10 inches
Steel; formed, fabricated
Photo by Renwick Gallery
Collection of Smithsonian American
Art Museum's Renwick Gallery

Opposite page:
Marc Maiorana
Wine Rack, 2009
32 x 6 x 4 inches
Steel; formed, fabricated
Photo by artist

The residency experience is an *all-in* kind of thing: you are either going to come out of this an artist or you're not. So you better give it all you've got or there's no point in being there. The first few months were awkward—everything was new. I was settling in far from home, trying to get equipment up and running. There was a lot of busyness. I worked hard and all the time. I wasn't even aware of the benefit auction at Penland when I arrived in May. Suddenly, there's this big event, and people are coming to my studio to see what I make, and all I could do was show off the newly constructed welding table and gallery walls. That first year was simply getting familiar with all things Penland—the summer sessions that segue into the longer concentrations; the transition into the quiet of winter; the segue into the excitement of summer classes again. It took me a year to get used to that rhythm.

• • •

My work in the beginning of my residency was where I'd left off during college—a lot of heavy forging in sculpture. I acquired a power hammer, my first big, expensive piece of equipment. I took the shapes I was making in undergrad and scaled them up a little bit. I shook that end of The Barns—literally. The resident above me, Miyuki Imai, collected specimens from nature that she used in her textile work. She had them arranged lab-like, all in neat rows on various tables. When I'd run the power hammer, her studio really shook, which made a mess of her collections!

I was getting out of my comfort zone, doing more fabricating, cutting and welding the metal. I never really left my blacksmithing roots, but I was collecting techniques to create sculpture.

• • •

Learning the business of the craft world was new to me. Luckily, Kathryn Gremley at the Penland Gallery was available and so helpful. Plus, when you're a Penland resident, people come and find you. Suddenly owners of Charlotte and Atlanta galleries came through, asking me for an exhibition. Soon I was able to sell my work, and I began to see the light—to see how this new life would develop. The school and the Penland community are a magnet: patrons from all over the country come to you. Collectors know how to find you. As a resident artist, you get the seal of approval.

Towards the middle of my residency, I had the opportunity to make some hardware for Penland, and later, the large staircase railing for the Pines Walk. I think a lot of people come into the resident artist program doing functional work with the intention to do more sculpture, but the experience tilted me the opposite way. The Penland commissions were all functional. I figured out early on that a railing doesn't have to be just straight line geometric and hold someone up—it can have the dynamic qualities of sculpture and still be functional.

• • •

In the third year of my residency, I had solo and group exhibitions in Charlotte, Atlanta, and at the Penland Gallery. Sculptural and functional commissions were adding up. Also, I had fallen in love with Robyn Raines, a core student and now my partner, and I tried to spend as much time as possible with her. I don't remember any idle time.

The functional work I did at Penland really influenced my work going forward. I think one of my strengths is that I figure out easily what is going on around me and adapt to the situation. The ideas I needed to execute when I came into the residency were best suited for sculpture. But I was content to work in both fields, learning from both. Looking back at my time at Penland, having had that diversity of experience has enabled me to keep going as a full-time artist.

I learned the heart of contemporary crafts during my immersion at Penland. Most importantly, I learned that I could contribute to it—make a living with the work I enjoyed. I went into the residency with uncertainty, and when I left, I was confident that I could create a life doing this.

MARK PEISER

RESIDENT ARTIST, 1967–1970

Mark Peiser is an innovator, a glass pioneer whose engagement with the material is unparalleled in his field. Since 1967, he has developed numerous technically challenging bodies of work—ingenuous, unorthodox methodologies and singular concepts: hot applied cane drawings in his early Paperweight Vases, cast and precision-cut sculptures for the Innerspace series, and the unprecedented technique of cold-stream cast glass for a series of sculptural vessel forms beginning in 2004. Peiser's Palomar series pays homage to the famous 200-inch telescope mirror cast in 1934 by Corning Glass Works for the Palomar Observatory in California. This body of work, begun in 2007, is the apex of both his skill and aesthetic vision. Peiser describes it this way: "The design of the Palomar disk was defined by physics. The negative space of its structure creates an environment revealing the physics of light. As a glassmaker, I strive to realize such spaces. And as an individual, I seek them as a sanctuary."

Peiser was the first glass resident at Penland School in 1967, during the earliest years of the American studio glass movement. Prior to arriving at Penland he had studied at Purdue University (IN) and received a BS in design from Illinois Institute of Technology. He is an honorary fellow of the American Craft Council (1988), a founder and honorary lifetime member of the Glass Art Society (2001), and a recipient of the Lifetime Achievement Award from the Art Alliance for Contemporary Glass (2004). In 2009, he received the North Carolina Award for his significant contributions to the state and nation in the field of fine arts. Internationally known, his work is in the collections of the Art Institute of Chicago, National Museum of American History (DC), Museum of Art Lucerne (Switzerland), Tokyo Museum of Modern Art, Asheville Art Museum (NC), and many others. He has been awarded grants from the National Endowment for the Arts and the Louis Comfort Tiffany Foundation.

Mark Peiser
Mount, Palomar Series 009, 2010
24½ x 23½ x 14½ inches
Glass; hot cast, phase separated
Photo by Steve Mann
Collection of the artist

IMPROVISATIONAL PIONEER

I started out to be an engineer. Early in my college studies, I changed gears and went to the Institute of Design at the Illinois Institute of Technology in Chicago, which was then the American incarnation of the Bauhaus, and that was a better fit. After graduation, I went into the army reserve and then got married. In the mid-1960s, I ran the model/prototype shop for a small manufacturing company. I was always good at making things.

I liked the work I was doing, but I had always wanted to be in music, so I quit and enrolled in the DePaul University School of Music. I started an industrial design/model-making business in my garage to finance my studies in piano and composition. I was twenty-seven then, and it was a little disheartening to see the eight-year-olds down the hall performing better than me! After a couple of years I knew I wasn't going to be a professional pianist, but I had nothing to replace my passion for music.

• • •

I made some display cabinets for Ray Williams, who opened the first serious attempt at a craft gallery in Chicago in the early '60s. Ray started to manufacture Tiffany lamp kits; he put a bunch of little pieces of colored glass, a soldering iron, and some lead into a box, and sold it. During that time, my wife, Jane, bought an old Tiffany table lamp for $15. One night as I contemplated my future, I imagined making and selling replica Tiffany lamps. In my typical fashion, I thought, "How hard can it be?" So I got some glass from Ray, and a few hours later I knew that this was not the way to make money. I spent an afternoon inhaling lead fumes and wound up with a small amount of glass stuck together.

• • •

My sister, who lived in Oakland, came to visit. Her husband was studying at the California College of Arts and Crafts (CCAC),[1] where she was secretary to the dean. She suggested I visit her and attend a glass class at CCAC that summer.

Mark Peiser
Opening, Palomar Series 008, 2010
27½ x 10¼ x 27¼ inches
Glass; hot cast, phase separated
Photo by Steve Mann
Private collection

Opposite page:
Photo by Robin Dreyer

Shortly after, I found a copy of *Craft Horizons*, which was then the publication of the American Craft Council. My wife, Jane, was a painter, but she had started to do ceramics. The text on the cover read, "Where to study this summer." CCAC, Minnesota State University–Mankato, Haystack, and Penland School were mentioned, and I wrote for information from them all. Penland didn't list any course descriptions, so I called to ask what the glass class was, and was told, it's whatever the instructor wants to do when he gets here! It seemed like a last resort, but I drove to Penland.

• • •

The first day after class, Roger Lang, the instructor, told us that although glass was just emerging, it was going to be a "growth industry." He also said that Penland had started a residency program; in exchange for fixing stuff up, you could have a studio. Intrigued, I went to meet Bill Brown and told him I thought Penland was an amazing place. He said, "Well, I don't do anything. I just hire the right people and they do it all." I expressed my interest in the residency and said I'd like to apply. I'd only taken one day of class so far. Bill said I could be a resident, but he thought it might be good if I took another class before the residency began! That was my experience of Penland in 1967, and the way it was for lots of people back then.

When Bill was running the school, one thing he did was to visit every class and say something positive to at least half the students. In all those years, I never heard him say anything negative about anyone's work or effort. He was an incredibly positive and reinforcing person. I think the basic thing I learned from my time at Penland as a resident was that if you extend trust to people, you will not be disappointed. As soon as you got out of your car at Penland, there was a sense that your future was your own responsibility. Bill and the instructors and staff were there to help you in any way they could, but it was up to you to show up. And everyone held up his or her end of the bargain. It was just the most wonderful thing ever.

• • •

In my first glass class and in just about every one I took or taught over the years, the teachers and students were learning together. So naturally, when the instructor demonstrated glassblowing that first time, and I saw how direct and simple and elegant the whole process was, I thought, "Well, I can do that." And I did.

In the winter of 1967, I started my residency. There was practically no one there—just two other residents on the whole campus. The Browns and the Fords lived down the street. Everything else was closed but not locked, so I was able to rummage for tools and materials. I was teaching myself how to blow glass. It seemed like everything I did was related to musical studies: there was timing and exercises. Over the years it became clear to me that glassblowing was also a performance in time—things needed to happen when they needed to happen, and if you had to go back and repeat part of it, it's not going to be right.

Mark Peiser
Passage 3, 2013
30¼ x 14 x 8¼ inches
Glass; hot cast, phase separated
Photo by Steve Mann
Private collection

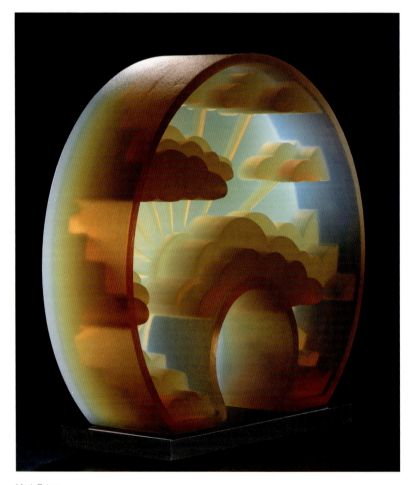

Mark Peiser
Passage 1, 2012
23¼ x 25 x 8½ inches
Glass; hot cast, phase separated
Photo by Steve Mann
Private collection

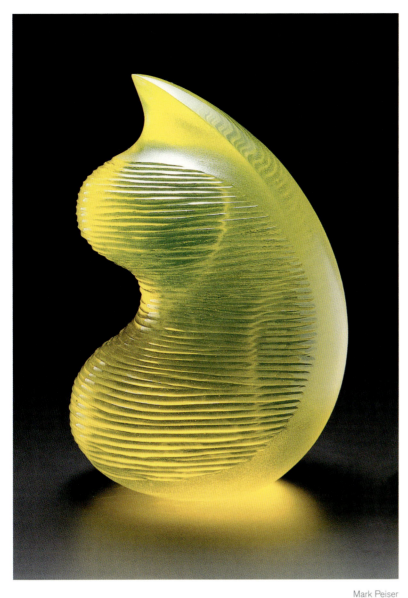

Mark Peiser
Anxiety, Forms of Consciousness Series 036.1901, 2003
14 ¾ x 10 x 8 ½ inches
Cast glass; carved, acid finished
Photo by Tom Mills
Collection of the artist

Mark Peiser
Passage 4, 2013
30 ¾ x 8 ¼ x 14 inches
Glass; hot cast, phase separated
Photo by Steve Mann
Private collection

That first Christmas, I packed up all these little bottles I'd blown, drove to Chicago, and put them on a shelf in the craft studio that Jane was part of. I priced them at $3.50 to $5.00 for a good one. I sold them all. A guy I knew from the design world said he wanted to be my agent. He explained he'd double the price and take half. I was pretty skeptical. I have never claimed to be an artist. I wanted to learn a trade, live in the woods, and escape from corporate life, but I knew the life of a maker wasn't a sure thing. In the '60s, there were three potters in America making a living—and those were production potters. This was the reality in which Penland was operating.

• • •

Penland's glass studio that first year was basically a tin roof held up with some four-by-fours—there were no walls. Sometimes snow blew into my face as I blew glass. The next summer, Bill said, "We're going to build you a studio on the back side of The Barns." And we did. I worked in that studio for two years. Then I built my own on the property and later donated it to the school. From those modest beginnings, I started to make a living as a glass artist.

The third day of class in 1967, Roger Lang described a technique that would work if we had a conical-shaped piece of wood. So I found the wood shop run by Skip Johnson—it was dark, with one light bulb. I asked if he had an engine lathe with a cross-feed to make the wood cones. Skip looked at me, paused, and said, "We got a band saw." I replied, "Okay, that's what we got, that's what we'll use."

That was a key lesson I learned from those first days as a student and those years as a resident: you use the tools you have—you improvise with what you've got. This has carried over into my work since then. One time, I built a bottom-pouring furnace so I could make certain pieces, and then I thought, what else could I do with this tool? And that led to another body of work.

I also learned from Bill, it's the work that's important. If you're doing it, throw everything you have at it to get it done.

1 Now called California College of the Arts.

CHRISTINA SHMIGEL
RESIDENT ARTIST, 1993–1994

Christina Shmigel's Foreigner's Cabinet of Chinese Curiosities *metaphorically illustrates her extensive and insatiable studio practice. Sixty-seven drawers in a one-hundred-year-old Chinese medicine cabinet each contain a curious memento— a carefully, thoughtfully fragmented view of life's puzzles and wonders in Shanghai. Her source material and technique arise from a deep creative wellspring, and converge as objects, installations, videos, literary compositions, and mentorship. Her recent works might be described as constructed tableaus that manifest her observations of the idiosyncrasies in her world.*

Shmigel received a BFA in painting from Rhode Island School of Design in 1980. She transitioned to sculpture for her MFA from Brooklyn College (NY), and a second MFA from Southern Illinois University–Carbondale (SIU–C), where she coupled technical craft skill with her conceptual art background. Leaving the Penland residency for a position at Webster University (MO), she continued to broaden her creative platform, exhibiting and teaching with an interdisciplinary approach, offering classes such as All About the Why *at Penland in 2010. A move to Shanghai, China, in 2004 has provided fuel for a body of work as a sculptor and installation artist. Projects include* This City, Daily Rising, *her 2010 solo exhibition at the Bruno David Gallery (St. Louis), and the iD TOWN International Arts District Residency in Shenzhen, China.*

SEEKING INCIDENTAL BEAUTY

I don't come from a craft tradition. At Rhode Island School of Design, I was a painter. In grad school, I studied sculpture. After teaching for several years, I went to grad school a second time to study blacksmithing and casting at Southern Illinois University because I wanted more technical skills. In my first MFA, the emphasis had been more conceptual. I hadn't learned to use materials and that felt like a handicap, both in terms of my work and my teaching. I went to SIU–C to study with Brent Kington, who was then chair of the metals program and taught Penland's first iron class in 1978. Because of Brent's involvement, the connection to Penland was so strong that we used to joke that after students graduated from SIU–C, they were put out to pasture at Penland. Metal sculptor Rick Smith, jeweler Doug Harling, glass artists Rick and Val Beck, blacksmith Marc Maiorana, jeweler Angela Bubash—so many of us continued on to the Penland residency.

• • •

The first time I came to Penland in 1992, the iron studio was pretty basic—wonderfully grungy with a dirt floor. Resident artist Rick Smith was also the studio coordinator. He pulled a Tom Sawyer, inviting the SIU–C grad students to come out to Penland for the weekend; he said, "We'll feed you and house you and you'll help the iron studio get in shape for spring concentration." He was so enthusiastic! A few of us drove the eleven hours on Friday, worked all weekend, and drove back Sunday night. That was my first experience of the physical place. I thought it was the most beautiful setting.

I came back to Penland during my last semester in 1993 to take a spring concentration with Rick—forging for metalsmiths—using both the metals and the iron studios. He finagled to have two studio assistants—Elizabeth Brim in iron and me in metals. Brent agreed to accept these two months as an independent study towards my MFA. Watching Rick and Elizabeth make work for two months was an amazing experience. I had already been accepted as a Penland resident artist for the fall, so the concentration felt like the beginning of my residency.

• • •

In some ways, I work in a very crafted, un-crafted way. Un-crafted means I'm interested in the kind of craft that I saw, for instance, in West Africa; you come across an old stool that had been broken, and someone had figured out some cobbled-together, practical way to repair it, and, inadvertently, the repair made

Christina Shmigel
Twenty Fifth (The Water Tower at Penland), 2010
20 x 9 x 9 inches
Bookboard, milk paint, bamboo in glass, wood vitrine
Collection of Laura and Bill Paulsen, NYC

Christina Shmigel
The City in Which I Love You, 2010
Variable dimensions
Galvanized steel, plastic, willow, poster board, found objects, sinamay, other materials
Photo by Bruno David
Courtesy Bruno David Gallery, St. Louis

Opposite page:
Photo by Dana Moore

Christina Shmigel
Shanghai Crown #1: Great World Reconstructed, 2011
42 x 24 x 24 inches
Bamboo, sinamay, plastic, ribbon, paint, pinwheels
Photo by Patrick Moreton

Opposite page:
Christina Shmigel
Foreigner's Cabinet of Chinese Curiosities (view of drawer interiors),
2005–2010
Each drawer: 5 x 4½ x 22 inches
Found traditional Chinese medicines (TCM) cabinet,
found materials, constructed, various media
Photo by Bruno David
Courtesy Bruno David Gallery, St. Louis

Christina Shmigel
This City, Daily Rising (installation view with the glass vitrines of
The View in Fragments on the left and the *Foreigner's Cabinet of
Chinese Curiosities* on the right.), 2005–2010
Variable; wooden cabinet: 80¼ x 60½ x 22½ inches
Bookboard constructions inside glass vitrines, traditional
Chinese medicines (TCM) cabinet; mixed media installations
Photo by Bruno David
Courtesy Bruno David Gallery, St. Louis

the object more beautiful. I love the human impulse to repair. I'm interested in that place where you make something, and you solve the problem with enough elegance so it "works"—it's a little sloppy and it has beauty, too. How do you get that accidental, improvisational quality, without getting precious about how you're doing it? So this question is interesting in the context of my experience at Penland. There I am, working alongside my fellow blacksmiths; I've made a weld, and I know it's not how my peers would do it, I know that I could work to that level of refinement, but I like this cruddy little line that I'm getting. There's the friction, for me, between the high standards of craft mastery and the desire to make something that expresses itself by virtue of simply being what it is. That's the line I'm walking. How do I bring that incidental beauty into my work?

• • •

I'm a pretty hermetic artist: I'm buoyed up by other people's creative energy and artistry, but I'm not particularly influenced by them in my artwork. I was definitely influenced by the resident artists in other ways, in terms of work ethic, discipline, and goal setting, which were not intrinsic to me. And I admired the residents who could mix creativity with running a business, who were able to make saleable work that felt integrated with who they were and what they believed.

I knew coming into the residency that I'd be an academic eventually, but I wanted to see what it would be like to be self-supporting as a studio artist. I had already started selling my water tower pieces in a gallery in New Orleans, so I had an idea that it might be possible to eke out a living while I was a resident. I didn't sell much out of The Barns, but I drove my work to galleries far off. In my second year, I was offered a job as assistant professor of sculpture at Webster University, and though it broke my heart to not stay at Penland for a third year, it was too good an opportunity to pass up.

Although I stayed focused on the water tower sculptures during my residency, I also did a series of crosshatch drawings that were a departure for me. I also took a book arts course because I was attracted to the containment of the book form. *The Foreigner's Cabinet of Chinese Curiosities* will, I hope, be a book someday, and that piece is definitely about containment. Making books opened up an important door to a craft and to people, like Julie Leonard, who remains a close friend. The friendships I made are a big part of what I value about my experience at Penland.

• • •

I loved the community at Penland. The value system there felt instinctive to me, and it doesn't exist in that way everywhere. Penland represents so much generosity—its values are "other" oriented. I think that's a craft trait. When you are making functional things for other people, you are always thinking about the "other"—where someone's hand will go on the cup you are making. I think there's an empathy built into craft, because it's traditionally for service. So I think craft attracts a certain kind of personality that is more open and empathetic, conscious of interdependence. Today I have a need—tomorrow you'll have one. I help you build a kiln—down the road you help me. People at Penland just pitched in like that, without expecting anything back.

• • •

One of my biggest life lessons happened at Penland when Elizabeth Brim and I were working as studio assistants in the iron studio. One day, she suddenly put her hammer down and left and stayed gone for quite a while. Finally, she returned and announced: "I quit my job"—her full-time paying job at a college. That was the moment when she decided to commit to the life that she lives now. She didn't have the financial means to do what she did, but she decided that if she was going to live the life she wanted, she just had to do it. To have that story in my head is like a miracle. I have dozens of stories about people choosing their lives while they were resident artists. And that's the biggest thing I've taken away from this place: having the courage to commit to the life you want. All the choices I've made since then pull from, and towards, that time at Penland.

EVON STREETMAN
RESIDENT ARTIST, 1971–1975

Synthesizing intellect, experimentation, and beauty, Evon Streetman's distinctive body of work is characterized by large color prints of ingeniously altered landscapes. Brilliantly distorting the physical world by enhancing recognizable milieu, Streetman compresses layers of visual information under the lens. Her magical images predate digital manipulation; instead they were created through careful construction in the landscape, often combined with hand alterations to the surface of the print. The results are exquisite and timeless visual tableaus, offering an invented reality.

Evon Streetman has received fellowships from the National Endowment for the Arts, and her work is held in public and private collections including those of the Polaroid Corporation and the White House. Black Boiled Coffee and the Cacophony of Frogs, *a catalog of her work, was published in 2000 by the Halsey Gallery, College of Charleston (SC); The Harn Museum (FL); the Southeast Museum of Photography (FL); and the High Museum (Atlanta) to accompany her retrospective exhibition. Streetman is professor emerita from the University of Florida where she taught from 1977 until she retired in 1999. She was a resident artist during the formative years of the program, and later a trustee and frequent instructor. With support from former Penland director Bill Brown, she was the driving force in developing Penland's photography program.*

Evon Streetman
Landscape for Edith, 1994
20 x 24 inches
Silver dye bleach print (cibachrome)

INTREPID PHOTOGRAPHER

I was running a successful commercial photography studio in Tallahassee, Florida, in the '60s, doing mostly portraiture. One day in 1964, Isabel, my receptionist, tells me there's a man calling me from North Carolina. His name is Bill Brown. I get on the phone, and he says he's seen some of my work in an exhibition and is very impressed. He's wondering if I might come to Penland and teach the instructors how to take their own slides so they'll have more success getting into exhibitions. I ask how long he'd want me there, and he says, "You must take a vacation in the summer anyway, and this would only be for two weeks." I'd had my studio for four or five years by then, and I'd never taken two consecutive days off! I ask about the pay, and he tells me, we don't pay anything. So I tell him, well, I wish you a whole lot of luck, but I can't do that. We said good-bye.

A week later, Bill calls again and we have a similar conversation. He keeps selling me along the lines of "this will be a free vacation." After the third call, Isabel tells me, "Evon, you need some time away. I think you should go." By then, I'd accepted that no money would be coming in for two weeks, but at least being at Penland wouldn't cost me anything.

...

The day I arrived at Penland, Bill announced my job at lunch. For the next two weeks, I would show instructors how to set up a tent, use a foolproof system of lighting, and work the camera to take the best pictures. Most of them took this seriously and began to take really nice photographs of their work. We used my equipment—the school didn't have any. After two weeks, I went home.

I came back every summer after that until 1970.

That first summer was an incredible vacation—I felt like a tramp at a banquet. I had started the photography department at Florida State University, my alma mater, back in the early '60s. I was doing that job on the side while running my studio, and then for two weeks every summer I came to Penland. The second year, Bill featured my job in the catalog as a regular two-week session of photography. Then he asked me to push the button and ring the bell on people I knew in the profession and start dragging them in to teach.

In the same way he leaned on potter Cynthia Bringle in the beginning with clay, Bill wanted me to help him develop a photography program. I'd call talented

Evon Streetman
Requiem for a Voyager, 1993
16 x 20 inches
Silver dye bleach print (cibachrome)
Collection of the artist

Opposite page:
Photo by Randy Batista

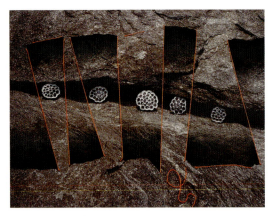

Evon Streetman
Falling Landscape XI, 1995
40 x 50 inches
Silver dye bleach print (cibachrome); multiplied, staged, manipulated
Collection of The Harn Museum Of Art

professionals and convince them that Penland was a wonderful place to teach and to hardly get paid! I would tell them in all honesty, if you come once, you're going to want to come back. We got some heavy hitters to teach at Penland—Aaron Siskind, Jerry Uelsmann—it was amazing.

• • •

On February 1, 1971, I moved to Penland and stayed for four years. I was already a successful professional, and my accountant wanted to send me to a shrink when I decided to sell my studio and move there!

My situation at Penland was so oddball. I wasn't a resident in the "regular" way. I was part of its evolution. I remember being there in 1967 when resident artists like Mark Peiser started showing up. I was part of the discussions with Bill about what he hoped to accomplish with the residency program, how much to charge for housing, studio space, etc.

Bill offered me a house and a studio and all my meals. He said, "Evon, I need a photographer—someone to take publicity photos and help with some books about Penland." So I wound up doing the photography for the pottery and the jewelry books Penland published. I photographed the first Glass Art Society conference hosted at the school. I ran the photographic studio. I would teach if I had to, but I was known as the person who invited you to teach or didn't invite you. I never would teach as long as I could get some really fine person to do it. But I was often that person's assistant—making sure the darkroom was prepped and the instructor had what he or she needed.

First I lived in The Barns and then in the house that we called Blue Haze, which became known as the photo house. The great photographer Emmet Gowin came to teach one year, and brought his wife, Edith, and I let them stay in Blue Haze. Later I put up a sign that said, "Emmet Gowin slept here."

• • •

Evon Streetman
Falling Landscape CXI, 1995
40 x 50 inches
Silver dye bleach print (cibachrome); multiplied, staged, manipulated
Collection of The Harn Museum of Art

There are two ways Penland changed me for life; first was all the lifelong friends I made—some of these people are like family to me. And the camaraderie and sharing of ideas about art were invaluable. Secondly, it was the first time in my photographic life that I didn't have to do commercial work and portraiture to buy groceries. I could make photographs just for my own personal reasons. A picture for picture's sake; it didn't have to meet someone else's needs. That had a tremendous impact on me. I had a dual degree in painting and graphic design, but I never took a photography class. I learned it myself when I was a design student and needed photographs of my work. Photography was like rolling off a log, it was so natural. As Bill Brown used to say, "Even a blind hog finds the occasional acorn." I always told my students that if you love something and want to learn, there are books you can read for technical information, but people are your spiritual and artistic inspiration.

Those years at Penland were an exploration for me as an artist. They gave me time. Most of the young craftspeople were there to improve their skills so they could make a living as an artist. I was there to quit making art for other people and learn to make it for myself. If I had to name one thing that wasn't a person that was the most important thing in my entire life, I would say Penland School of Crafts. And I'm among thousands of students who would tell you the same thing, which is what makes it so truthful.

Jerry Uelsmann was the reason I finally left Penland: he offered me a teaching job with tenure back in Florida. I needed to move on—my time on Magic Mountain had run its course. I knew if I stayed at Penland any longer, I was having too much dessert, and it was gonna make me fat and lazy. And, I needed to get back to Florida to fish!

I continued to teach at Penland during some of the summers. I taught for the last time with my dear friend Alida Fish in 2004—a session called Photographic Magic. I've reached an age when—you know, like with singers—you don't want to go out when your voice is crackin'. It's time for the younger people to do it. If you teach well, your students wind up being so much better than you are.

Evon Streetman
Rocks and Bluets, Mt. Mitchell, 1982
24 x 20 inches
Silver dye bleach print (cibachrome): hand painting

AMY TAVERN
RESIDENT ARTIST, 2009–2012

Amy Tavern has created a holistic studio practice embracing material, place, transiency, and social media—wrapping self-observation with accomplished craftsmanship. A spare aesthetic defined Tavern's early jewelry—line drawings in silver that became increasingly complex and dimensional. Lately, deliberate distillation and an observational habit have moved her work toward content and material freedom. Work from the exhibitions This is How I Remember It *(2011) and* I Live Here Now *(2013–2014) source contemplation and ritual as conceptual material. A necklace contains dirt collected from friends; fragments of a concrete foundation are set as stones; and her mother's deconstructed wedding dress begets a necklace.*

Tavern has a BA in arts administration from the State University of New York–Fredonia and a BFA in metals from the University of Washington. Before, during, and after the Penland residency, Tavern's studio practice has also included extensive teaching and lecturing. Residencies in Iceland initiated new directions in and out of the studio—investigating process, memory, and accumulation. Three solo exhibitions at Four (Sweden), Beyond Fashion (Belgium), and Velvet da Vinci in San Francisco (CA) have provided a forum for new works and installations.

COLLECTOR OF MEMORIES

I started to play the French horn when I was ten. I chose it because I liked it, but also because all the girls played flute or clarinet and I didn't want to be like all the other girls. Then I started singing and studying voice and decided to go to college to be an opera singer. After one semester, I realized it wasn't for me because I'm too much of an introvert. Although I didn't consider myself an artist, I wanted to be involved in the arts in some way, so I studied arts administration. In my senior year at Fredonia, I took studio art classes because I thought, if someday I'm going to own an art gallery and work with artists, I should know something about artistic process. I took drawing, painting, and sculpture, along with a concentration in ceramics, but I didn't think of myself as an artist. I had an interest in metalsmithing, too, and I started to think of jewelry as small-scale sculpture.

· · ·

After I graduated from college, I had the chance to study with Barbara Crocker, who was offering private metalsmithing lessons in Great Barrington, Massachusetts, near where I was living. She taught me all the basics and helped me build my portfolio so I could start applying to school for jewelry.

At Barbara's urging, in 1999, as a work-study student, I took a casting class at Penland taught by Heather White van Stolk. The class reinforced my love of metalsmithing and introduced me to Penland, where I was surrounded by people who were hardworking, creative, fun, and who thought like me. Being a work-study student gave me such a sense of purpose, in addition to the purpose of taking a class. I was there to help Penland, and I felt honored to be part of the school in that way. I loved being there.

I took another metals class at Penland the following year taught by Lori Talcott. Then I started working on my BFA. In the summer of 2005, I went back to Penland as studio assistant to Joanna Gollberg, who was teaching a metals class. We had met at Penland during the class with Lori in 2000, when we were both students, and we have been friends ever since. Later, I moved to Asheville from Seattle in 2007 and shared a studio with Joanna. By then, I was a full-time jeweler, making mostly production work, which I sold in shops around the country.

· · ·

After doing production work for a couple of years, I realized it just wasn't enough for me. My work then was simple and structured. It had this modern elegance to it and I liked the designs, but it wasn't technically or conceptually challenging. I went back to Penland in fall 2007 as a studio assistant to

Amy Tavern
Silently (I Saw a Robin Today), View 1, 2014
14 x 14 x 6 inches
The lining of my mother's wedding dress, cotton string, sterling silver, spray paint
Photo by Hank Drew

Amy Tavern
Silently (I Saw a Robin Today), View 2, 2014
96 x 9 x 4 inches
The lining of my mother's wedding dress, cotton string, sterling silver, spray paint
Photo by Hank Drew

Opposite page:
Photo by Dana Moore

Amy Tavern
Since 1882, Since 1976, 2014
18 x 1½ x ¾ inches
Stones from the foundation of my childhood home, sterling silver, vintage velvet jewelry box; fabricated, oxidized
Photo by Hank Drew

Amy Tavern
In Between, 2014
25 x 5 x 9 feet
Paper, monofilament
Photo by Leslie Williamson

Opposite page:
Amy Tavern
Forget Me Not, 2014
21¼ x 3¾ x ¼ inches
Sterling silver, spray paint, photograph of my father, my father's hair, acrylic; fabricated, painted, scratched, oxidized
Photos by Hank Drew

Raïssa Bump, who was teaching a metals concentration. I found myself at a crossroads then, and I expressed my frustrations to her. Raïssa encouraged me to get back into one-of-a-kind work, so I began a new series called *Line Drawings*. This work showed me it was time to make a change, and I felt the Resident Artist Program would be a good vehicle for my intentions. Even after a two-week class at Penland, I always left feeling like I had moved forward in a big way. So I knew that in three years as a resident artist I could do something really big. I'm self-directed and motivated, and I knew I'd use the time to my advantage.

• • •

I started as a resident artist at Penland in 2009, and my goal was to figure out what my one-of-a-kind work would look like. When I was working on my application, I made lists of all the things I could do to figure that out—different ways I would work, how I would reach out to instructors. And I did that a lot as a resident: I asked instructors to come to my studio and critique my work. I learned something important from everyone. One instructor said my work didn't have enough intention. Another suggested I make work that is purposefully "ugly" or in a different scale. I was criticized for being too subtle. Someone else suggested working outside of my medium. All of this feedback was influential. One instructor told me that in order to create new, one-of-a-kind jewelry, I needed to stop all my production work, which I was still doing to support myself. I retired all my original production work permanently, and that decision was one of best things I ever did.

• • •

The lack of privacy in my studio was challenging for me. I'm private when I'm making my work. I'm not private when I'm talking about it. I'm happy to reveal what it's about, or how I make it, because I want people to understand. My main goal as an artist is to communicate and connect, but when I'm making the work, I really like being alone. I had a lot of visitors in my studio, especially in the summer and fall, and these visits often happened during the moments when I didn't want to be interrupted. Even a five-minute interruption was challenging; sometimes it's so hard to "get there," and an interruption can throw me off. I had to learn to let go and be more resilient. This was a good skill to develop. I learned to take a deep breath and to remember that this was a big part of what being a resident artist was about, and then I was able to enjoy these experiences and the people I met.

Living at Penland as a resident artist means your private life is not private. Some visitors would actually peek through the windows into the apartment where I lived. One day I was vacuuming, and a visitor got lost and walked into my house. I had to escort him out and give him directions. Carving out private time was hard, but necessary. I learned to love the winter with its isolation. I learned that I needed the winter to get through the summer and I needed the summer to get through the winter.

• • •

The most important thing I discovered at Penland is that my work is about memory. I'm an incredibly sentimental person and I hold on very tightly to my memories. My work is narrative and autobiographical and my ideas come from mining my memory, and what do I know better than my own personal experience?

Today I was thinking about the transitory life I lead—I travel a lot to create, teach, and do exhibitions. I didn't expect my life to look like this, but I'm learning to live without planning too far ahead. This is a deliberate choice and I'm okay with it. Alongside this transitory life, Penland has been a constant for me, and I know my relationship with that place is going to continue. I started something there in 1999 and it just keeps growing. At Penland, everything became so familiar that I could literally and figuratively walk around in the dark and not get lost.

CORE FELLOWS, 1971–2016

Currently, core fellows arrive in late February of year one and complete their two-year residency in early February following their second core year. Although we attempted to reach all former core fellows, some dates are still unknown. We welcome your feedback to make the list as accurate as possible. Visit penland.org/corefellows to see an ongoing list of former core fellows with examples of their work.

James B. Abbott	1975–1976	Sondra Dorn	1992–1994
Eleanor Anderson	2016–2018	Day Dotson	2003–2005
L. John Andrew	1999–2001	Karen Downing	1985–1986
Benares Angeley	2000–2002	Jennifer Drum	1992–1994
Ele Annand	2010–2012	Lauren Dyer	1997–1999
Brian Barber	2000	Peggy Dysart	1973–1974
Cyndy Barbone	1979–1980	Angela Eastman	2013–2015
Nancy Barnett	1996–1997	Jon Ellenbogen	1974–1975
Daniel T. Beck	2010–2012	Daniel Essig	1992–1994
Audrey Bell	2013–2015	Doug Eubank*	1985–1986
Bob Biddlestone	2011–2013	Susan Feagin	1998–2000
Dorothe Bohringer*		Dana Fehsenfeld	2007–2009
Zee Boudreaux	2012–2014	Kenneth Fischer	2005
Christina Boy	2008–2010	Alida Fish	1971–1973
Meredith Brickell	2000–2002	Geralyn Flick	1982–1983
Elizabeth Brim	1983–1985	Kristen Flournoy	2006–2008
Doreen Brinkerhoff	1987–1988	Audrey Fontaine	1989–1990
Marilyn Brogan	2005–2007	Nita Forde	1985–1986
Sarah Rachel Brown	2013–2015	April Franklin	2001–2003
Belinda Bruns	1987–1988	Debra Frasier	1977–1978
Andy Buck	1989–1990	Leah Frost	2009–2011
Jason Bige Burnett	2009–2011	Elmar Fujita	2015–2017
Carie Cable	1975–1976	Aran Galligan	2006–2008
Geoff Calabrese	1996–1997	Rachel K. Garceau	2011–2013
Critz Campbell	1994–1996	Paula Garrett*	1979–1980
Thomas Campbell	2016–2018	Daniel Garver	2015–2017
Marion Carter	1989–1990	Alexandra Geske	2007
Rebecca Carter	1999–2001	Mary Gager Godfrey	1987–1988
Frances Castelli	1986–1987	Eleanor Gould	1999–2001
Jake Chamberlain	1995–1997	Seth Gould	2011–2013
Jim Charneski	1982–1983	Celia Gray	2001–2003
Anna Child	2005–2007	Kathryn Gremley	1983
Susan Chin	1983–1984	John Hagy	1998–2000
Janet Coghenaur		Holly Hanessian	1984–1985
Sharon Cohen	1979–1980	Douglas Harling	1987–1989
Thomas Judd Cook	1977–1978	Jana Harper	1995–1997
Georgianne Cowan	1975–1976	Jane Hatcher	1972–1973
Linda J. Crabill	1989–1990	Andrew Hayes	2007–2009
Natalie Craig	1973–1974	Jessica Heikes	2009–2011
Cindy Cribbs		Sarah Heimann	1989–1990
Rick Cronin	1971–1972	Ian Henderson	2010–2012
Andy Crum	1984–1985	James Henkel	1974–1976
Marianne Dages	2008–2010	James Herring	1984–1985
Shane Darwent	2007–2009	Morgan Hill	2015–2017
Sharon Dascomb	1971–1972	Troy Hines	1997–1999
Jesse Davenport	1989–1990	Michael Hunt	1996–1998
Bruce Davis		Susan Hutchinson	1990–1991
Paige Hamilton Davis	1977–1978	Karen Hylinsky	1985–1986
Terry Davis	1983–1984	Kara Ikenberry	1998–2000
Julie Oehlerking Decaen	1994–1996	Carla Illanes	1989–1990
Eric Dekker	2001–2003	Shawn Ireland	1993–1995
Chuck DeWolfe	1991	Amy Jacobs	2004–2006
Courtney Dodd	2006–2008	Annalisa Jensen	2003–2005
Tom Dorais	1984–1985	Jennifer Joyce-Kasten	
Elizabeth Dorbad	1996–1998	Jamie Karolich	2014–2016

Deborah Kaye	1983–1984	Robyn Raines	2005–2007
Rachel Kedinger	2016–2018	Douglass Rankin	1976–1977
Jane Kellar	1975–1976	John T. Renick, III	1994–1996
Linnie Kendrick	2002–2004	Joan N. Riemer	1986–1987
Maren Kloppmann	1986–1987	Linda Foard Roberts	1982–1983
Liz Koerner	2012–2014	Christopher Robinson	1996–1997
Joshua Kovarik	2014–2016	Marjorie Robinson	1985–1986
Mike Krupiarz	2012–2014	Michael Robinson	1973–1974
Joshua Kuensting	2008–2010	Emily Rogstad	2014–2016
Kyle Kulchar	2016–2018	Cynthia Rohrer	2004–2006
Kim Kulow–Jones	1987	Bird Ross	1986–1987
Michael Lamar	1981–1982	Sharon Royal	1980–1981
Peter Lane	1979–1980	Rosina Saqib	2010–2012
James Lawton	1977–1978	Beth Schaible	2008–2010
Will Lentz	2013–2015	Mare Schelz	1990–1991
Julie Leonard	1989–1990	Rosie Sharpe	1990–1992
Clarence Lewis		Jon T Shearin	2006–2008
Duncan Lewis	1979–1981	Jane Shellenbarger	1987–1988
Tibi Light	1974–1975	Susan Shipman	1996–1997
Suze Lindsay	1987–1988	Michael Siede*	1974–1975
Melissa Sullivan Linney	2003–2005	Susan Silver	1974–1975
Sarah Loertscher	2005–2007	Chuck Smith	1989–1990
Virginia Mahoney	1976–1977	Katherine Smith	
Darryl Maleike	2000–2002	McKenzie Smith	1985–1986
Jeannine Marchand	2001–2003	Aaron Sober	2004–2006
Meghan Martin	2014–2016	Molly Kite Spadone	2012–2014
E. Vincent Martinez	1988–1989	Liz Sparks	1998–2000
Jack Mauch	2011–2013	David Sperry	
Rachel Mauser	2012–2014	Peter Spider	
Tom McCarthy	1984–1985	Brook Spurlock	2002–2004
Alexandra McClay	2016–2018	Andi Steele	1998–2000
Brian McGee	2003–2005	Wes Stitt	2008–2010
Beth McLaughlin	1987–1988	Elizabeth Stokes	2003–2005
Kreh Mellick	2007–2009	Tyler Stoll	2014–2016
Jenny Mendes	1984–1985	Laurencia Strauss	2000
Kirk Meyer		Erika Strecker	1993–1994
Caverly Morgan	1997–1999	Steven Tatar	1984–1985
Jenny Nadler–Allerman		Amanda Thatch	2010–2012
John Neff*	1994–1996	Matthew Thomason	2001–2003
Karen Newgard	1993–1995	Mark Tomczak	1991–1992
Lilith Eberle Nielander	1987–1989	Natalie Tornatore	2005–2007
Kurt Nielsen	1992–1993	Mary Trechsel–Smyer	1988–1989
Zack Noble	1999–2001	Leigh Tsujino	1987–1988
Leslie Noell	1994–1996	Maria Venezia	1985–1986
Whitney Nye	1989–1990	Kevin Waddell	2002–2004
Kelly O'Briant	2001–2003	Holly Walker	1979–1981
Gretchen Oubre	1990–1991	Bradley Walters	1991–1992
Marsha Owen	1981–1982	Mark Warren	2009–2011
Bryan Parnham	2015–2017	Jerry Wesson*	1986–1987
Neil Patterson	1986–1987	Christy Wilcox	1984–1985
Todd Pearson	1982	Michael Winsor*	
Jenny Peck	1982–1983	Dave Wofford	1995–1996
Ronan Peterson	2000–2002	Marthanna Yater	1985–1986
Greg Pitts	1978–1979	Robert Young	2003–2005
Geraldine Plato	1984–1985		
John Podlipec	1992–1994	*Deceased	
Robin Pokorny			
Dan Price	1997–1999		
IlaSahai Prouty	1994–1996		
Kimberly Grey Purser	1993–1995		

RESIDENT ARTISTS, 1963–2016

Although we attempted to reach all former resident artists, some dates are still unknown. We welcome your feedback to make the list as accurate as possible. Visit penland.org/residents to see an ongoing list of former resident artists with examples of their work.

Peter Adams	1979–1984	Debra Frasier	1980–1983
Adela Akers	1968–1970	Steve Gamza	1979–1983
Vernon Allen	1968–1969	Susie Ganch	1999–2002
Dean Allison	2015–2018	Ron Garfinkle	1969–1972
Stanley Mace Andersen	1979–1983	Ruth Kelly Gaynes	1974–1976
Ann Arick		Terry Gess	1995–1998
Junichiro Baba	1998–2000	Seth Gould	2015–2018
Pamela K. Babcock	1989–1990	Kathryn Gremley	1984–1987
Dan W. Bailey	1980	Carmen Grier	1994–1996
Bruce Bangert	1965	Deborah Groover	1992–1994
Pat Bangert	1965	Hoss Haley	1997–2000
Rick Beck	1992–1994	Douglas Harling	1992–1994
Valerie Beck	1992–1994	Jane Hatcher	1975
Vivian Beer	2005–2008	Andrew Hayes	2014–2017
Paulus Berensohn^		James Henkel	1974–1976
Katherine Bernstein	1968–1970	James Herring	1986–1989
William Bernstein	1968–1970	Yoko Higuchi	1989–1992
Cynthia Bringle	1971–1975	Martha Holt	
Edwina Bringle	1969–1972	Cynthia Fick Homire	1969
Ed Brinkman	1963–1964	Paul Hudgins*	1966–1968
Judith Brinkman*	1964	Miyuki Imai	2001–2004
William Craig Brouillard	1976–1978	Shawn Ireland	1996–1999
Bill Brown, Jr.	1978–1980	Tom Jaszczak	2015–2018
Angela Bubash	2004–2007	Mercedes Jelinek	2014–2017
George Bucquet	1985–1988	Skip Johnson*	1963–1965
Jennifer Bueno	2004–2007	Robin Johnston	2011–2014
Thor Bueno	2004–2007	Cary Emile Jordan	1984–1986
Devin Burgess	2008–2011	Mark Jordan	1983–1986
Ron Burke	1964–1965	Bart Kasten	1989–1992
Geraldine Calone	1969–1972	David Keator	1975–1978
Kathleen Campbell	1988–1989	Matt Kelleher	2005–2008
Ken Carder	1984–1988	True Kelly	1970–1971
Alice Carroll	1992–1994	Ann Marie Kennedy	2001–2004
David Chatt	2008–2011	Alicia Keshishian	1989–1990
John Clark	1986–1988	Michael Kline	1998–2001
Margaret Cogswell	2008–2010	Ebba Kosick–Hance*	
Don Cohen	1973	James Lawton	1983–1985
Cristina Córdova	2002–2005	Jeong Ju Lee	2009–2012
David Cornell	1967–1970	Anne Lemanski	2004–2007
Judith Cornell*^	1969–1970	Cathy Lenox	
Cindy Cribbs		Julie Leonard	1990–1993
Sondra Dorn	1997–2001	Rob Levin	1976–1980
J. Doster	1995	Suze Lindsay	1992–1995
Kathleen Doyle	1979–1982	Marc Maiorana	2002–2005
Fritz Dreisbach		Daniel Marinelli	2009–2012
Rick Eckerd	1988–1991	Sarah Martin	2008–2011
Stephen Dee Edwards	1980–1983	James McBride	
David Eichelberger	2011–2014	Rachel Meginnes	2012–2015
Rostislav Eismont	1973–1975	Jenny Mendes	2004–2007
Micah Evans	2012–2015	Ellen Craib Mitchell	1978–1980
Annie Evelyn	2014–2017	Jaydan Moore	2014–2017
Dustin Farnsworth	2012–2015	Catherine Morony*	1968
Greg Fidler	2001–2004	Harris Nathan	1984–1987
Maggie Finlayson	2015–2018	Jack Neff*	1972–1976

186 INSPIRED

Joe Nielander	1994–1996
Harold O'Connor	1966
Hideo Okino*	1970
Ed O'Reilly	1978–1983
Marsha Owen	1984–1985
Jill Peek	
Jane Peiser	1970–1973
Mark Peiser	1967–1970
Meg Peterson	1996–1999
Jennifer Price	
Ron Propst	1967–1970
IlaSahai Prouty	2001–2004
Louise Radochonski	1998–2001
Richard Ritter	1972–1976
Sally Rogers	1989–1992
JoAnn Schnabel	1987–1989
Norman Schulman*^	1971
Tom Shields	2011–2014
Christina Shmigel	1993–1994
Randy Shull	1989–1990
Ben Simmons	1978–1982
Gay Smith	1987
Rick Smith	1991–1994
John Snyder	1996–1999
Mark Stanitz	
Cynthia Stone	1996–1999
Evon Streetman	1971–1975
Tom Suomalainen	1967–1969
Amy Tavern	2009–2012
Janet Taylor	1983–1984
Shoko Teruyama	2005–2008
George Thiewes	1983
Travis Townsend	2000–2001
Jerilyn Virden	2001–2004
Eileen Wallace	1999–2000
Jan Williams	1976–1977
Jonathan Williams*	
Phyllis Yacopino*	1970–1973
gwendolyn yoppolo	2011–2013
Suzanne Yowell	1977–1980
Ed Zucca	1969–1971

*Deceased
^Funded by the NEA as a special six-month residency

INSPIRING INSTRUCTORS AND COMMUNITY ARTISTS

Our thanks go to the many instructors, community members, and other artists who have supported, encouraged, and inspired Penland's resident artists and core fellows through the years. This group includes, but is not limited to, the people listed below. We asked all former program participants to name a few people who were important to them during their time at Penland. This list was compiled from their responses.

Hank Adams
Peter Adams
Cathy Adelman
Krishna Amin-Patel
Linda Arbuckle
Dan Bailey
Bryan Baker
Dorothy Gill Barnes
Mary Barringer
Vivian Beer
Chris Benfey
Paulus Berensohn
Doug Beube
Lisa Blackburn
Brian Boggs
Joy Boutrup
Joe Bova
George Bowes
Elizabeth Brim
Cynthia Bringle
Jon Brooks
Lola Brooks
William Brouillard
Bill Brown
Donna Brown
Curtis Buchanan
Jim Buonaccorsi
Klaus Bürgel
Devin Burgess
Jay Burnham-Kidwell
David Butler
Joseph Campbell
Susan Goethel Campbell
Helen Carnac
Kenny Carter
Macy Chadwick
Natalie Chanin
David Chatt
Julie Chen
Linda Christianson
John Clark
Dan Clayman
John Cogswell
Sas Colby
Kat Cole
Jim Cooper
Louise Todd Cope
Cristina Córdova
Maria Cristalli
Jim Croft
Rick Cronin
Bill Daley
Randall Darwall
Elisa DiFeo
Michael Dixon

Eddie Domingez
Sondra Dorn
Fritz Dreisbach
Donna Jean Dreyer
Kyle Durrie
Bob Ebendorf
Margot Ecke
David Eichelberger
John Ehle
Jon Ellenbogen
Catharine Ellis
Bridget Elmer
Heather Mae Erickson
Daniel Essig
Dan Estabrook
Annie Evelyn
Dustin Farnsworth
Jim Fawcett
Bernie Ficek-Swenson
John Ficek-Swenson
Angela Fina
Dan Finnegan
Alida Fish
Penelope Fleming
Bonnie Ford
Rebekkah Frank
Debra Frasier
Jeffrey Funk
Aran Galligan
Susie Ganch
Joanna Gollberg
Arthur Gonzalez
Jeff Goodman
Silvie Granatelli
Kathryn Gremley
Pearl Grindstaff
Hoss Haley
Audrey Handler
Bobby Hansson
Mary Hark
Julia Harrison
Del Harrow
John Hartom
Jane Hatcher
Luke Haynes
Wayne Henderson
Doug Hendrickson
Chuck Hindes
Japheth Howard
Katie Hudnall
Michael Hurwitz
Clary Illian
Marvin Jensen
Gary Jobe
Nick Joerling

Skip Johnson
Aimee Joyaux
Karen Karnes
Jane Kaufman
Amos Kennedy
Kathy King
Lisa Klakulak
Michael Kline
George Kokis
Charlotte Kwon
Sophena Kwon
Hedi Kyle
Stoney Lamar
Cay Lang
James Lawton
Leah Leitson
Mary Jane Leland
Julie Leonard
Marthe LeVan
Rob Levin
Suze Lindsay
Sarah Loertscher
Carman Lozar
Deborah Luster
Marcia MacDonald
Warren Mackenzie
Richard Mafong
Paul Marioni
Ann Matlock
Barbara Mauriello
Richard Mawdsley
Robert May
Tom McCarthy
Josiah McElheney
Chaffe McIlhenny
Linda McFarling
Jenny Mendes
Ron Meyers
Daniel Michalik
Edjohnetta Miller
Ellen Craib Mitchell
LeeAnn Mitchell
Dana Moore
Clarence Morgan
Joan Morris
Bob Mueller
Jack Neff
Thomas Neff
Bea Nettles
Sammie Nicely
Leslie Noell
Gary Noffke
Matt Nolen
Nance O'Banion
Jeff Oestreich

Betty Oliver
Jere Osgood
Jane Peiser
Mark Peiser
Flossie Perisho
David Peterson
Meg Peterson
David Pimentel
Geraldine Plato
Becky Plummer
Ron Propst
Martin Puryear
Michael Puryear
Douglass Rankin
Neal Rantoul
Brian Reid
Dick Rice
Mattie Rice
Richard Ritter
Jan-Erik Ritzman
Holly Roberts
Mary Roehm
Christine Rolik
Peter Ross
Mike Rossi
Will Ruggles
Ismini Samanidou
Phil Sanders
Paul Sasso
Norm Schulman
John Scott
Shawn Sheehy
Jessie Sheffrin
Jane Shellenbarger
Piper Shepard
Tom Shields
Carol Shinn
Christina Shmigel
Randy Shull
Doug Sigler
Linda Sikora
Michael Simon
Sandy Simon
Brent Skidmore
Clarissa Sligh
Dolph Smith
McKenzie Smith
Phil Smith
Pablo Soto
Jerry Spagnoli
Rory Sparks
Tom Spleth
Joan Sterrenburg
Tal Streeter
Evon Streetman
Billie Ruth Sudduth
Tom Suomalainen
Toshiko Takaezu
Mina Takahashi
Akio Takamore

Tim Tate
Amy Tavern
Byron Temple
Steve Tengelsen
Pam Thompson
Anna Tomczak
Bob Trotman
Marlene True
Robert Turner
Roy Underhill
Clare Verstegan
Jerilyn Virden
Eileen Wallace
Kiwon Wang
Marguerite Wildenhain
Jan Williams
Rob Williams
Doug Wilson
Hiroko Yamada
Bhakti Ziek
Mark Zirpel

ACKNOWLEDGMENTS

Documenting the history of the Core Fellowship and Resident Artist programs is long overdue. Both programs represent truly innovative and model support systems for artists and serve as test-worthy guides for the growth of artistic communities. We are indebted to Bill and Jane Brown for envisioning these programs and to Robyn Horn and the Windgate Charitable Foundation for believing that the story of the programs needed to be told. We also thank Windgate for endowing the programs to ensure that artists, long into the future, will be able to experience Penland as the educational resource they need for transitions in their creative lives.

Many artists have passed through these programs and will for years to come. We thank each artist who contributed their time and memories to this book and those who participated in the programs but were not featured in our profiles. Many talented staff members also devoted years of their lives to working with the core and resident programs. We thank them for dedicated service and assistance. We are also grateful that many Penland trustees have taken so many core fellows and resident artists under their wings—to purchase and commission new work, introduce them to gallerists and collectors, and encourage them along their paths.

Specifically we want to thank Charlotte Vestal Wainwright for her initial research and work on this publication. We thank Dana Moore, who served on our original staff planning team. Jasmin McFayden undertook hours of organizing records, contacting artists, and gathering material in archives. We thank Penland's former archivist Michelle Francis for her fact-checking and Penland's current archivist Carey Hedlund for additional archival and photographic research. All uncredited photographs are from the Jane Kessler Memorial Archive at Penland School of Crafts. Devoting long hours to discussion, planning, writing, reading, and editing, Kathryn Gremley, Leslie Noell, and Robin Dreyer are to be commended for creativity, ingenuity, passion, and commitment. Special thanks go to Kathryn Gremley for her introductions to each artist conversation, to Robin Dreyer for his history of Penland, and to Caitlin Strokosch for her overview of artists' residencies. We also recognize and thank Rob Pulleyn who guided us behind the scenes and provided invaluable feedback at each requested turn.

We thank the team that brought this publication to press—Deborah Morgenthal, Kathy Sheldon, Ele Annand, and Todd Kaderabek. Deborah ran with our redefined vision of the publication—telling the story of the programs through the voices of participating artists. She interviewed each artist profiled in this book, edited the excerpts from those conversations, and wrote an overview chapter for each program. We enthusiastically thank her for patience, tenacity, and belief in the power of these programs. Kathy has served as the project manager. She has done her best to keep us on schedule and we are truly grateful for her attention to the many dates and details behind an undertaking such as this. Ele, a former core fellow herself, was our art director and book designer, making the book as beautiful to look at as it is to read. And Todd expertly navigated the printing process for us.

Now we thank you, the reader, for spending time with our stories and for the support you provide to the artists in your everyday lives.

Jean W. McLaughlin
Executive Director
Penland School of Crafts

INDEX

Page numbers in italics refer to photographs.

Adams, Ansel, 71
Adams, Peter, 26, 120–123
Addams, Jane, 12
Akers, Adela, (quote) 25, *30*, 124–127
Alliance of Artists Communities, 6
American Craft Council, 8, 20, 65, 79, 125, 169, 170
Andersen, Stanley Mace, 31, (quote) 33, 128–131
Anderson Ranch Arts Center, 8, 22
Angeley, Benares, (quote) 39, *42*, 51
Annand, Ele, *43*, 190
Appalachian School, 11, 12, 13, 17, *31*, 31
Archie Bray Foundation for the Ceramic Arts, 112
Arrowmont School of Arts and Crafts, 8, 22, 35, 103
Artist residencies: and artists' needs, 8; growth and purposes of, 6–7
Baba, Junichiro, 132–135
Bailey, Dan, *21*, 27, 108, 121
Bangert, Bruce, *25*, 30
Bangert, Pat, *25*, 30
Barnes, Dorothy Gill, 69
Barrett, Tim, 93
Barrow, Judith, 30
Beck, Daniel, *46*
Beck, Rick, 173
Beck, Val, 173
Beer, Vivian, (quote) 27, *28*, 30, 136–139
Berea Academy and College, 12, 13
Berensohn, Paulus, 92, 113, 115, 122, 141
Bernat, Paul, 22
Bernstein, Katherine 31, 146
Bernstein, William (Billy) 31, 146
Beube, Doug, 84
Bishop, Mary, 14
Blackburn, Lisa, *21*, 88
Botnick, Ken, 20, 21, 33, 46, 112
Bottero, Claudio, 76
Boudreaux, Zee, *37*
Bova, Joe, 158
Boy, Christina, *38*
Boyd, Mark, 45
Boysen, Bill, *16*, 16
Brickell, Meredith, *42*, 54–57, 105
Brim, Elizabeth, (quote) 11, *36*, 84, 173, 174
Bringle, Cynthia, *18*, 19, 22, 31, 113, 129, 141, 143, 158, 177
Bringle, Edwina, 19
Brinkman, Ed, 17, 30, 31
Brouillard, Bill, 158
Brown, Bill, 8, 14, *15*, 16, 17, 19, 20, *25*, 30, 31, 45, 64, 71, 107, 108, 121, 122, 125, 129, 145, 158, 170, 171, 177, 178, 190
Brown, Bill, Jr., *15*, 16, 121
Brown, Jane, 9, 14, *15*, 16, 17, 19, 20, 22, 45, 48, 63, 64, 108, 111, 129, 157, 190
Brown, Jerry, *15*
Brown, Sarah Rachel, 48
Bubash, Angela, *28*, 173
Bueno, Jennifer, *28*
Bueno, Thor, *28*

Bump, Raïssa, 182
Burke, Ron, *25*, 30
Burnett, Jason Bige, *38*, 45
Campbell, Critz, 58–61, 116
Campbell, Susan Goethel, 96
Carder, Kenny, 133
Carter, Marion, 91
Castle, Wendell, *17*
Center for Furniture Craftsmanship, 99
Chamberlain, Jake, *40*
Chatt, David, 25, *27*, 138
Chiarito, Robert, 45
Chin, Susan, (quote) 45, 62–65
Chown, Joyce, 125
Clark, Jimmy, 141
Clay Studio (Philadelphia), 55
Concentration program at Penland, 19
Córdova, Arturo, 22
Córdova, Cristina, 22, 30, (quote) 51, 138, 140–143
Core Student Program (Core Fellowship): annual show, 42; beginning of, 19, 72; financial support, 39; history of, 45
Crocker, Barbara, 181
Cronin, Rick, 71
Dages, Marianne, *38*, (quote) 42
Daley, Bill, 117
Davis, Paige, 65, 84
Dekker, Eric, *42*
DeWolfe, Chuck, 45
Dieu Donné, 87, 89
Dodd, Courtney, 45
Dohner, Andy, 83
Doster, J., *118*
Doyle, Kathleen, 63
Dreisbach, Fritz, 146
Eastman, Angela, *9, back cover*
Edwards, Stephen Dee, (quote) 34, 144–147
Eichelberger, David, *32*
Ellenbogen, Jon, 111, 113
EMMA International Collaboration, 83, 84
Essig, Daniel, (quote) 38, 66–69, 88, 93
Ethical Metalsmiths, 149
Evans, Micah, 35
Evergreen, Charlie, *22*
Farnsworth, Dustin, 7
Fehsenfeld, Dana, (quote) 43
Fenster, Fred, 149, 151
Fidler, Greg, 142
Fidler, Lisa, 95
Fina, Angela, 157
Fish, Alida, *9*, 46, 70–73, 108, 178
Forbes-deSoule, Steven, 103
Ford, Bonnie Willis, 12, 13, 16, 22
Ford, Howard (Toni), *12*, 12, 13
Forde, Nita, 45, 79, 92
Francis, Michelle, 190
Franklin, April, *42*
Frasier, Debra, 121, 122
Frost, Leah, *38*, 49
Fujita, Elmar, *44*
Ganch, Susie, 148–151

Garceau, Rachel, *41*, 45
Garfinkle, Ron, 72
Garrett, Paula, 79
Garver, Daniel, *39*
Gernandt, Suzanne, 87
Gess, Terry, *118*
GI Bill, 14
Glass Art Society, 16, 145, 169, 178
Gollberg, Joanna, 181
Gordon, Lida, 87
Gosin, Susan, 88
Gould, Seth, 74–77, 100
Gowin, Emmet, 178
Granatelli, Silvie, 56
Gray, Celia, *42*
Gremley, Kathryn, 26, 27, 42, 46, 51, 104, 105, 112, 150, 166
Grier, Carmen, 88, *118*
Grindstaff, Pearl, 130, 158
Groover, Deb, 59
Hahn, Betty, 72, 73
Haley, Hoss, 25, 83, 85, 117, 134, 150, 152–155
Hamilton, Ann, 87
Hanes, Gordon, 31, 35
Hanes, Philip, 17, 31, 35
Hansson, Bobby, 84
Hark, Mary, 88
Harling, Douglas, 78–81, 173
Harper, Bill, 157
Harper, Jana, 116
Harris, Edwin F., 21
Hatcher, Jane, 113
Hayes, Andrew, 82–85`
Haystack Mountain School of Crafts, 8, 14, 16, 17, 22, 35, 87, 89, 107, 108, 158, 170
Hedlund, Carey, 190
Heart of Los Angeles (HOLA), 26, 35
Heikes, Jessica, *38*
Heiman, Sarah, 91
Henderson, Ian, *43*, 76
Hermanovski, Mila, 95, 97
Hindes, Chuck, 99, 112, 129
Holzman, Warren, 83
Horn, John, *21*
Horn, Robyn, 34, 37, 190
Hosaluk, Michael, 84
Howard, Japheth, 76
Hutchinson, Susan, 45
Ikenberry, Kara, 104, 105
Illanes, Carla, 91
Imai, Miyuki, 166
Jacobs, Amy, 86–89
James G. Hanes Memorial Fund, 17, 31
Janecky, Martin, *20*
Jelinek, Mercedes, *34*
Jensen, Marvin, 108
Joerling, Nick, 56
John C. Campbell Folk School, 22, 103
John Michael Kohler Arts Center, 63, 153, 161
Johnson, Beth Ross, 37
Johnson, C. R. (Skip), *17*, 17, *25*, 30, 121, 171

INDEX 191

INDEX CONTINUED

Jones, Carola, 22
Jones, Harold, 158
Joyce, Jennifer, *45*
Joyce, Tom, 153, 154
Kadis, Bobby, 158
Karolich, Jamie, *39*, 47
Keator, David, 158
Kelleher, Matt, *28*
Kelly, True, 71, 72
Kennedy, Amos, 117
Kennedy, Ann Marie, *33*
Kariher, Hunter, 20, 33
Kim, Grace, *23*
King, Kathy, 104
Kington, Brent, 16, 80, 173
Kitner, Harold, 92
Klein, Scott, *21*
Koerner, Liz, (quote) 40
Kuensting, Joshua, *38*
Labino, Dominick, 16
Lane, Stacey, 47
Lang, Roger, 170, 171
Larson, Susan, 22
Lathrop, Julia, 12
Lawton, James, (quote) 35, 59, 156–159
Leach, Bernard, 157
Lemanski, Anne, (quote) 26, *28*, 138, 139, 160–163
Lentz, Will, 43
Leonard, Julie, 67, 68, 90–93, 174
Levin, Rob, 31, 145, 146
Lindsay, Suze, 55, 56, *118*
Littleton, Harvey, 16, 146
Lloyd, Frances, 67
Loertscher, Sarah, 94–97
Louis Comfort Tiffany Foundation, 169
MacArthur Foundation, 6
Macdonald, Marcia, 149
Maiorana, Marc, 26, (quote) 28, 30, 137, 164–167, 173
Maleike, Darryl, *42*
Marchand, Jeannine, *42*
Martin, Meghan, *52*
Mauch, Jack, (quote) 48, 76, 98–101
Mauriello, Barbara, 104
Mawdsley, Richard, 80
McCarthy, Tom, 79, 80
McFayden, Jasmin, 190
McKinney, Jessie, 13
McLaughlin, Jean, 8, 20, *21*, 21, 33, 34, *42*, 46, 47, 108, 190
Meginnes, Rachel, *24*, 35
Mellick, Kreh, *7*, 84
Menapace, John, 108
Mendes, Jenny, *28*, 65, 138
Merritt, Francis, 14, 16, 17, 107
Miller, Steve, *21*
Mint Museum of Craft + Design, 79, 107, 141, 153, 157, 161
Miura, Tini, 91
Moore, Dana, 20, *21*, 33, 34, 46, 115, 137, 151, 161
Morgan, Clarence, 60
Morgan, Lucy, 8, *10*, *12*, 11–13, 14, 16, 21, 22, 43, 88
Morgan, Rufus, 11, 12, 43

Morgenthal, Deborah, 25, 37, 51, 190
National Endowment for the Arts, 45, 59, 71, 79, 121, 126, 145, 157, 169, 177
National Ornamental Metal Museum, 75, 83, 137, 154, 165
Nelson, Patricia, 95
Nettles, Bea, *16*
Nielander, Joe, *118*
Niffenegger, Audrey, 88
Noble, Zack, 46
Noell, Leslie, 27, 34, 38–40, 43, 47, 85, 88, 116
Noffke, Gary, 11
Nordness, Lee, 126
North Carolina Artist Fellowship, 67, 79, 107, 141, 161
Nye, Whitney, *45*
O'Briant, Kelly, *42*
Oubre, Gretchen, *45*
Ox-Bow School of Art and Artists' Residency, 6, 87, 161
Page, Mike, 22
Peiser, Jane, 31, 126, 170
Peiser, Mark, (quote) 31, 126, 146, 168–171, 178
Penland School of Crafts: history of, 11–22; impact of, 7; institutional affiliations of, 8
Penland Weavers, 11–13
Perkins, Sarah, 80
Peterson, Meg, 112, 116
Peterson, Ronan, *42*, (quote) 46, *51*, 102–105
Peters Valley School of Craft, 8, 22
Pfahl, John, 72, 73
Pierantozzi, Sandi, 57
Pierobon, Peter, 137
Pilchuck Glass School, 8, 22
Plato, Geraldine, 45, 46, 150
Plummer, Becky, 111, 113
Pollock-Krasner Foundation, 125
Raines, Robyn, *48*, 166
Rais, John, 83
Reitz, Don, 130
Renwick Gallery of the Smithsonian American Art Museum, 30, 67, 125, 137, 141, 145, 157, 165, 166
Resident Artist Program: beginning of, 17; financial support, 26; history of, 30; program requirements, 28
Rice, Richardson, 45
Ritter, Richard, *29*, 31
Roberts, Linda Foard, 45, 106–109
Sanchez, Angel, 95, 97
Sasso, Paul, 84
Schaible, Beth, *38*
Schelz, Mare, *45*
Schiavone, Joanne, 91
Schulman, Norm, 31, 129
Sharpe, Rosie, *45*
Shellenbarger, Jane, 57
Shelton, Taylor, 38, 39
Shields, Tom, *front cover*
Shipp, Tony, 115
Shmigel, Christina, 47, 92, 172–175
Sigler, Doug, 22
Simmons, Ben, 107, 108
Simon, Michael, 91, 157
Simon, Sandy, 157
Siskind, Aaron, 178

Smersh, John and Frances, 96, 97
Smith, Dolph, 69
Smith, Keith, 91
Smith, Lulu, 96, 97
Smith, McKenzie, 103
Smith, Rick, 153, 173
Snipes, Kevin, *21*
Soto, Pablo, 141
Spadone, Molly, *41*
Spleth, Tom, 57
Stanford, Joy, 45, 79
Stanford, Verne, 20, 45, 65, 79
Starr, Ellen Gates, 12
Stevenson, Charlie, 158
Stitt, Wes, (quote) 37, *38*
Stokes, Elizabeth, 47
Streetman, Evon, 16, (quote) 30, 72, 176–179
Strokosch, Caitlin, 6, 190
Suh, Do-Ho, 87, 89
Swedlund, Chuck, 67
Takahashi, Mina, 89
Talcott, Lori, 181
Tavern, Amy, 180–183
Tawney, Lenore, 126
Temple, Byron, 157
Teruyama, Shoko, *9*, *28*
Thomason, Matthew, *42*
Thomson, Frank, 33
Taipale, Martta, 126
Tipton, Cordie, 130
Toe River Arts Council, 30
Tomczak, Mark, *45*
Touchstone Center for Crafts, 141
Troy, Jack, 99
Turner, Robert, *19*, 60
Uelsmann, Jerry, 178
USA Artist Fellowship, 141
van Stolk, Heather White, 181
Veness, Tim, 45, 68
Verdin, Jerilyn, *26*
Voorhees, David, 103
Wagle, Kate, 149
Wainwright, Charlotte Vestal, 190
Walker, Holly, (quote) 48, 110–113
Walters, Bradley, *45*
Wang, Kiwon, 95
Warren, Mark, *38*
Watershed Center for the Ceramic Arts, 55, 111, 112
Way, Laura, 47
White, Minor, 71
Williams, Jan, 31
Willis, Adeline, 12
Wilson, Doug, 11
Windgate Charitable Foundation, 25, 34, 37, 48, 137, 161, 190
Wofford, Dave, 55, 114–117
Wong, Paul, 89
Wood, John, 72
Worst, Edward F., *13*, 13, 22
Yamada, Hiroko, 76
Young, Doris, 158
Yusko, Steve, 165